MUSIC, LATE AND SOON

T0159960

SCHIRMER'S LIBRARY
OF MUSICAL CLASSICS

Vol. 1

BEETHOVEN
SONATAS
For the Piano

IN TWO BOOKS

Book I

(BÜLOW-LEBERT)

INTERNATIONAL MUSIC STORE LIMITED
1334 ST. CATHERINE ST. WEST
MONTREAL

MUSIC, LATE AND SOON

A MEMOIR

ROBYN SARAH

Biblioasis
Windsor, Ontario

FIRST EDITION
10 9 8 7 6 5 4 3 2 1

Library and Archives Canada Cataloguing in Publication

Title: Music, late and soon / Robyn Sarah.
Names: Sarah, Robyn, author.
Identifiers: Canadiana (print) 20210221275 | Canadiana (ebook) 20210221763 | ISBN 9781771963565 (softcover) | ISBN 9781771963572 (ebook)
Subjects: LCSH: Sarah, Robyn. | LCSH: Pianists—Canada—Biography. | LCSH: Clarinetists—Canada—Biography. | CSH: Authors, Canadian (English)—20th century—Biography. | LCSH: Teacher-student relationships. | LCGFT: Autobiographies.
Classification: LCC ML417.S243 A3 2021 | DDC 786.2092—dc23

Edited by Daniel Wells
Copyedited by Linda Pruessen
Text and cover designed by Michel Vrana

All persons who appear in this book are real. For different reasons, names of a few have been changed.

Published with the generous assistance of the Canada Council for the Arts, which last year invested $153 million to bring the arts to Canadians throughout the country, and the financial support of the Government of Canada. Biblioasis also acknowledges the support of the Ontario Arts Council (OAC), an agency of the Government of Ontario, which last year funded 1,709 individual artists and 1,078 organizations in 204 communities across Ontario, for a total of $52.1 million, and the contribution of the Government of Ontario through the Ontario Book Publishing Tax Credit and Ontario Creates.

PRINTED AND BOUND IN CANADA

The world is too much with us; late and soon,
getting and spending, we lay waste our powers ...
—William Wordsworth

Early in life, at the hands of an unworldly music teacher, I learned that there are worlds within this world. I found one in music—a pursuit that replenished my powers instead of wasting them, a bulwark against the hustle of getting and spending. Late in life, I found it again.

Da Capo al Fine
A musical directive to repeat from the beginning and continue until you reach a point in the music marked "Fine" (end).

For my mother,

whose interest and belief in me helped me to find my path

and spur me to keep following the music.

PART ONE: *DA CAPO*

1

I   BEGINNINGS

Prelude: The Idea

I WAS LATE FOR MY PIANO LESSON. THIRTY-FIVE YEARS late, to be exact. I stood at the bus stop in the mild end-of-winter sunshine casting anxious glances at my watch—furious at myself for not leaving the house earlier, making no allowance for missed buses, late buses, slow traffic. Such an auspicious moment and here I was, off to a bad start. I wanted to arrive serene and composed, not frazzled and sweaty, for my first piano lesson in three and a half decades.

"Don't you feel like a little kid?" my sister had asked me when I told her what I was doing that afternoon. On the bus, contemplating my pile of piano books with their frayed covers, loose bindings, and yellowing pages, I thought about that. Did I feel like a kid? Were piano lessons a kid thing? What I was doing felt quite natural and familiar; also, deeply improbable and a bit scary. *Do I even remember what a piano lesson is? How will it feel to play for a stranger's ears,* knowledgeable *ears—and to play for a teacher I've never met—after all of this time playing for my own ears, at home, in my slippers? Am I ready to re-enter this world? Is it a little crazy?* I was fifty-nine years old. Something was driving me.

In due course I turned up the front walk of a modest town-house whose address matched the one I had pencilled on a Post-It Note stuck to the cover of my old Schirmer's Beethoven Sonatas. It was on a quiet, block-long street tucked away from the traffic and noise of major arteries. In the front yard, crocuses were pushing up through the melting snow. I rang the doorbell, feeling an odd mixture of trepidation and reckless-ness. From a distance I could hear the shouts of kids at recess in the playground of the primary school down the block—a school my grown children had once attended. Pieces of my past were colliding.

The woman who came to the door was petite, attractive, around ten years my junior. Waving away my apologies for being late, she showed me into what would have been the din-ing room had it not been taken over almost completely by a Steinway baby grand. Her demeanour was gracious, alert, and inquisitive. We knew next to nothing about each other, but had spoken, briefly, on the phone to arrange this first meeting. We had studied with the same teacher, though not during the same years; she came recommended by him. She had made her life in music, while I had lapsed, early on, and taken a different path. And now, here we were.

"Well, here I am," I said, more gamely than I felt. "I come to you with my chapped hands, my raggedy piano books, and my hopeful heart." And so began a new page in my life—a page that is still unfolding.

"What made you decide to take piano lessons again?" people have been asking me since. In the same period, the question I have asked myself is "Why did it take me so long?" Lurking beneath that is another question, "Why did I stop in the first place?"—and this last, I know I am not alone in ask-ing. The world is full of lapsed pianists who wish they hadn't. Three real questions, not one of which has a simple answer. I can only address them by tracking a very individual musical journey. Human stories are complicated. This is a human story.

※

In January of 1968, when I performed as guest soloist with the Montreal Symphony Orchestra in a concert series featuring young artists, my performance was not on piano. I was eighteen, a fifth-year student at Quebec's Conservatoire de musique et d'art dramatique, majoring in clarinet while also a philosophy major at McGill. The *Matinée Symphonique* at which I played a movement of Mozart's clarinet concerto was in Ottawa—convenient for my family, who had moved there from Montreal while I was finishing high school, leaving me in care of my grandparents so I could graduate with my class and continue my musical studies. The previous March, I had performed on clarinet in the Sarah Fischer recital series at the Ritz-Carlton in Montreal (sharing the program—as I was surprised to note recently on unearthing a yellowed newspaper review—with celebrated pianist André Laplante, also then seventeen). Together these two events constituted my musical debut—standard first steps, in Montreal at the time, for a young professional-track musician. For such I had somehow, willy-nilly, become.

Performing as soloist with the MSO, a professional orchestra, should have been major for me—a milestone moment. I don't remember it that way. The event was coloured by disappointment from the start, with my matinée scheduled, anomalously, in Ottawa. Montreal had a dazzling new concert hall; Ottawa's National Arts Centre was in its last year at the old Capitol Theatre, a venue designed for cinema and vaudeville. I would miss out on the thrill of playing in Place des Arts. And all my friends were in Montreal.

In a daze of nerves through the performance itself, I came off stage with a palpable sense of letdown, hyper-aware of every glitch, every passage that hadn't come off as well as it could have. It felt like a missed chance. In the wings, my parents and excited younger siblings were waiting, unaware that I had not given the performance I'd hoped to. Also waiting were a photographer and a female arts reporter from the *Ottawa Journal,* who wanted to talk about my studies in philosophy, my prospects as a woman wind player—things that struck me as irrelevant to the moment, prompting irrelevancies in reply. Soon after, in company of the orchestra, I boarded a train to return to Montreal. The symphony musicians, in those years nearly all men, settled down with newspaper sports sections and decks of cards; some dozed off. This was all in a day's work for them. No one seemed interested in engaging with the clarinet soloist, whose moment in the sun seemed to be over.

Fidgety in my seat as the train lurched homeward, I hatched an idea for a short story I could write: a deeply conflicted young musician realizes, in the immediate aftermath of her debut, that she cannot continue on this path. Suddenly, with a stab of grief, she knows that her debut will prove to be her swan song. I saw I could use some of the details of the train ride; the character could have this flash insight on the train. Of course the story wasn't about *me,* I reassured myself; I was only stepping into this character's shoes. I was committed to a life in music. I had been playing principal clarinet in the Conservatoire Orchestra since the age of fifteen, a position conferred on me after a mere two years on the instrument. There would be many more chances to perform as soloist with an orchestra, and they would be different.

Was I fooling myself, or was I prescient? Though I continued on the path for another four years—long enough to graduate from the Conservatoire with a Concours *Premier Prix* in performance on clarinet—in essence my debut was my swan song.

%

For most of my adult life, I've been a word person—a poet, writer, and literary editor; for twenty years a college English teacher. I have always been a word person; I began writing stories and poems almost as soon as I could hold a pencil. But music was central to my formative years, and for nearly a decade I entertained a notion that I could one day support a writing habit by playing clarinet in an orchestra. My mother's sage advice that I take an academic degree concurrently with my Conservatoire studies, so as to have "something to fall back on," was to be expected from a parent widowed at twenty-seven with two children. The advice served me well but failed to recognize that when one has something to fall back on, one is likely to fall back on it.

Missing from this picture is the piano. Piano was my first instrument; I'd had private lessons from childhood and kept them up all through high school, even after clarinet supplanted piano as the focus of my time and attention. But I never thought of playing piano professionally. In all those years I never played in a student recital or even took an exam (my teacher didn't believe in them). By the time I entered university at seventeen, piano lessons had become irregular and soon lapsed, though I returned to them briefly in my early twenties.

I was twenty-four when I finally abandoned thoughts of a musical career and quit studying both instruments. It was becoming apparent I could not juggle a career in music with the needs of literary creation: music would take all. And the pull of words had become urgent. Of course I told myself I would still play, and of course that didn't work out. Clarinet fell by the wayside quickly: the embouchure has a low tolerance for fickleness, and without the pressure of scheduled rehearsals and performances, there was no motivation to practise daily to stay in shape. The limitations of the instrument didn't foster much desire to keep it up alone: unlike a keyboard instrument, a clarinet cannot play more than one note at a time—it cannot play chords to accompany a melody, nor a second part to harmonize with one. My Conservatoire friends, bent on careers and beginning to freelance, had no time for recreational music-making. It proved hard to find amateurs advanced enough to play chamber repertoire I would find satisfying, harder still to schedule mutually convenient rehearsal times. I soon gave up trying. Then, for a number of years, I found myself without a piano. By the time my life was rooted enough to own one again, I had two preschoolers and a job as a college English teacher.

My two professional-quality clarinets languished unplayed in their dusty cases. No one knew me as a musician anymore. But I had a piano. So began my thirty-five years as a closet pianist on a part-time, self-coached, on-again, off-again maintenance regime.

%

What brought me to emerge from that closet at an age when any possibility of a musical career was long behind me? What made me decide I needed a teacher again, after half a lifetime's desultory piano-playing on my own? There was a dream I once had—one that I periodically found myself remembering—that seems, obscurely, to hold an answer.

It was one of those dreams where at first you're not sure if you're remembering a dream or something that really happened: I was back in my early twenties, the period when I had last taken piano lessons. It was a warm spring afternoon and I was running uphill from the bus stop towards my piano teacher's house, late for a lesson I had nearly forgotten about— remembering, with a jolt, when there was just a bare chance of getting there on time if I left immediately. A lesson, moreover, for which I had hardly practised and which I had already postponed once for that reason. In the dream I had recently resumed lessons after a lapse, but despite my best intentions I was not practising regularly, and this was not the first time

I would be showing up flagrantly unprepared. On top of it all I was late. How could I excuse myself? Would my teacher decide I was wasting his time? His response to my last return had been distinctly cool, his voice on the phone reserved; I felt he was taking me back on sufferance. His wife answered the door and seemed surprised to see me. She went into the next room to speak to him, then came back and told me I was mistaken—my lesson wasn't until this time next week. Relief flooded me: I had been granted a second chance. I wasn't late for my lesson after all; I hadn't utterly disgraced myself; I had a whole week to prepare now. At which point I woke up.

Only the fact that the house in the dream was no house my piano teacher ever lived in tells me that this was a dream. The rest is all too true to life: my ambivalence, my fits and starts, the angst and self-disgust that went with them. I loved the piano. I wanted the lessons badly. But I had too many other irons in the fire to apply myself consistently.

At this distance in time, dream and memory have run together and it seems to me that in real life I did not seize that second chance: I never showed up for the next lesson. What I did around this time, along with my young first husband, was to pack my life into storage and head for the West Coast on a one-way ticket. The piano we had been boarding for a friend passed into another friend's keeping. We assigned the lease on our flat, distributed furniture here and there on long-term loan, shipped a trunk of books and a manual typewriter to await us in Vancouver, and got on the train with nothing but knapsacks. My plans, which included writing a book, were open-ended. I must have told my teacher I was leaving, though I probably put off telling him for as long as I could. We must have said goodbye. There must have been a last lesson, either before or after I told him. I have no recollection of it.

The persistence of the dream, though—the way it kept coming back to me—tells me I must all along have felt there was some unfinished business in my life attached to the piano. And the tenor of the dream was not unhopeful: it left a door open. It was not an ending, as it threatened to be, but a deferment.

※

A deferment of what, exactly? I had never performed or aspired to perform on piano: there were no failed ambitions to address. Though I was playing repertoire considered advanced when I stopped studying, I never thought of myself as a pianist. When the piano came back into my life—that is, when after five years without an instrument, I suddenly had one under my roof again—it came as a gift from my parents, with my children in mind. It didn't occur to me to take lessons again myself. I was nearly thirty; who took piano lessons at thirty? It was enough to sit down for a few minutes after supper, while the kids wound down towards bedtime, and see what my fingers might have retained of my repertoire, trying one old favourite or another from memory until I got stuck and had to dig up the score. That I could remember as much as I did was gratifying, but I was lazy about relearning passages I'd forgotten—generally ones I'd been lazy about getting down solidly in the first place. There wasn't a piece that didn't have at least one black hole in it—a spot where I was bound to trip up, usually past hope of recovery.

Still, playing was pleasurable. I didn't get much chance to do it uninterrupted. Weeks might go by when I didn't play at all because of family or work pressures, or because the piano had gone off pitch and I couldn't afford another tuning so soon. When I was off teaching, I played quite a lot, reviving repertoire in rotation: a summer of Bach preludes and fugues; a summer of Chopin mazurkas; a summer on a full Beethoven sonata—a few years later I would have to learn them all over again. For a long time I played only music I had played before, mistrusting my ability to approach a new piece without guidance. When I did, it was always with the feeling I was getting away with something: maybe I could learn all the notes, even achieve some fluency, but surely I must be missing something essential?

Well, yes. I was missing my teacher. But did I need his permission to learn a new piece? Had I not, over the years of study, internalized enough to carry on by myself—trusting his voice in my head, remembered watchwords, positions, and movements; trusting the acute awareness of touch and its relation to sound he had cultivated in me, that activated itself the instant I sat down at the keyboard? So I argued with myself when, from time to time, nostalgia for piano lessons washed over me. *Time to grow up, kiddo. It's not as though you were one of those people who always dreamed of playing an instrument but never had the chance as a kid, or who took lessons for two or three years and then quit, to regret it later. You had close to ten years of lessons with a master teacher. If at your stage you need a teacher to start you on a new piece of music, there will be no end of needing a teacher.* Besides—where was my teacher? I couldn't imagine studying piano with anyone else, but even if I had seriously wanted to return, it didn't seem an option. The years were taking me farther and farther from a plausible point of re-entry. If at thirty it had already felt too late, what was I to tell myself at thirty-eight? at forty-five?

Still the thought kept returning: I had let something precious slip away; something wasn't finished. If I had not decided at fifteen to make clarinet my primary instrument, what might I have achieved on piano? There were moments when I knew I was playing well. Sometimes, in a moment of disillusionment with the literary world and arrant musical bravado, I'd joke that I might just pack it in as a writer, go back to studying piano, and hit the concert stage for a few years. The older I got, the sillier it sounded, yet underneath I couldn't help wondering how far I might get if I were in a position to throw everything else over and make the piano my primary focus. Could I make up for lost time? Could I cross over into another life—one I had prepared for but abandoned before I began to live it? Ah, but that preparation was on another instrument. And I had struggled with performance issues: bad nerves, memory lapses, a discomfort with the spotlight—almost never did I play my best under pressure. If at twenty-three I could not perform on clarinet to my satisfaction, what hope of emerging as a middle-aged Jill-come-lately on piano? I would be lucky to get replacement gigs accompanying children's ballet classes.

It wasn't the performing I missed about the life, but the preparation. It was the singleness of purpose, the clarity of focus, the long hours of absorption in practice. The simplicity of waking up every day knowing exactly what I had to do: having a score in front of me, instead of the blank page or blank screen that faces a writer; having a schedule of practice, lessons, and rehearsals to give structure to my week, instead of random sessions shadowboxing with the Muse. Not least, it was having a teacher—by turns a guide, a coach, a guru—and not being alone with the work, the way a writer is alone with the work. There were times, especially when I felt blocked in my writing, when those early years in music felt like a paradise lost. Why did it seem one couldn't have these things unless the goal was performance? But it did seem that way. They went together. The daily life of a serious musician was preparation for performance.

%

In the years after my children moved out on their own, I found myself playing a fair amount of piano for somebody who wasn't a pianist. Progress remained Sisyphean as other commitments took me away from the keyboard for days or weeks at a time, but something was changing. I had begun to make demands on myself. I wanted to be able to get through pieces without stopping. I wanted to clean up the black holes in my repertoire—nail down the notes in passages I'd never properly learned; see if I could figure out what was hanging me up in spots where I chronically derailed. I wanted to work up a few pieces to a level where I could perform them reliably from beginning to end, at least for family or friends. The music itself seemed to be demanding this. The better I played, the more it wanted to be shared.

Gradually, thoughts about "what might have been" shifted to thoughts about what might still be. Thoughts coalesced into an idea: maybe I could devote some time—a year, say—to studying piano intensively, with the goal of playing a small recital on my sixtieth birthday. And then write a book about it. Rumour had it my old teacher was still around: I had heard of sightings at the university where he was professor emeritus, engaged in continuing research. If I approached him with the project, might he be willing to help me prepare? Even just to lend me his ears from time to time? Suddenly this seemed, quite simply, to be what I was supposed to do next. To pick up where I had left off with the piano and take it to its logical conclusion: a performance. To set myself that challenge and give myself that gift—the gift of one year. A time-limited commitment. If the goal was a performance, I could be allowed to have lessons again. If it was in the interests of writing a book, I could justify the expense to myself, the hours spent at the instrument. I would have an excuse. Why I thought I needed one is an interesting question.

The idea quickly became The Idea, the thing in my life I was most excited about. It was there, irradiating the very air when I woke in the morning. Sometimes it was more like "the *idea!*" (do I mean this? or is it just some manic fantasy, the caprice of an aging woman?) But already it was moving from idea to intention. I had the piano tuned. I cleaned out the piano bench, sorting my classical sheet music from my son's jazz charts. I took stock of my repertoire, making lists: current, lapsed, "kept up," learned on my own, never finished learning. What if my teacher wasn't available, or wasn't interested? I'd done the math: he must be at least eighty. Even if he was in good health, he could be excused for not wanting to oversee the possibly hare-brained project of a long-lapsed former pupil, herself hurtling towards sixty. But already I was thinking if I had to, I could find another teacher—The Idea didn't depend on him. His web page at the university listed contact information, but the page was ten years old. I procrastinated for a week, then dialed his extension; it accessed an active voicemail box. The recorded greeting was his voice. I listened, froze, and hung up; decided to email instead.

When my teacher phoned a week later, the strangest thing about hearing his voice again was hearing his voice again— live, this time, on the other end of the line. He sounded as he always had—as if I'd been away for a month, rather than thirty-five years. Could it be that all this time he was only a phone call away? Then why did I feel, all those years, as if he existed only in my head—or as if he were on the other side of a wall—in a different dimension, or a different world?

Slowly it dawned on me that *I* was the wall.

Fugue: Finding Middle C

My first piano was a toy. A grand piano in miniature, painted red, it could sit on the floor or on a table, and it had more than two chromatic octaves with real black keys. Other kids had toy pianos whose "black keys" were just painted onto the white ones; if you tried to pick out a tune by ear, there were notes that, mystifyingly, weren't to be found. I don't remember how soon I started picking out one-finger tunes on that little piano, but I remember vividly the thin yet echoey resonance of a struck note, the loose lightness and faint clicking of the key action. When I began coming home from kindergarten and picking my way through each new song we learned in class, my mother decided we should get a real piano and lessons for me.

On the installment plan, she purchased a brand new (circa 1950) Mason & Risch apartment-style upright in a light wood finish. I don't remember huge excitement on my part about the acquisition. I remember her showing me how many more keys I now had at my disposal: on this piano I would never run out of notes for the tunes I taught myself by ear, as sometimes happened on the little red piano. Then, reading from a dog-eared album of *Everybody's Favourite Piano Pieces,* she played me some tunes of her own, resurrected from lessons she'd had as an adolescent: Für Elise, Blue Danube, Volga Boat Man.

Much as I admired what my mother could do at this giant keyboard, I preferred my toy piano, which I could transport from room to room and play sitting on the floor. Having to leave my child-domain for a high bench in the living room posed a barrier to my bonding with the new instrument, which was more a piece of furniture than a toy, and which wasn't only mine. It belonged to the house; it was something that had come to live with us, a presence. Every morning my grandmother dusted the keys with a soft flannel dampened in vinegar solution—first from treble to bass, *pleek! plink, plink, plink, plank, plank, plonk,* PLUNK, PLUNK, **THUNK, THRUNK, THUD!**— and then back again, **THUD!** THRUNK, THUNK, PLUNK, PLUNK, *plonk, plank, plank, plink, plink, plink, pleek!* After my mother remarried, we were to move house four times with that piano, changing cities once. Three out of five children had their crack at lessons.

The Mason & Risch came to live with me again when I was twenty-nine, pregnant with my own second child; my parents shipped it from Ottawa. For an apartment-style upright, it isn't a bad instrument; it has a sweet tone and an even action. It is still my piano today.

Around the time I began regular lessons, a professional photographer came to the house to do portraits of my brother and me. I still have the two he made of me: one standing demurely by the piano, the other seated, serenely playing—or

so it appears. Asked to play, I launched into a piece I was learning from Couperin's *First Lessons* but kept faltering and starting over. My expression of tense concentration as I craned at
the music didn't suit the photographer, who finally told me to
rest my hands on any old keys and just pretend I was playing.
The photos were duly framed and displayed on the mantel, but
I bore a long grudge against the second one, knowing it for a
lie. Still, there is the Mason & Risch, pristine, and there am I,
a rabbit-toothed eight-year-old in the nearly outgrown party
dress my grandmother made for my seventh birthday. The
beginning of a long relationship is captured there.

%

My arts education began early and inauspiciously. Old Mrs.
Silverman gave me my first taste of piano instruction at five.
She lived, conveniently, in the duplex below ours, mother-in-
law to the younger Mrs. Silverman, our landlady. Old Mrs.
Silverman had white hair in a bun and glasses on a chain. She
gave group lessons to neighbourhood children after school,
four or five girls of kindergarten age. We sat in a semicircle on
the carpet and waited our turn to be called up to the piano. In
the meantime, we each had a lesson sheet with a picture of the
keyboard to colour with crayons. Musical "notation" on these
sheets was in the form of colour-coded dots corresponding to
piano keys. Middle C was a pink dot, D was a green dot, E was
a yellow dot—each dot had an arrow pointing to a key we were
to colour accordingly. I felt cheated. I knew, from having seen
my mother's piano books, this was not how music was written.
I wanted to read real notes. And I wanted to play the way my
mother did—not just a one-finger tune, but what I thought of
as real music, a mysterious business that I knew entailed playing with both hands.

One by one we took our turn on the bench beside Old Mrs.
Silverman and placed our right thumb on middle C, which we

were taught to locate for ourselves on the keyboard. The other fingers were to be placed on adjacent keys, one to a key, with our left hand, for now, *non grata*. Then we were expected to "read" a row of coloured dots and strike the corresponding key for each, using the appropriate finger. This did not translate into anything that sounded like music, and I didn't see how it could lead to playing with both hands. I had no patience for sitting cross-legged on the carpet, staring out the Silvermans' big front window at the waning afternoon while one child after another, with much starting and stopping, plunked out her few notes. Nor did my few minutes at the keyboard seem worth the wait. Despite my facility playing by ear, I was no better than the other girls at hitting the right notes with the right fingers, and before I could try again, my turn was up. I don't think I lasted more than a few weeks at this sorry exercise. My mother's next move was to find me a private teacher who would come to our home.

Mr. Emenitov lasted hardly longer. He had been my mother's own piano teacher in adolescence. (I was intrigued to come across his name in a biography of Montreal poet A.M. Klein; he seems to have been the piano teacher of choice for children of local immigrant Jews.) I remember him as a smallish, rumpled man with uncombed hair, stained fingers, and musty breath; he was missing most of his teeth. His dark jacket was too large and hung askew.

Emenitov came with prizes in his pockets—trinkets that would be mine to keep if I performed well at my lesson. I remember one in particular, a pair of miniature ballerinas with magnets inside. Set at the end of the keyboard, they twirled magically when moved near each other. There they sat while I tried to do whatever it was Emenitov was trying to get me to do; if I did it right, I would get to see them dance again. But if I made a mistake, or if my fingers lost their prescribed arch, he might tap the back of my hand with a little ruler—not hard, just a reminder. Still, it was an affront. At the end of the lesson he pocketed the ballerinas; perhaps, he said encouragingly, I would earn them next time. I smelled a rat.

My mother didn't approve of the little ruler and told Emenitov not to use it. But I was significantly unexcited about "next time" and soon gave her to know I didn't want to take piano lessons anymore. Concluding that I might be too young for formal instruction, or that Emenitov was not the right teacher for me, she put my musical education on hold.

Today my mother doesn't remember the ruler. She started her own lessons with Emenitov at fourteen, and her recollection of his teaching is only that he was, in her words, "overly intense"—she imitated how he would lean close and suck his breath in sharply and noisily as she approached a difficult passage, then hold it until she was in the clear. She also told me a story that went around about him. According to it, he came from an upper-class family in Russia, and when he was a child, the Bolsheviks came to the door, dragged the family out of the house, and shot both parents before his eyes. It leaves me with a different feeling about the slightly dishevelled Russian Jew who went from home to home in Montreal during the 1940s and '50s, teaching children to play piano. An internet search brought up only one reference to Vladimir Emenitov: he was an early teacher of the Canadian composer Samuel Dolin.

Since piano hadn't worked out, my mother signed me up for ballet, for which I had zero aptitude and which I disliked because of the bother of having to change clothes (I was also disappointed in the costume, a crinkly black leotard with tights that sagged—nothing like the floaty dresses of picture-book ballerinas). The next semester she tried me in drama, where kids sat on the floor with eyes closed while the teacher asked us to imagine we were turning into a rain cloud, or a tree, or an elephant. Then we had to open our eyes, stand up, and "be" that thing. I had no idea how to effect such a transformation, and mostly stood like a lump, watching other kids make vague gestures with their arms and bodies. They looked like kids twirling and weaving their arms around—nothing like rain clouds or trees or elephants—which seemed to vindicate my refusal to attempt the thing at all. When I showed no enthusiasm for going back to drama the following year, my mother, determined that I do some after-school activity, suggested piano lessons with a different teacher. I brightened at the suggestion. Learning piano felt like a new idea, a not unwelcome one. So it was that at the age of eight I began lessons with my first "real" teacher, the one who taught me to play with both hands.

%

Lorna T. was a school friend of my mother's who had studied at the Quebec Conservatoire. I took the bus by myself to her sunny lower duplex a few blocks away. Her little daughter played with toys in the adjacent den while I had my lesson. A tall, thin, nervous woman, Lorna wore glasses with lenses so thick they looked like slabs of ice. What I got from her over the next three years was a solid, conservative grounding in classical piano, tailored to a child, but with a minimum of talking down. Once again, we began by locating middle C—this time placing both thumbs on that key, positioning the hands so the knuckles weren't flat: "Make a little house with your hand. Or pretend you're holding an apple." We worked our way selectively through a standard primer, Couperin's *First Lessons for the Pianoforte* (it was news to me that the word *piano* was short for this Italian coinage meaning "soft-loud"). A classic, still in print today, it introduced new concepts systematically and arrived at "playing with both hands" mercifully early. There was a second book called *Finger Tricks: Technic at the Piano* (sic), which I disliked because the pieces had babyish titles like "Hippity Hop," "Pitter Patter," and "Busy Bee." But we hardly used this before moving on to *First Lessons in Bach*, the beginning of my collection of Schirmer's editions with their trademark yellow covers and ornate dark borders.

With Lorna I did the standard things. I counted out loud, reluctant and self-conscious, when told to do so (embarrassed because I found it impossible to count and play simultaneously without *singing* the count.) I learned my pieces "hands separately," then "hands together." I learned scales and arpeggios. I sat down after school to practise a prescribed half-hour, not always happily, and not always lasting the full half-hour. But I was content to stay with the lessons until Lorna gave up teaching when her second child was born.

Who can say why certain moments catch in memory's sieve while the rest slide by like water? Of the three-year period I studied with Lorna, only three specific instances have stayed with me. Interestingly, the first had to do with music as emotional expression, the second with music as performance, and the third with music as science.

The first moment came not long after I began lessons. I was practising at home, struggling with a new "both hands" piece called Parade of the Elephants and ready to abandon ship, but the clock on top of the piano said my half-hour wasn't even half over. When my mother insisted I persevere a little longer, I vented frustration by launching back into it angrily, banging out the notes and no longer even trying to get the right ones. It was aimed at showing her I couldn't play this piece, it was too hard, and if she wanted me to keep trying, she was going to suffer (*smash, smash*)—but then something happened. The loudness and the anger somehow fused. My fingers were finding the right notes as if of their own accord, there was a resonance coming up from the keys into my fingers, and the pounding rhythm of the descending four-note figure, repeated bar after bar in the bass, seemed to vibrate through my whole body. Here came the elephants! It was as if I could feel their tread shaking the floor.

I remember playing the piece over and over, no longer banging but very robustly, impressed at the power of my anger to animate the music, and the power of the music to absorb my anger and transform it into something that felt wonderful. I think of this moment as my musical birth. I had so far forgotten my initial motive that when my mother appeared in the doorway and remarked, "The piano sounds beautiful, I've never heard you play like that before," it didn't even bother me that my fit of pique had backfired. I knew she was right.

Around a year later came a less happy *moment musical*. I was in fourth grade when our local public school decided to hold an across-the-grades talent show. It wouldn't have occurred to me to volunteer, but my mother and Lorna thought I should play a piano piece, the familiar G major Minuet from Bach's Anna Magdalena Notebook, which I could by then play practically with my eyes closed. My classroom teacher was enthusiastic. Not many children in our school were learning musical instruments: most of the acts were songs, recitations, skits, or acrobatics. Looking back on it, I wonder at Lorna for encouraging this step. Was it mostly my mother's idea? I was an introverted, hypersensitive, perfectionistic nine-year-old, and to my memory, nothing was done to prepare me for playing in public—not a hint that it might feel different from playing at home or at my lesson; no instruction on what to do if I made a mistake or lost my place. It was taken for granted I would simply get up on stage and play the little minuet, a piece I had played by heart hundreds of times. Perhaps Lorna didn't want to set me up for nervousness by warning me that anything could go amiss.

Walking up the middle aisle when called—past the rows of parents expectant in their chairs on one side, the junior grades seated with their teachers on the other—I felt alone, exposed, strange. The piano, a full-sized upright in dark wood, looked foreign and forbidding (a Pianoforte?) and the round stool felt wobbly. Happily the keyboard was familiar. I began the minuet. My fingers moved automatically, but I felt curiously disconnected from them. As I approached the cadence at the end of the first section, I tripped over a note—something minor; it did not stop me from concluding the section. But a couple of bars into the next, inexplicably, my left hand forgot where it was supposed to go. I faltered, stricken, and began the section again while the teacher serving as emcee hovered, making encouraging noises: once, twice, three times—but it was no use. Bewilderingly, each time, I got stuck in the same place. "I can't," I said finally, on the edge of tears, and was reprieved—allowed to abort my act and return to my seat in the audience.

The talent show continued. To humiliate me further, a girl in fifth grade got up soon after and played a piece on the piano without mishap, curtseying to applause. That was what was supposed to happen! I could do that too! Why hadn't I done it? And how would anybody know I could do it if I hadn't done it? I've sometimes wondered whether this first experience of musical performance set the stage for me, literally, for all future performances. Did it create an association between performance and failure, leaving me vulnerable from day one to the knowledge that my hands and my memory could betray me, the fear that they would?

The third memory is of a discovery I made one day before my lesson while I waited for Lorna to put in a load of laundry. I had noticed I could play one of my pieces, a little melody in C major, beginning five notes higher, but it required that I use one black key. Then I discovered I could repeat the trick beginning five notes higher again. Continuing the process (eventually, of course, I had to skip down to a lower octave), I found that with each new starting note, I had to use more and more black keys, until the starting note itself was a black key. Just as I was beginning to feel I'd entered a pathless wood, the process slowly reversed itself, requiring fewer and fewer black keys, until—as I had begun to anticipate—"five notes higher" brought me back to the key of C, where I could again play the melody on white keys only.

When I looked up, Lorna was standing quietly in the doorway watching me. "You've found the circle of fifths. Good for you!" I was not to hear the term again until music theory class in high school, when instead of the mysterious and intriguing phenomenon I'd chanced upon, it referred to a sequence of major and minor keys, and a fixed order of sharps and flats— just one more set of things to memorize for an exam.

※

Where things would have gone had Lorna continued to teach me, I cannot guess. But it is thanks to Lorna that I went next to a teacher who was to be a profound influence on me, not only musically but as a life mentor. When she decided to stop teaching, she gave my mother the names of two well-regarded piano teachers who might take up where she had left off. One was a local organist. The second was Philip Cohen, who, like herself, had been a student of Yvonne Hubert, and eventually Hubert's assistant at the Conservatoire—"but he's very busy these days, he might not be taking any new students." I don't think it would be an exaggeration to say that the rest of my life has been shaped by the fact that my mother dialed Philip Cohen first.

II   STARTING OVER

Prelude: Doing the Undramatic

THE MOMENTOUS PHONE CALL, WHEN IT CAME, TOOK me down to earth a bit. A conversation in the middle of the living room, with my husband and grown daughter attendant on it and a chicken roasting in the oven. Ambient noise, food smells wafting from the kitchen, broccoli turning to mush in the steamer—not the circumstances I had imagined for this signal exchange: my message in a bottle, tossed across thirty-five years of water under the bridge, had been picked up. On the other end of the phone, the man who had taught me piano from the age of eleven to seventeen, and again from twenty-one to twenty-four, was saying that the next two months were impossibly busy, but after that we could meet and talk, figure out what might be possible.

Could we really? Was it that simple? I was still awash in amazement at the miracle of hearing his voice again, the fact that he had responded at all. In my email, I had set out the project as I envisaged it: to spend a year bringing a few pieces to performance level, with the goal of playing a small recital and of writing a book about the process. I did not ask to take lessons again, since I had no idea if he was still teaching, but I wondered if he would be willing to meet with me now and then and lend his ears.

Now he was saying he didn't understand why I was fixated on the idea of performing, and especially with a deadline. Why would I not just start working again and see where it led? He said he occasionally did have older students make comebacks—he mentioned an eighty-year-old man from Texas returning to piano after thirty years, who actually did perform again—but he reminded me that playing the piano was like any art form, any creative process: "It can't be forced, it doesn't work by deadline."

I knew this. Hearing it spoken so matter-of-factly, I felt at once foolish and relieved. This was a teacher whose private pupils were spared the ordeal of an annual recital, who did not have them play standard exams unless their parents insisted on it. For years I had come to him weekly to make music for its own sake, with no goal but to explore all the ways of bringing out what was beautiful in a piano piece, what was sublime. He created a space in which this became the most important thing in the world, the *only* thing. At home, at the keyboard, I attempted daily to recreate that space. It was a process without end, a timeless unfolding.

Suddenly I was bursting with questions, things I'd never thought to ask back then and had wondered about since. Why were there days when the piano sounded wonderful and I just seemed to *know* what to do, and other days when my fingers were ornery and stupid, the sound dead, no matter what I tried? What was the magic at work on those "blessed" days? Was it something that could be accessed at will? And why was it that with too much repetition, a piece would not only stop improving but begin to fall apart, my fingers seeming to forget what they'd known, even to sabotage it of their own volition?

I ventured to ask only the last. He said he thought it had to do with boredom. "If you repeat something mindlessly, it becomes facile and automatic. Your fingers go somewhere else because they're bored. Working on a piece should be different all the time, trying different things, like the sketches of a creative artist—like the literally thousands of sketches found among Beethoven's papers, among Michelangelo's. Think of practising as sketching. Creative practice isn't playing the piece over and over, but playing with it. Isolating parts of it, playing it out of time on purpose, leaving out some of the voices, even playing it backwards ..."

When I put down the phone, The Idea had had some wind taken out of its sails but it seemed I had returned to my piano teacher. The "why" wasn't clear, but it didn't need to be.

٪

Two months. I had two months to get ready. In four weeks, my pianist friend Alan Fraser, an ex-pat now living and teaching in Novi Sad, Serbia, would be coming to Montreal. I had not seen Al in two decades, but we were back in touch thanks to my new project. I had emailed him about it, hoping he might still be in contact with Phil Cohen, who had taught him in university. Al thought it was a wonderful idea—"not only doable, but a must-do." He had not spoken to Phil for a few years but said there was no reason to believe he wasn't still at the university—"Just pick up the phone and call him!" So I'd have four weeks on my own, then some input from Al, and four more weeks to prepare before playing for the man my husband had taken to calling "Mr. Big." In the meantime, buoyed, I began spending more time at the keyboard.

A couple of days later, Phil Cohen called again: he knew a woman he thought could help me, someone he recommended highly. My heart sank. Did he mean *instead* of meeting with me in April, or *until*? Was he passing me on to some gorgeous young competition-winning doctoral graduate, beside whom I would feel geriatric and hopeless? He gave me to understand he was still willing to meet with me; he just thought I might want to get started sooner. I hesitated, then said I would keep her coordinates handy. Pamela Korman; I took down the number. But by the end of a week, my journal was recording second thoughts about the entire enterprise:

Our conversation was somehow frustrating—this is true of the last one, too. "It's not about that" is his response to anything I say about my struggles with inaccuracy: missed notes, wrong notes, fuzzed notes. To believe him, none of this matters, it's about the shape of a phrase, making it an aesthetic experience, it's about "getting something serious happening." And I both do and do not understand him. SOMETIMES *one has to come down to earth. He works from such a lofty, mystical place. That's what I loved in his teaching, but I wonder if it isn't also what messed me up? I could never sustain those heights. I could never please him, or myself, once I felt his standards. Didn't it seem as if I could never get anything right? And now I can't even* SAY *anything right. It felt as if we were talking past each other.*

Am I going to revert to a timorous KID, *if I go back to taking lessons? Already I feel that the fragile confidence I have built up over years of playing untutored is crumbling. When I said I've never properly finished anything, he said, "You can never finish anything— we* DON'T *finish pieces." Of course I know that—in the sense* HE *means it. But he seems not to know what* I *mean: that I never achieve real fluency, because I never tackle the last bugaboos.*

And have I become confirmed in bad, amateurish habits of thinking and practising? Too much mindless repetition? Aiming for a higher plateau for each piece, instead of an ongoing, ever-evolving experience? I think that's right. But he doesn't understand that I'm stuck in

my old, old problem with just basic continuity. AND I
WANT TO SOLVE IT.

*Only I'm not solving it. Since I've begun practising
again, it has gotten worse. My confidence is gone. My
simple happiness at the keyboard is gone. I didn't used
to have to think about what to do when I sat down at the
piano—I would just start playing something I felt like
playing. If it wasn't going well, I would call it a bad day
& go do other things; if it was sounding good, I might
work on a passage that needed cleaning up, maybe read
a bit of something new, relearn a bit of something old.
My practising was entirely intuitive and self-generating.
Now it has become complicated.*

*Well—do I or do I not trust my old teacher? If I do,
maybe I should call this woman.*

*I know part of what's hanging me up right now is
a reluctance to give up the autonomy, freedom, and
uncomplicated pleasures of being an amateur. But Phil
today pronounced the word "amateur" as though it
referred to a lower order of being—as opposed to "getting something serious going." I'm digging in my heels at
the thought of that seriousness, what I know it takes to be
on that path of "not finishing." Of never allowing oneself to be satisfied. Of every piece being forever an open
file. Of one's relation to the instrument being forever an
open file. Of going to a teacher not for validation but to
be challenged.*

Can one be HAPPY *without being satisfied?*

A few days later I dialed the number I had jotted down by
the telephone and set up a lesson with Pamela K.

%

"To be serious about a thing is to be willing to do the undramatic." Those words were spoken by the second great teacher I was blessed to have in my life: Professor David Hartman, an orthodox rabbi who taught in the philosophy department while I was at McGill. They came back to me powerfully as I became a piano student again.

Pamela's Steinway had a stiff action and a brighter sound than I generally like, besides being the first piano other than my own that I had played on in a long time. Disoriented by this and by the unaccustomed situation of playing for a stranger who was also a professional pianist, I hardly had to remind her, that first afternoon, of what my problems were. Launching nervously into the first movement of Beethoven's Pathétique Sonata, I proceeded to deliver what could have been a textbook illustration of the full range. The expected clinkers and notes that didn't sound were everywhere (not) to be heard—not only in anticipated trouble spots but in places that were normally solid and confident. Suddenly I wasn't sure how a phrase began; I'd come to a standstill, doubting, and then take a stab that turned out to be not even in the right key! My fingers did such inexplicably perverse things that I could only laugh in incredulity. It was worse when I tried the opening of Chopin's "Revolutionary" Étude, which I had decided I wanted to learn as my first new piece because it appeared to be the last thing my teacher assigned before I took off for the West Coast (his pencilled x at the bottom of the second page suggesting he wanted me to read to this point for the next lesson that never happened). I had no recollection of having done any work on the piece back then, with or without him, but had recently managed on my own to get two pages down at something less than half speed. But now, in front of Pamela, I derailed repeatedly before I was even off the ground, muffing the dramatic opening chords in the right hand—chords that should ring out like an alarm. It felt like a bad comedy act.

The things Pamela showed me that day were simple, practical, and helpful. Moreover, as I brought them home and began practising, they blossomed. It seemed I might now be able to learn at the piano in a way that I couldn't before. Suddenly I was able to see *solvable problems* where I used to see mysterious, bewildering impasses. And sometimes the solutions were mind-bogglingly simple: a change of fingering, a relinquishing of the idea that I must connect certain notes by holding them, when I could let go and leave it to the pedal. The reminders I wrote to sum up what I had learned at that first lesson were things so basic it was hard to believe I could have forgotten them—unless it was that I had never made them fully conscious before:

Piano technique should be based on FINDING WHAT WORKS *in a passage. What works for one person may not work for another, it depends on hand size and shape, body type, etc. Look for fingerings, positions, and movements that minimize tension and maximize economy of motion. Concentrate in different ways: now listening, now looking (to check your hand position, position on the keyboard, hand and arm movement), now feeling (the natural surges of the music, the tension-and-release as your body enacts them).*

To keep a freshness in performance, it's important to keep getting to know the music in new ways—hearing it better and understanding it better. Don't forget that the melody isn't the whole thing. Isolate different voices and play them individually so that you learn to hear moving lines, not just changing chords. Look at how the inner voices move, see and feel each one as a melodic line in its own right. Don't think "note by note"; look where each note in the line is moving to, where the phrase is leading.

A week later, my journal had this to say:

Second piano lesson. We worked mostly on the Pathétique first movement. On small sections. Pamela says, "Look! Make sure you know where you're going." And I think: How terrific! Why did I not know I was allowed to look at my hands? Or how did I forget?

She tells me Phil says even the smallest excerpt can be regarded as a piece of music. "Even a four-bar phrase has a beginning, a phrase arc, inner voices, an ending. We can practise trouble spots that way, thinking of them as whole pieces. We can try to make them beautiful."

I don't know how I ever stopped playing piano seriously. How I did not even know I missed it. (Did I know? I must have known.) The piano was my heart.

Fugue: The Bottom of the Key

"He sounds very nice. Such a soft-spoken man," said my mother as she put down the phone, conjuring in my mind a distinguished-looking gentleman, tall and grave, with wavy dark-blond hair and a small, neat mustache. Philip Cohen. I was dubious about having a new piano teacher. My mother was matter-of-fact. "We have an appointment to meet him on Thursday. If he thinks you're at the right level, you can start lessons with him this month."

The soft-spoken man looked not at all as I'd imagined. He was of average height and had black hair and glasses. His glance was darting, sidelong, and a bit sardonic. His shirt was open at the neck. In the front room of his first-floor flat which, like our own home, showed the wear and tear of young children, the three of us stood by the Knabe baby grand as he examined my eleven-year-old hands, turning them over and over in seeming fascination. "I won't say her hands were made for playing piano," he remarked to my mother, "because after all, nobody's were—but *hers* actually might have been."

A small boy in socks wandered into the room, retrieved a toy from beneath the piano, and wandered out again. Mr. Cohen took no notice. He asked me to play something for him, and I flipped open my Sonatina Album to the piece Lorna had suggested I prepare for this meeting. I played two movements of a Beethoven sonatina, rapidly and a little nervously. As I began the second movement, the Andante, he exclaimed, "Hold it— *hold* it! That's another movement. Don't rush into it—stop for a moment, relax!"

But he must have liked what he heard. He agreed to take me for a three-month trial; we could begin next week. I was to bring whatever music I'd been working on with Lorna, and— very important—a notebook and pencil, so I could keep a record of what we had done at each lesson and what I was to work on at home that week.

I arrived for my first lesson with the entire pile of piano books I'd accumulated in three years with Lorna. Couperin was in the pile; so was the embarrassing and seldom-used *Finger Tricks*. My new teacher flipped through the lot, setting aside one or two items of immediate interest. He said we could hold on to this and hold on to that for the time being; others I could put away, and when he came to *Finger Tricks*—"As for this," he remarked dryly, "you can take it home and wipe your *tukhes* with it, as they say in Greek." The sidelong sardonic look. (Was that a Greek word, too? I didn't *think* it was ...)

A piano lesson followed, unlike any I'd had before. Mr. Cohen never even opened a piano book. He neither asked to hear a scale or arpeggio, nor assigned one for me to learn. Instead, he guided me through a series of strange exercises that seemed more appropriate to swimming than playing the piano—exercises that involved my whole arm and slow, dreamy, fluid movements, like movements under water. He had me raise my arm above the keyboard to shoulder height, letting the hand dangle from a relaxed bent wrist; I was then to let this dangling hand fall slowly until my index finger touched the surface of a key, any key, and allow the finger to sink smoothly to the bottom of the keybed along with the key. To *sink into* the key rather than striking it—minimizing any sense of impact. When the note sounded, I was to maintain finger contact with the key but continue the downward movement of hand and arm, allowing the hand to drop down, the wrist to sink below the level of the keyboard as far as it could, until my relaxed hand was hanging from my fingertip. Then I was to reverse the movement, slowly bringing the hand back up, rolling forward on the fingertip and pushing gently up off the bottom of the key, letting my arm float back upward with bent wrist and hand again loosely dangling.

The upward movement reminded me of pushing off against the side of a swimming pool with my feet. It was as if the piano key was propelling my arm upward. When momentum ran out, I was to repeat the sequence, again letting my hand fall slowly, this time to land on a different key, with a different finger. It didn't matter what note I landed on. It didn't even matter if the note didn't sound, as long as the key was depressed—in fact, I could also try doing this silently. What mattered was to keep the movement smooth, fluid, and continuous, and to feel it was the piano that was guiding it. This was my week's assignment: to practise this exercise with both hands, separately and together, using different fingers.

"How did it go?" my mother wanted to know when I got home. "Is there a new piece he wants you to work on?" How to explain that I had spent the better part of an hour making swimming movements in air and playing random single notes? I can still see her face as she puzzled over Mr. Cohen's almost indecipherable scrawl in my little blue notebook: "Keep arm relaxed at all times as *piano plays you*," she read aloud, mystified. "As piano plays *you*?" She laughed. "What does he mean? Is that what it really says?" I nodded. I felt defensive of my new teacher. I knew what he meant, even if it sounded funny.

I knew there was a purpose to it all; already, on some level, I even understood the purpose. It was there in the movement itself and in the sensations it activated. There weren't words for it, but "as piano plays you" came close.

※

And here I must digress to say a little about this teacher into whose hands I had fortuitously fallen. At the time I came to him, in 1960, he was studying physiology and neuropsychology in the interests of how they might be applied to piano pedagogy. Eclectic, he was versed in Eastern philosophy and mysticism—this before they were popularized in the West. A father of three boys, the oldest seven, the youngest around two, he was facing one of the hardest passages life can deal a parent: the previous year his middle son, then four, had been diagnosed with terminal leukemia. Mr. Cohen had taken leave from a university post to be home with the boy, who confounded the doctors by living another two years—twice the initial prognosis. (A round-faced sprite with dark curly hair and lively eyes, Gordie was a sociable and gifted child who liked to run into the front room between lessons, scramble up on the piano stool, and attempt by ear a few phrases of whatever he had just heard being played. Once, while I was waiting my turn in the small study adjacent, Gordie came in and asked if I would like him to read me a Greek myth. I assented, expecting he would "read" from a favourite picture book as my littlest siblings liked to do, turning the pages and using the illustrations to cue them as they recited words they knew by heart. Gordie climbed on a chair and took a book of Greek mythology down from the shelf—not a children's book at all— and to my astonishment, opened it and began to read fluently aloud in a perfectly inflected, happily animated voice.)

How much I appreciated of my teacher's situation at the time I don't recall, but it wasn't hidden from me. Mr. Cohen made no secret of it, talking to my mother about Gordie in front of me in a matter-of-fact voice. Privately she told me a little about leukemia, and I wondered how a child could have such a terrible illness but be up and about the house, not visibly sick. Other words new to me came up in connection: at one point a blue mat appeared in the study and I remember Mr. Cohen telling me he and Gordie were learning yoga together, special exercises to counteract stiffness caused by a drug, cortisone, that the little boy had to take.

Gordie Cohen died before he was seven. My mother took me to the funeral, the first funeral I ever attended—a child's funeral, in December. It was snowing that day, a thick wet snow. Outside the funeral parlour, Mr. Cohen's wife was weeping. My teacher stood with his arm around her, paternal, protective, even while stilled by grief. He radiated strength and calm, but his head was down. For years that pose, that gesture, so full of humility yet so abounding in human dignity, remained with me. I was twelve.

※

It was around all this, a private drama I had only glimpses of, that the next stage of my musical education began, on Saturday afternoons in the little dark flat on Mountain Sights. The shadowy front room with its glass-paned door; white curtains always drawn on the window giving on the street; wine-red carpet with threadbare spots; floor lamp beside the piano. The baby grand pretty much filled the room; the walls were bare except for a curious trio of bas-reliefs on the wall above the piano. In soapstone or some similar medium, they depicted in tones of dark grey and white a simpering ponytailed teenage girl with a pet dachshund—a mystifying (in context) piece of kitsch that I recognized as such, though I didn't know there was a word for it. At this little triptych, for reasons unknown, I used to stare while my teacher saw his previous pupil to the door; and if during the lesson tears welled in my eyes because it seemed to me he was asking the impossible, I would fix on it until I regained enough composure to try the passage again. Once, when he caught me looking at it, he remarked, deadpan, "Isn't that something? A real work of art, don't you think?" I sensed irony. But if he didn't think it was art, why had he put it on the wall? As a private joke? So as not to offend the giver, if it was a gift? Could he be serious? I could never tell, at times like this. To be safe, I'd keep my counsel but give him a cautious half-smile—smile in case he was joking, half in case he was not. I don't know what he made of this half-smile, which was possibly as enigmatic to him as such remarks of his were to me.

In the same anteroom where Gordie read to me from the Greek myths, Mr. Cohen introduced me to Chinese poetry in English free-verse translation, putting the book into my hands before going back to the pupil he was teaching. A lesson could go a whole hour overtime, and often did. Always if it was to be a long wait, he'd put a book in my hands—anything from *New World Short Stories* to *Teachings of Lao-Tse* to *Impossible: Yet It Happened!* (a pocket paperback whose title he intoned theatrically, with a droll glance as he handed it to me). The Chinese poems were a revelation; my own next poems were unrhymed imitations of them, a leap forward from the formulaic, conventional rhyming stanzas I had been writing.

At the start of a lesson Mr. Cohen often had other things to toss at me—a drawing by one of his kids; a curious fact (did I know that in Zen archery, one practises holding and drawing the bow, with proper breathing, for months or years before releasing an arrow?); a maxim ("You know what the Chinese say? A mistake is a danger—and an opportunity"). Once, it was a cartoon from *Saturday Review*: a man inside a cube-shaped frame with three open sides. The fourth side was also open, but it had two closely spaced vertical bars in the middle. The man had chosen to stand in front of these, gripping a bar in each hand and staring mournfully out between them. The message—that we make cages for ourselves where no cage is—was not lost on me; over the years, in a variety of forms, it was one my teacher would give me again and again. It showed up early on in a little story of two men who had each tried three times to perform a task: "The first man said, 'I'm a failure.' The second one said, 'I failed three times.'"

Sometimes it took the form of a practical suggestion. At times when I was discouraged and resistant to practising, he had a revolutionary prescription: "Don't tell yourself you have to practise for an hour, or that you have to hammer away at a thing until you get it. Put a clock on the piano, set the alarm to ring in ten minutes, and tell yourself you'll work on it just until the alarm rings." Why was this transformative? It freed something in me. By the time the alarm rang, I had become involved and didn't want to stop. "When we sit down at the piano," he used to say, "we should begin by saying *I know nothing*. What we *think* we know is a trap."

I cannot forget the lesson when he wouldn't let me cry. For once he remained unmoved, would not allow me to give in to my own defeatism; no reprieve that day, no gentle turning to a different page for the rest of the lesson. Again and again his quiet, even voice told me to play the passage that had reduced me to tears—to play it from beginning to end, badly or not— while I shook with silent sobs. Finally he said it was enough. Still his face showed no sympathy, only steel-nerved patience. I wasn't yet thirteen, but I knew that he was struggling, that his impassivity was costing a lot. As I walked up Mountain Sights afterwards, still smarting inwardly, I understood the lesson was a watershed. He meant for me to take charge of my own emotions, not let them rule the day. I knew he had behaved as he had for my sake.

%

In the year after Gordie died, a new baby girl was born to the Cohens and the family moved to an apartment building on Queen Mary Road, a few blocks away. (At the last lesson in the old flat, I heard the girl before me asking Mr. Cohen what they were going to name the baby. I *thought* I could detect a jesting undertone, but couldn't be entirely sure, when he replied, "We were thinking of Hortense. Isn't that a nice name?"—the question as apparently innocent as "Don't you think it's a great work of art?" To my relief they named the child Glennis.)

The new apartment in the Chantilly had no anteroom. The apartment door opened into an entrance hall directly facing the arched doorway of the living room that served again as piano studio. One waited for one's lesson at a telephone table in the hall, very much party to the lesson in progress as well as to comings and goings—Warren, the oldest boy, arriving with schoolbag on his back; his mother coming home laden with groceries. In the studio, the red rug was gone, replaced by a piece of tweedy broadloom. I recall books lined up on the floor along the wall for months (years?) awaiting shelving that failed to materialize. Things that were important in other houses seemed not to be important here. The hall had carpet padding (for soundproofing, perhaps?) but no carpet. Magazines fell down behind the radiator and stayed there, poking out at the bottom, for weeks. On the telephone table, mail piled up unopened. One day I arrived to find a bead curtain hanging in the studio's open arch—a token gesture towards privacy? Mr. Cohen parted the strands and mock-bowed to me: "Welcome to my den of iniquity."

Years of lessons in that room. For a long time my lesson was at nine on Saturday mornings, first pupil of the day, my teacher sometimes still in pyjamas when I arrived. He would come into the room in haste, buttoning his shirt. Mrs. Cohen kept herself in the background, had a smile and a "hello" for the pupil but nothing more. One would catch glimpses of her in the dim hallway, gathering laundry from room to room or bending slowly to pick up a toy from the floor. Sometimes she would come into the studio with a glass of water for her husband, or set a plate of toast and jam and a cup of coffee down on the piano top. Little Dougie, in sleepers, wandered in and out of the room, and unless he was noisy, Mr. Cohen took no notice. If his wife was out on errands or teaching (she was a singer) he sometimes taught my lesson with the baby on his shoulder, unfazed if from time to time she burped a cheesy waterfall down the back of his shirt. Neither was I fazed; we had babies at home.

Money embarrassed him. Once a month I brought a cheque, carried them sticking out of a piano book so I would remember to give them to him. He would spot the green piece of paper and say, in a tone of feigned innocence, "What's this?"

"That's for you," I would reply, at which he would thank me and extract it, but almost invariably allow it to slip through his fingers and flutter to the floor. I would get down on my hands and knees under the piano to retrieve it, then say, "Where should I put it?"

"Oh, anywhere!" and he'd take it himself and put it down absently on the piano-top. Sometimes during the lesson the turning of a page would send it flying again.

If he was delayed by breakfast or a phone call, he would call to me from somewhere in the mysterious Rest-of-the-House, "Robyn, why don't you play some exercises?" But somehow, alone in the living room—or, oftener, with Dougie standing by the piano watching me curiously—I was constrained. After a half-hearted stab at Pischna I'd lapse back into daydream, communing with the soapstone girl until he came in hurriedly and switched the lamp on, talking in his quiet, matter-of-fact, confidential manner—"*Sorry*. I have to knock off early today, too—there's someone I have to see at eleven. Okay. What were we working on last week?"

Each lesson began with the ordeal of having to play something through for him; each time, I got off to a shaky start and things went downhill from there. How hard it always was to

launch, cold, into the piece or movement I'd worked on all
week—or neglected to work on; it seemed to make no difference. Always there were false starts, falterings, my tone thin
and pinched, no warmth or roundness to it. If only he would
let me start over! I could give so much better an account of
myself on second try!—but no, it was always, "Continue!
Keep going!" until I made it to the end or (more usually)
foundered somewhere. "All right," he'd say quietly, and there
would be a moment's silence during which—defiant, humili-
ated, defeated—I'd glare through barely contained tears at the
simpering soapstone girl.

"Really, that wasn't bad," Mr. Cohen would say then, in
what I learned to recognize as a ritual courtesy before his let's-
get-cracking signal: "*However ...*" I'd begin to smile inwardly
in anticipation of that word, even knowing what was in store:
seeing my fragile edifice tumble down under the wrecking ball
of his observations.

But then we'd rebuild. I would play again while he watched
and listened, patient, serious, attentive; soon he'd stop me
with the words, "Okay. Here's the bit," and there would be
some new principle to grasp—a new way to move, a new way to
hear the rhythm of a certain phrase or the character of a phrase
ending. It might take a dozen tries for me to approximate what
he was demonstrating, but suddenly something would click,
it would feel *right*, and he'd dart me a triumphant look just
as I shot him a questioning one. Our swift exchange of smiles
confirmed what I already knew as he spoke the magic words:
"You've got it."

I was hooked on this magic that happened at lessons. It
had nothing to do with getting the right notes. It had to do
with some mysterious shift—a turning point when movement,
touch, and sound fused into one, and the sounds coming from
the piano synchronized perfectly with what I was hearing in my
head and wanted to hear. That simultaneous flash glance we'd
exchange was proof that what had happened here was real, that

my teacher had heard it too. This was where he had been leading me—to this moment of lift, this quickening. Test: could I
repeat the effect?—and yes, I could. "That's it. You've got it."

At home I had to go straight to the piano to try it again.
What if this only worked on Mr. Cohen's baby grand? But it
worked on my piano too. I could repeat it the next day, and the
next. Yet as the week wore on, it seemed to fade—first becoming a pale imitation of itself, and then something I'd try to
talk myself into believing I could still hear, when in fact I had
reverted to the way I used to play the passage, when the notes
were just the notes. At the next lesson it was like starting from
scratch again, though we'd get to it faster. But whatever it was
I'd suddenly been able to do, it seemed I couldn't maintain it
without follow-up and reinforcement.

So a lesson would progress, with tears, laughs, efforts,
interruptions, glasses of water, digressions, repetitions—till
it ended, always with the same abrupt words, sometimes following an allusion to having to "knock off" but oftenest out
of nowhere, accompanied by the gesture of closing my piano
books: "All right, it's coming along. And now—scram, kiddo!"
At first this alarmed me. I would think I had angered him, and
hastily gathering my belongings, would scurry out of the room,
dropping items on the way. At the door his wife would give me
her kind smile, with an undertone of amusement at my taking
the brusque dismissal so to heart.

％

Why is it that a good music teacher, in formative years, so
often becomes more than a music teacher: a life mentor, a role
model, an artistic parent-figure? During these years, musical
substance comes entwined with a broader kind of influence, not
just cultural but *integral*, a fusion of intellectual, emotional,
and spiritual discovery. While I vividly remember the music I
worked on during this period, in retrospect something larger

was going on for me between the ages of eleven and seventeen in the form of exposure to a unique personality. Almost unconsciously I absorbed Mr. Cohen's aesthetic sensibility, beliefs, and attitudes; the ambience he created at lessons became my musical abode and the cradle for an evolving sense of self.

How to separate the music from my teacher's warmth, intensity, insight, and humour? Insights I carried home like touchstones; crazy humour that could make me laugh aloud weeks later, on a bus, suddenly recalling something he said or a face he made. Yet beneath it, always, a seriousness, a deep humility that was in no way passive but came paired with a stance of unflagging engagement. What I learned with him at the keyboard was transferable to so many other areas of my life, both then and later. It had to do with purity of intent, with work as its own reward, detached from ideas of gain or acclaim. It was about the giving-over of self to the task at hand without doubting its importance. I remember him once saying, "If I ever start questioning what I'm doing in the world—sitting here day after day teaching people to play the piano—I could make myself crazy! The trouble nowadays is that people don't believe in themselves anymore." He taught me to believe in myself. He taught me not to compete—to find musical fulfillment without comparing myself to others; he gave me to understand the real challenge was always to come closer to the heart of the music, to play something more beautifully than I played it yesterday. What happened at lessons had a validity detached from any thought of where it might lead. He taught me to care, he taught me passion. When we worked on a piece together, to "get the music" took on cosmic proportions.

Sometimes school classmates who also took piano lessons would ask me what grade I was in on piano, and express surprise that I did not take yearly exams, as though this were the purpose of lessons and the only possible measure of musical achievement. There were other things I didn't do that they found equally strange: we never used a metronome, and I was never required to learn scales and arpeggios in all the keys and practise them by rote. For a couple of years in my early teens I was assigned an exercise from Pischna each week, but scale and arpeggio practice took the form of exercises based on passages in the music I was learning, so that I never played them independently of a musical context. Mr. Cohen excoriated the whole idea of standardized piano exams, and he was withering about the grading of piano pieces by level of difficulty: "What does that mean, a Grade Three piece? a Grade Eight piece? Who decides this is a Grade Three piece? Who decides this one is easy, that one is hard? There are no 'easy pieces.' That's not what music is about."

Once, when I was around fourteen, he invited me with a few other pupils to audit a rehearsal of a Beethoven concerto at the home of an older student preparing to perform it. There we saw a different Mr. Cohen. We didn't exist for him that day; his focus was wholly on the girl at the piano and on the Beethoven. He was working with Sharon; he was the music, they were the music. As she played, he conducted, shouted prompts and encouragement; his entire body moved to the music, he sang and roared. I remember him dropping suddenly to a squat, rolling on his heels, listening. And Sharon played as if he were drawing the music from her. Before the cadenza he stood up, shirt and hair wet, and said to Sharon's mother, "Bring a glass of water. We'll take a break now." It was a glimpse of the role of coach and of what it was to prepare for performance. Afterwards, I left in company of a girl I hadn't met before. Like me, she played in her high-school band and had become more motivated at the piano since taking up a second instrument. We walked to the bus together, a little subdued and pensive, exchanging impressions of our teacher and of the afternoon's performance. We both felt we had witnessed something sublime. In Sharon's living room Mr. Cohen's uninhibitedness, his passion, had almost embarrassed me, but awe overrode discomfiture. I felt small and far away from him that afternoon; also privileged.

%

It would be dishonest to pretend I have only good memories of those years. There were periods of unhappiness and ambivalence. Double levels were characteristic not only of my teacher's sense of humour but of his very nature. There was a dark secrecy in him, an unknowable core; his actions often seemed based on a master plan whose tenets were a mystery, whose wisdom one could neither be sure of nor dare risk questioning. Times of intimacy and rapport alternated with times of cool, impersonal distance. One might get the feeling, from casual allusions to activities of other students, that one was on the periphery of some favoured inner circle: the mentions tantalized, hinted that one might ultimately be admitted to it oneself, but in the end it seemed the hints were as close as one would ever get (if it even existed). There were also times when I felt something else going on at the lessons, something besides the music, that generated painful emotion: a sense that I was thwarting his expectations, that he was trying to show me something I couldn't see, that he was masking disappointment, that I had hurt? was hurting? him. The girl I'd met at the rehearsal confessed to similar feelings, even wondered if he was trying to get her to quit. Yet when she asked directly, he was surprised and injured.

Enigmas ... but what endured was the wholeness, love, seriousness, humour. The self-sufficiency I learned. For thirty-five years those lessons were like a room I could go back to in my head. Rainy afternoons; light of the brass floor lamp warm on the piano keys; the glass of water atop the piano, water trembling a little, shimmering in the lamplight as the glass picked up vibrations of bass notes. The flow of Mr. Cohen's very quiet, very kind voice revealing hidden truths about music and life—bringing life into the music, bringing the music to life. "The thing you have to understand about this variation[1]—in fact, you could say it about a lot of great art—is that it walks a tightrope between the profound and the absurd. That's what makes it so difficult to perform. You have to walk that tightrope. You mustn't fall off on *either* side." And: "Focus on where you're going, not on where you went off track. What interferes with life is backward motion." If you were waiting in the next room, hearing someone else's lesson, you could only make out the occasional word, but the rise and fall of that voice was its own language. You heard the subtext: deep peace with an undercurrent of excitement and secrecy, the transmission of a musical Kabbalah that was also, in code, a guide for how to live well in the world.

Years later, in my early thirties, a few years into my self-imposed exile from that room and from any kind of active musicianship, I invoked the essence of the experience in a poem—a long sequence in which I grappled for the first time with the subject of mortality. In it, I named a familiar fulcrum—the home ground from which *piano plays you*—as a metaphorical place of repose, spiritual centering, and embarkation:

At the bottom of the key
fullness hangs
on a fingertip. See,
a moon-sliver, the blanched
rim of the nail.
Blood presses
against it. At rest
like this, sunk
in a tuned stillness
the hand becomes
capable of motion.

1   Beethoven, Sonata in A flat major Op. 26, first movement, 2nd variation

III INTERMEZZO

(THREE VARIATIONS)

1. November 22, 1963

IT HAS BEEN A TRUISM FOR TWO GENERATIONS THAT everyone who was old enough at the time remembers exactly where they were and what they were doing when they heard that Kennedy was shot. I was in my ninth-grade high-school homeroom, writing a French mid-term. It was a Friday, last period of the day—a gloomy overcast afternoon, the classroom lights blazing. I had a piano lesson after school. First in the room to finish writing, I glanced over my exam one last time, then raised my hand to signal I was done so I could leave early. But our teacher motioned me to stay put. "May I have your attention please, class. No one is to leave this room before the end of the period," she said as she walked over to collect my paper herself. "If you finish early, you may hand in your exam, but please return to your seat until everyone is finished writing. Miss Henry will be coming in to make an announcement before you're dismissed today."

Miss Henry was Vice Principal. Moments before the bell, she knocked on the classroom door and conferred briefly, inaudibly, in the doorway with our teacher. When the bell rang, the last students turned in their papers and we sat at our desks, waiting and wondering, as they re-entered the room together. The vice-principal announced that she had sad news. The president of the United States had been shot: John F. Kennedy was dead. Staff had been following the reports and thought it would be better for us to hear this before we left the building, because we might encounter people who were distraught. She suggested we go directly home.

I could not go directly home, nor could I linger. At a moment when I might have huddled with friends in the schoolyard to process the news, I had to take a bus across town to my piano lesson. It did not occur to me to do otherwise or even to call home from a pay phone. The sky was dark and smoky-looking. It was very quiet on the bus; no one was talking. A few people seemed to be crying silently. In those days when TV still felt new and brought the world into our living rooms, everyone liked the young, handsome US president with his glamorous wife and their two little children. People saw him as a family man, candid, personable, unpretentious— someone we could identify with. To Canadians too, he represented hope and optimism in that postwar era. He was the country's first Catholic president. If a Catholic could become president, my parents speculated, why not a Jew some day? Now he was dead.

I was buzzed in to the Chantilly; Mr. Cohen opened to my knock and waved me straight in to the studio—the pupil before me had cancelled unexpectedly. No one else seemed to be home. Was it raining out, he wanted to know as I took off my coat. He didn't say a word about the president. As I fished piano scores out of my schoolbag, I looked at him cautiously; his face was unreadable. Was he protecting me—thinking I hadn't heard yet, thinking it wasn't for him to tell me? Should I say something to let him know I'd heard? Then we would

have to talk about it. Maybe he thought it was better to proceed with the lesson and talk afterwards. But—was it possible *he* didn't know yet? In which case, shouldn't I tell him?
Shouldn't it at least be acknowledged that this had happened?
I felt tongue-tied. Was the assassination of the US president
important enough to override a piano lesson? Or was it news
that could wait? My teacher resolved the dilemma by flipping
open one of the albums I'd placed on the music rack. "Let's
hear this today, shall we?"

I don't remember what piece we worked on during that
surreal hour. I just remember how I kept going back and
forth in my mind: *He knows but thinks I haven't heard yet,
so he's chosen not to mention it, and it's best if I go along—*
or, *he doesn't know yet, and hadn't I better tell him?* It was
hard to concentrate. When the lesson ended, I waited for
him to say something, but again he didn't. And again his face
told me nothing—which should have told me *something*. It
should have told me he didn't know yet. But if that were true,
how could I explain my having waited out the whole lesson,
knowing and not saying anything? It was too embarrassing.
Unhappily, I swallowed the words I hadn't spoken and went
out into the early dark. People on the street and on the bus
were talking about what had happened now, trading bits of
information; strangers on the bus were talking to each other.

It seems oddly appropriate that my memory of a landmark
moment, a central trauma of our time, should be bound up
with my piano teacher: that he should have been the first person I interacted with after hearing the news, even though I did
not hear it from him or in his presence, and even though we
did not speak of it. (He hadn't heard yet, as I later found out;
he was stunned to learn that I'd known yet kept silent.) What
I chiefly remember of the event is my curious dance of discon-
nection with him that afternoon, a dance of second-guessing.
Neither the first such dance, nor the last.

2. I had a stepbrother

When I was seven my mother, widowed before I turned four, remarried. My stepdad had also been married before, and had a son, two years my junior and a year older than my little brother, who lived with his mother a few blocks away. For the first year or two I was only vaguely aware of this child's existence; our stepdad visited him separately, picking him up in the car from his mother's house on Sunday afternoons and taking him on outings. As our new family grew, my mother suggested that instead, Sheldon should visit his dad at our house and get to know my brother and me and his new half-siblings. It was an arrangement that never felt comfortable and did not last very long. I mostly ignored the visitor and went about my business, while my shy brother, never very social, would soon retreat to his room and close the door. But for perhaps a year of Sundays, the gangling boy with the tightly curly brown hair was an uneasy adjunct to our household, playing chess with his dad (*our* dad) in a corner of the living room, or chasing my little sisters up and down the hall on his hands and knees, pretending to be a dog: barking was easier than trying to think of things to say.

He was a child of brief, intense, serial enthusiasms: chess, stamp collecting, ham radio, writing his own newspaper. Each was pursued exhaustively for a few weeks or months, only to be abandoned in favour of a new interest, so when he announced— shortly before the awkward Sunday visits ended—that he wanted piano lessons, I didn't expect them to last long. His mother found him a teacher and we heard indirectly of his progress, which was predictably rapid as he threw himself into this latest passion. But this time the obsession didn't flag. Over the months, my stepdad proudly shared the reports he got from his ex-wife when he dropped off their son after taking him downtown to browse and buy records and sheet music. Sheldon had learned to read music in record time. Sheldon was practising two hours a day. Sheldon had completed three grades of piano in half a year. Sheldon was composing his own pieces and trying to write them down. Sheldon's piano teacher thought he needed to study with somebody who could teach him on a more advanced level. Sheldon had a wonderful new piano teacher who was amazed at his abilities. Sheldon had written a symphony. Sheldon had written three symphonies.

At this I balked. I was just beginning to pore over symphonic scores as I listened to classical recordings. I was hard pressed to write even a few bars of music. A symphonic score, as I had discovered, was an astonishingly complex thing, each single line of the music occupying a whole page, with the different instrumental parts notated on parallel staves. Was I supposed to believe that this gawky kid who'd just started lessons a year or two ago was writing symphonies? Were they *really* symphonies? Was he just writing little tunes and calling them symphonies? And who was his new teacher?

A troubling suspicion crossed my mind. "Who is Sheldon's new piano teacher?" I asked my stepdad. He looked uncomfortable. "Oh, just somebody his mother heard about somewhere. I haven't met him."

"Is it Mr. Cohen?" I asked.

"No, no."

A year or more was to pass before I found out that it was.

3. A conversation on the stairs

On the eve of his departure for Europe to play a series of piano recitals there—his first real tour, in his late twenties—my friend Al Fraser knocked on our door, having heard through the grapevine that we were being evicted from our flat in a rapidly gentrifying neighbourhood and would have to vacate six weeks before the start of a new lease we'd signed for July 1. Around the corner just two blocks away, Al needed a house-sitter and dog-sitter for a period that almost exactly coincided.

Besides conveniently solving both of our problems, this bit of lucky synchronicity brought me back in touch with Al, who until then had been mostly peripheral, a friend of friends in the neighbourhood, though I'd known him in an earlier life as the kid brother of a close friend in high school. I knew he was musically gifted on piano but something of a late starter, drifting from one teacher to another and playing in a rock band before finally getting serious in his mid-twenties and applying to the new performance program where Phil Cohen was teaching.

A day or two before he was to fly to England, I arrived in company of my kids to move a few belongings for our family of four into Al's rather crammed flat—just the things we needed for the six weeks until we could relocate and reclaim our household effects from storage. I'd brought the kids' clothes, schoolbooks, and some favourite toys and games over in an old baby carriage. The arrangement began rockily, with Jason, the golden retriever, plucking my daughter's oldest doll out of the carriage by its rubber head and absconding with it to the back balcony. But once this had been smoothed over and our property secured, kids and dog set about making friends while Al and I sat out on the front stairs in spring sunshine, reminiscing about piano lessons with the teacher we'd had in common, though at different times and in very different circumstances. It had then been several years since I had seen Mr. Cohen. I was out of the loop with everybody I'd known in what I thought of as my "music days" and had not heard of his sojourns to teach abroad.

"When he said he was going on sabbatical, I thought it would be the end for me," Al confessed. "I was so dependent. I thought I couldn't play without his help."

This was startling for me to hear. It resonated. Why did I keep wishing I could take lessons again? Why was I so dubious about trying any new repertoire on my own, as though my old teacher was the keeper of the keys and only he could show me the way in?

"Why do you think you felt that way?" I asked.

"Well, I had so much un-learning to do when I came to him. I really had to start over from scratch. So I had all these insecurities. But even then, he could get me to do things none of my other teachers could. Amazing things would happen at lessons—I could do things that I never would have gotten on my own at that stage of my pianistic development. I don't know how he got me to do them. I don't think *he* even knew how he did it."

The magic! I thought. "Oh! I know what you mean. That used to happen to me too. And I could still do the thing when I went home, but after a few days it would sort of wear off ..."

"Exactly! Sometimes I used to wonder if he hypnotized me at my lessons. Like, was I playing in a state of post-hypnotic suggestion and once it wore off, I needed him again?"

No such thought had ever occurred to me, but it was hard to dismiss. This was disquieting: hypnosis wasn't something I trusted. But why should "magic" be easier to trust?

"The point is," Al went on, "whatever it is that he does, in his teaching—I don't think it's something that translates into words. It's funny, because he said he was writing a book on piano pedagogy. Sometimes in the middle of a lesson, he would say, 'Stop! I have to get this down for my book,' and he would turn on a little tape recorder that he kept on top of the piano and start talking into it. But I couldn't believe what would come out of his mouth. It was all in this convoluted, hyper-intellectualized language that had *nothing whatever* to do with the magical thing that had just happened."

"But the book?" I was excited about the book. "Did he ever finish the book?"

"Not that I know of. He had a wonderful title for it, though. He was going to call it *The Mindful Hand.*"

IV   GETTING IN DEEPER

Prelude: Breaking the Chain

WHEN AL FRASER ARRIVED IN MONTREAL IN THE SPRING
of 2009, twenty-five years had passed since our conversation
on the stairs. Left dangling for a quarter of a century, that conversation was to resume with scarcely a missed beat, but first
we had catching up to do.

I had last seen Alan in the late 1980s. I attended his MMus
graduation recital at McGill in 1987, and for a year or two after
that he taught my son piano. Around this time, he had begun to
pursue an interest in physical movement, studying tai chi and
training as a practitioner of Feldenkrais Method, an approach
to movement based on principles of physics, neurology, physiology, and the martial arts. In 1988 he heard the Yugoslavian
pianist Kemal Gekić perform at the International Piano
Competition in Montreal, an experience that was to prove
life-changing. Electrified by the performance, and scandalized
when Gekić was not named a finalist, he approached the pianist, arranged a recital for him in Montreal, and inquired about
studying with him. "Come to Novi Sad," was the response,

"but you'd better come soon, because there's going to be a war in Yugoslavia. You want to get there before it starts."

Alan left Montreal in 1990 to study at the Arts Academy of Novi Sad, stayed through the war that began a year later, found life in the newly named Serbia more to his liking than life in North America, and decided to relocate permanently. Now himself teaching at the academy, he was in Montreal for a few days before going on to the United States to collaborate on a recording project with Gekić, who in an ironic reversal had accepted a teaching position in Miami. Alan had brought something to show me: his soon-to-be-reissued manual and accompanying DVD, *The Craft of Piano Playing*. It summed up the pianistic philosophy and system of teaching he had developed, drawing on some aspects of Cohen's approach, but primarily adapting and applying Feldenkrais principles to piano technique. Since the book's publication in 2003, he had built up something of a following, travelling to give master classes in the United States and Europe, and he was near to completing a sequel volume.

I looked through the book, simultaneously intrigued and intimidated. The tone was refreshingly conversational but the demonstrations and exercises had their basis in a knowledge of the skeletal structure and musculature of hand and arm that I didn't possess. Subject and terminology alike were unfamiliar. I doubted whether I would have the patience or motivation to make my way through this material. Thinking back to my lessons as an adolescent and young adult, I could not remember Mr. Cohen talking about things like distal phalanges or metacarpal-phalangeal joints. I did remember him using terms like "double anchorage" and using metaphors to talk about physiological aspects of piano playing—"Think of finger and shoulder as two points of stability ... think of the arm as a rope swinging loosely between them ..." But the directions in Al's book were much more detailed and anatomically precise.

He sensed my ambivalence. "I think you'll find some powerful help if you go through the DVD step by step, on your own time, and actually try the exercises," he said. "Of course, technical input of any kind is just a tool. As Kemal says, you can't make music when you're thinking about your shoulder. But we can talk later ... let's hear you play something."

One thing that had gone out the window as soon as I decided to take lessons again was any perspective on my own playing. It was instructive that some of Al's observations were similar to Pamela's, while others were in contradiction: in the second movement of the Pathétique Sonata, Pamela thought I was overemphasizing the melody notes; Al thought I wasn't emphasizing them enough. Pamela had wanted to hear the inner voices more; Al wanted them more subservient. Was this a matter of different interpretational priorities, or had I gone from one extreme to another in trying to apply her input? I couldn't tell. But Al said he was fascinated to hear me play, because he could see I embodied Phil Cohen's teaching at its purest, arrested when I was in my early twenties and evolving over decades as I applied it uncoached, with no later teacher's influence to modify or interfere with it. "It's like seeing Phil's teaching in a petri dish. And your performances have a kind of naïveté that's very touching. There's a freshness that's delightful, a lack of sophistication—on some level your playing is still a child's playing. It's entirely emotional and intuitive, not tempered by intellect or analysis ..."

Was this good or bad? Again, I couldn't tell. I had never been big on analysis; I spent high school fighting with my English teachers over their insistence that we "pick apart" poems. There was something chastening in hearing that at fifty-nine my playing was like a child's, but before I could think further, Al was on to the next thing: a single technical problem he thought could account for ninety percent of what was holding me back at the piano.

"It's your thumbs. It's a common problem, a codependency, where the thumb isn't differentiated from the hand. It makes totally unnecessary, sympathetic movements—as if it wanted to help the hand, when the hand needs no help and the tension in the thumb actually interferes with it. Or where the arch of the hand collapses in response to the thumb's falling into a key." He demonstrated. "You can improve your accuracy and control by playing *actively* with your thumbs, making them behave more like the other fingers. Stand up on them on impact, make them more autonomous. I call it achieving independence of hand and thumb."

The hours we spent at the keyboard over the next two days did serve to show me that adjustments to hand position could make powerful differences to my sound and sense of security. And it was validating to be listened to with such engagement and lively interest. Away from the piano, we had some long talks about Phil Cohen's teaching. In contrast to my private training, begun in childhood and continuing over a decade of formative years, Al's experience had begun as an adult and was relatively brief but intensive, in the context of a university program and sometimes in a group setting. His three years with Cohen were preceded by work with several other teachers (two of them former Cohen students) and were followed by private study, master classes, and pedagogical exchanges in several countries.

"Nobody in the piano world today, nobody I've worked with or observed or heard about through the grapevine, is doing anything like what Phil does," he remarked at one point. "He's in a category by himself. If you've never had an adult-level lesson with anyone but Phil, you don't even know what a normal piano lesson is. He cultivates an awareness of sound and physical sensation that's so refined, so far beyond where piano instruction usually takes people, that you can't even describe it to them."

"How do other piano teachers teach?" I asked, a little nonplussed.

"Different ways. But not with that focus on minute subtleties of touch and tone colour, where you can spend an hour on a single phrase, on the exact way a finger has to make contact with the key to get a particular sound—concentrating on feeling the vibration of the key in the fingertip—finding the exact movement of the hand that both follows and helps shape the phrase. With normal piano teachers it's more like—play this part louder, or play that part faster, here you should slow down, there you need more contrast, give the repeat a different character ..."

"Like stage directions?"

"Something like that. It can be more imaginative. Kemal and I do a lot of visualizations and verbalizations of the programmatic, dramatic content of the music. Like trying to come up with the exact adjective to describe the character of sound we want for a particular opening chord or melodic entry ... or imagining a storyline, a narrative that can be applied to the different passages and transitions in the music. We talk a lot about the meaning of the music."

"But isn't the music its own meaning?" I felt oddly resistant to the idea of using words to find a way into the music. "I think music is my vacation from words. I spend my life with words—they're my artistic medium and my livelihood. I need a break from them sometimes. That's part of the attraction music has for me ... it's a way of getting *away* from words, away from *thinking* in words. It gets me out of my head and takes me somewhere else."

He looked interested. "I hear you. But to get back to Phil ... I think there's something in the way he teaches that fosters a dependency. For a long time—as I've said—I felt I couldn't play without him. I was desperate for whatever it was I was getting from him. I used to play badly at my lessons on purpose, because then I knew I would get an inspired lesson. Thank goodness he went on sabbatical or I might never have realized I could play. You know, other students of his have had problems similar to yours—performance breakdowns, insecurities. I think it's because his teaching process is so intensely inward-focused ..."

"That's a good description. I remember I used to close my eyes sometimes at lessons—not because he told me to, it would just happen."

"Same here. We needed to do that, to concentrate on the sensations and sounds he was prompting us to focus on. But the kind of work he likes to do doesn't involve much conscious process. It's highly intuitive and works in mysterious ways. He gets you to do incredible things, but you don't know intellectually how you're doing them, and that puts you on thin ice."

Thin ice was the perfect description for how I felt when I was playing really well. As if I might fall through at any minute. As if what was happening was too good to be true, as if I couldn't trust it and was therefore *bound* to fall through.

Al said, "I spent years, both on my own and with Kemal, trying to work through intellectually what I learned from Phil—to make it concrete, to compensate for its deficits."

"But—what are you saying? You supported my going back to him. You told me where I could reach him! Did you not think he was a good teacher?"

He looked at me in amazement. "He was a *fantastic* teacher. He was like a father to me in terms of my relationship to the piano. He was my other father."

One week later, Alan emailed from Miami:

> I have many thoughts about our work together and your playing as I observed it. You have that evolved, seemingly-specific-to-Phil facility I recognize and value highly: your fingers work effectively and easily, and they behave

intelligently. As for the question of musical shaping and naïveté, program or instinct, I realize now that your process is not verbal and it needs to be non-verbal, not just because you spend your life with words and want a break from them, but because that direct musical expression is central to how you experience a piece. As we worked and you played, I noticed there were times when you would go very far into the music, you could keep playing even as you absorbed my technical input and applied it.

Not only do I think it worthwhile for you to pursue this further, I believe it is a necessity for you. Something in you needs very much to end your long period of musical cold turkey. You have been making tentative sorties but I sense a need in you now to do more than that, to really make a return to the world you love and to which you belong. It is an emotional, physical, spiritual and soul need in you, one that I really honour.

Sometimes an inner truth only hits home when we hear it voiced by somebody else. I read those words—"the world you love and to which you belong"—and felt some kind of fight go out of me, a decades-old subterranean struggle to defend and buttress my choice not to pursue a life in music. It didn't matter that it was now too late to choose the other way. The words were in the present tense. What mattered was that I was still a musician—had never ceased to be one—and perhaps no longer needed to pretend otherwise to protect myself from sadness, regret, or shame.

%

Fourth and fifth lesson with Pamela. I'm starting to get more of a sense of why I derail so easily. It's a hypersensitivity to the unexpected: if a note comes out louder than I intended, or I hit a note that's slightly out of tune, it throws me and there's a domino effect—I begin playing wrong notes or losing it in other ways. It can even happen when I'm playing really well: then it's how *good* it sounds that throws me. And I don't know how to stop the chain reaction. Pamela thinks it has to do with relying too much on muscle memory, not being secure enough in my knowledge of the music to back it up with solid spatial awareness. She says she sees me casting and reaching unnecessarily, as though I think the next note is much farther away than it actually is—an indication that I'm not sure where I'm going.

I say, "But if I don't know where I'm going, how do I get there when I do get there?"

"You get there, it's true," she acknowledges, "but sometimes it's like sliding into home plate, the way you get there."

In the Chopin, we are working on small groups of notes that precede transitions—reinforcing my awareness of where the shift is, so I can anticipate and prepare for it. In the Beethoven, she alerts me to many details in the interest of playing it less romantically, with more rhythmic precision and structural clarity. Things I'm grateful to have her point out.

I have left a voicemail with Phil: "Maybe you were hoping I would go away, but I'm still here and it's the middle of April now." A day later I come home to one from him: no, he was not hoping I would disappear; he looks forward to our meeting and will soon call to set up a time. And I feel—what? Elation, excitement, gratitude, nervousness, peace? All of those.

Pamela thinks if Phil decides to work with me, he will want me to lay aside the music we've been working on. "He won't want you playing anything you've played before, anything with what he calls ghosts in it." The idea of a recital is slipping farther and farther out of reach: I can revive old repertoire fairly quickly, but it has always taken me a long time to learn anything new from scratch. It could take me a few years to build up fluency in a half-hour's worth of new repertoire—barely

enough for a program. And I no longer feel at a level to think
of performing even old repertoire. Then what exactly am I
embarked on here?

But the promised phone call comes. The naming of a day,
a time, a place when I will meet with my old teacher and "see
what might be possible." Whatever it is I'm embarked on,
things are moving forward.

%

How strange to think we've both been in Montreal all this time,
yet our paths have never once crossed. When I see Phil Cohen
again, waiting by the door of Hingston Hall to lead the way to
the piano studio he refers to as "the Project," I recognize him
instantly; I would have recognized him anywhere (he says the
same of me). He has aged, but he doesn't look old; the years
have not changed the familiar contours of his face, the classic
Semitic profile and extraordinary slope of forehead. His hair
isn't even all grey—just streaked, like mine. He's shorter than
I remembered, and a little stooped. He is wearing sunglasses.
I realize I don't remember what colour his eyes are—brown?
blue? green? But just as when I heard his voice on the phone,
what shocks me about this face-to-face encounter is its ordin-
ariness. It's as if we last saw each other only a month or two
ago. It is oddly anticlimactic.

I follow him down the hallway, through two sets of double
doors and into the rear wing of the low-rise 1960s-style university building on Concordia's Loyola Campus. As he fumbles
with the keys to the studio, I remember his curious ineptness
with anything mechanical. The room he finally manages to
unlock is unprepossessing, a soulless institutional space—
fluorescent lighting, water-stained acoustic ceiling tile, some
removed to reveal pipes that must have leaked; a single narrow
window of a sort that can't be opened. The piano, a concert

grand bearing the name "Falcone" in Gothic gilt lettering, occupies the front third. Pushed towards the far wall are some sticks of classroom furniture—a Formica study table, two or three chairs with cushioned seats, several moulded plastic ones haphazardly stacked. A few items interrupt the blankness of the walls—three small unframed paintings, clearly by the same artist; posters for concerts long past; a series of photographs of a piano under construction. Seeing me notice these, he remarks that the piano is the one in front of us—a prototype Falcone, one of the first the maker built. "The guy's an Italian who worked rebuilding Steinways and got the idea to build pianos of his own. He made some very good instruments and then decided to do something else. Now he makes chocolate, what can I say." That old droll sidelong glance—"It's really good chocolate."

His very quiet, almost conspiratorial voice and manner are exactly as I remember. He seems a little hard of hearing, and he speaks so softly that I have trouble hearing him, too; we both have to ask each other to repeat things. Positioning his chair a few feet away from the piano stool where he motioned me to sit, he asks me some questions about what I've been doing at the piano and listens intently to my answers but does not engage. I feel I'm prattling on—backtracking, rephrasing myself, suddenly a lot less sure of what I really have to say, or what matters enough to mention. Then he wants to hear me play.

Though the stakes feel higher, it isn't such a cold plunge after a few weeks with Pamela and then playing for Al. Besides, I'm excited to try the piano; I can't remember when I last played on a full-sized grand. Right from the opening chord of the Pathétique Sonata, the richness of sound is so new and absorbing that I almost forget I have an audience. Adjusting my touch to the unexpectedly light action, experimenting with tone colour, trying different things with the pedal, I'm gratified to make it through the whole first movement without derailing.

As the final chords die out I glance warily over at my old teacher, waiting for a verdict. He is quiet for a long moment, face inscrutable, hands in his lap. The fingers of one hand tap against the back of the other. Then he says, almost inaudibly, "I see. So the question is, what are you going to do with the talent." After a moment he moves his chair closer and flips ahead a few pages in the album on the music rack. "Have you done the second movement?"

Ah. The real test—something slow, with a long singing line. "I've relearned all three, but I haven't worked much on the others yet."

"Let's hear the opening."

I know what he's listening for and what I, too, want to hear. But I feel myself muddying the beautiful melody, unable to make it sing out over the other voices, then drowning it with too much pedal, from bad to worse! He stops me after half a page. "This movement is another story. It's actually very unpianistic; that's what makes it so challenging to play well. What else have you been working on?"

"I started learning the Revolutionary Étude. Just reading it, I mean. You gave it to me to start reading, one of the last lessons I had with you. I've been working on it with Pamela."

"Go ahead."

"It's not up to tempo," I warn. "And it isn't fluent yet."

"Never mind, let's hear it."

I make it through two pages, keeping it slow and deliberate, solidly placed, stumbling here and there nonetheless, but surprised elsewhere when something difficult comes across with unwonted facility, thanks to the responsiveness of the instrument.

"That's as far as I've gotten from memory."

"It's not a bad start. Of course, it's supposed to be about four times the speed, but you understand the music. Another time I'll show you how to get that opening—to get the connections between those chords so they make a dramatic statement, to give them their character." *Another time.* Can this mean he might accept me as a student again?

The verdict on my playing is so reticent it makes me laugh: "Nothing was unmusical."

"Well, I should hope not!"

He ignores that. "You have to understand, I don't give piano lessons anymore."

My hopes plummet. But it doesn't mean what I thought it did, for he goes on, "What I do is give feedback, I work creatively with musicians. I do sessions; I don't call them lessons. There are things I can show you to help you use your time at the piano more effectively—things that have to do with creating an aesthetic experience, making each phrase beautiful, getting to know the music the way the composer does. Breaking it down different ways to hear the individual voice lines, the orchestration. I don't think of what I do as teaching. It's not about 'learning to play the piano better'—that's a trap. People want me to explain my approach, to talk about technique—I won't do it, I don't like the word. I've had to ditch a lot of terminology and find new ways to talk about musical process. I don't use the word 'practising' anymore. What we associate with that word—'playing it over and over,' 'trying to get it right'—doesn't make sense as a way of working. There are no answers and there's no right way."

But isn't this semantics? a part of me protests inwardly. *Learning is a real thing. If my aim is not to play the piano better, why bother? "Creating an aesthetic experience, making each phrase beautiful"—aren't these the values I internalized before I turned eighteen? They're still my guiding spirit, they go without saying. But why should they be incompatible with goals I've identified for myself more recently, like playing more continuously? more accurately? more reliably? Like finally finishing a few pieces to a level where I could perform them?*

"There's a cartoon I once saw." His expression hasn't changed, but I have the oddest sense he heard my inner objection. And now I think, *A cartoon? Am I in a time warp? Is it going to be the same one—the man in the cage?*

"There are two frames. In the first one, you see a man in a smoking jacket, out in the garden. He's standing in the sunshine, puffing away on his pipe, happy as can be. Then you notice he has a ball and chain on his leg. In the second frame, he looks down, sees that someone has cut the chain—and suddenly, panic!—he's all in a sweat, he drops his pipe ..."

Not the same one. But the same one.

"You're going to have to break the chain," he says, solemnly. "Got it?"

The inner objector is still on alert. *That's a little facile. It's a great line, but what's he getting at? In what way am I chained? I don't feel chained.*

"Well, but what *is* the chain?" I know it's a hopelessly flat-footed question, but stubbornly, I want something a little more specific.

He doesn't answer. Is he pretending he didn't hear me? Is this a dodge, or a deliberate refusal to spell it out? (And why should a poet, of all people, be asking to have a metaphor spelled out?) I flash back to Pamela, a lesson or two ago, when I told her Phil had finally called to arrange a meeting: "I have so many questions for him. So many things I've wondered about for so long." She warned, "Phil won't give you answers. You know that about him, right—you have to be ready for that, it can be frustrating. He'll never answer your questions."

The quiet voice continues now: "For many years, I've been involved in research on creativity, work that brings me in contact with very interesting people. It's a long-term study I initiated, the Leonardo Project. I've worked with high-level performing artists and with musicians who have impediments—sometimes psychological, sometimes physical, musicians with injuries or handicaps. I've worked with a blind pianist and a pianist with two fingers, a baritone with asthma. There was a prodigy, a kid who'd been pushed by his daddy— there wasn't a thing this kid couldn't do technically but he played like a machine, with a total absence of emotion. How do you teach somebody to feel the music? I have hours of film footage tracking the work I did with these people, sometimes over years, and it's the ones with the handicaps I learned the most from—watching them invent ways to overcome their problems. The high-level ones, the concert artists—what distinguishes them is they never play a piece the same way twice. There's an expressive variability to their performances, subtle differences in timing that can be measured. It's that variability that makes a great performer. It's a good sign never to be satisfied, always to feel there's more we can do with a piece. If we become self-satisfied, we stop being creative. It's not about finishing something. It's about keeping it alive."

The objector has slunk off. I sit listening, hands folded in my lap, feeling like a good schoolgirl. Like the schoolgirl I still was when last in the presence of this man.

"People think of the creative arts and the performing arts as two different things. They think there are two kinds of artist, one who creates and one who interprets. I don't draw that distinction. Performing is as much a creative art as composing or writing. A performance is a creation. Playing a piece of music is a creative act, not an interpretive act. The composer creates the music. The performer creates an *experience* of the music. It's the listener who interprets."

How can I have forgotten my teacher's penchant for monologue—how the talk is a bit mystifying, as if secret knowledge is being handed down, something he alone is privy to, something you will need him to unlock for you. Now it comes back: the screed delivered in low tones, unrushed, hardly above a murmur but infused with moment; the sense that you are getting only the chapter headings here, the rest will be revealed over time. *Is it really the listener who interprets? What does that mean, exactly? That would bespeak a very active kind of listener, wouldn't it—a participant in the music, not just a recipient* ... My head has already begun to wrestle with the idea, as it has wrestled with other of his pronouncements over the years, enigmatic statements that feel true but that "resist the intelligence / almost successfully"—to borrow a phrase from Wallace Stevens, who maintained this is what a poem must do. I'm remembering another one now: "Actually we learn by imagination, not by experience." *How old was I when he said that, maybe fifteen? and I've thought about it ever since... I still turn it over in my mind from time to time, trying to fathom how it applies—like a stone I've carried around in my pocket all these years* ...

Somehow two hours have gone by when we get up to leave. His decision seems to be that he will do an introductory session with me "soon"—maybe as early as next week—and then have Pamela continue to work with me, reinforcing what he wants me to be doing, "until I have more time. Right now there are big things happening ..." *What big things? When will he have more time?* The subject of an eventual recital—my declared goal—hasn't come up. He asks if I can do him a favour—help him to close the piano, then go underneath and lock together the three looped ends of the vinyl cover that protects it. "Please. I hope you don't mind . . . it's hard for me, I have a pacemaker ..." On my hands and knees under the Falcone I smile, remembering crawling under the Knabe as a child to retrieve my mother's cheques.

On the way out he draws my attention to a small framed portrait on the table, a photograph of celebrated pianist Alfred Cortot, autographed and inscribed to Yvonne Hubert. "Cortot gave this to Yvonne, to my teacher. It passed to me when she died—she left her whole archive to the Leonardo Project. You know she studied with him in Paris, right? He called her his best pupil. I keep a few of her things here ... the rest is in storage with the department."

We are taking the same bus, it turns out, so there's time to talk as we wait, but we're both a little cautious, circumspect. He doesn't ask me anything about my personal life. We are both with different partners than when we last saw each other—in his case, I know as much from Al, but does he know the same is true of me? A lot happens to people in thirty-five years, a dismaying amount; do we need to get into all that? Of his current life, he volunteers only that he'll be going to New York soon: his ten-year-old grandson Graham, Warren's son, has just won a Morton Gould award for composition, the youngest-ever recipient, and there's going to be a presentation and press conference. I realize this must be the big thing he was referring to.

"That's wonderful! Why didn't you tell me before?"

"Oh—I thought you knew." *How would I know?*

He tells me Graham is named for Gordie—"for my little boy who died—it was Gordie's middle name"—and adds that this grandson is very like his namesake: a genius child of eclectic interests, a musical prodigy.

"I remember Gordie," I tell him. "He once read me a Greek myth. I remember you doing yoga with him."

This seems to open a door. He begins to reminisce about the years when Gordie was ill, the doctors' surprise at how long the boy held out—"It was because there were so many things he was interested in, things he loved to do." He describes the days he spent at the hospital playing with his son, reading to him, finding him projects: "The staff gave me carte blanche to do anything I wanted to keep Gordie happy. In his last week he conducted the nurses' choir for their Christmas concert ..." A transitory softening of his face as he recalls this.

I ask about his other children. Warren is a conductor, he tells me with pride; Dougie a psychologist, Glennis a painter.

None are in Montreal. I cannot bring myself to ask about their mother. Perhaps he assumes I know the story, whatever it is. And now I am feeling the years. "I didn't know if I would find you again," I confess. "I thought you would be retired."

"Retired? No." He shakes his head. "Why would I retire? I love music, it's my life. I love my work. I'll do it as long as I can, I don't see why I would want to stick around otherwise."

The bus we board together is the 51, eastbound. It's the same bus I took from school to my piano lesson the day Kennedy was shot—number unchanged since I was in high school, route barely altered, though some street names have changed in a move to give the city more of a French face (Édouard-Montpetit, the street the bus is named for, used to be Maplewood). Phil Cohen gets off a few stops later. He waves to me through the window before turning to walk on, a small-ish man in a beige windbreaker, strolling slowly east along Fielding in the late afternoon sunshine. I settle back in my seat for the long, zigzag ride home. Along Queen Mary Road, as the grand old homes of Hampstead begin to give way to the rough-and-scrabble commerce of Snowdon's main drag, the bus goes past Mountain Sights, the street where I had my first lessons with him, and then past the Chantilly, long missing its name. What happened to the silver script letters above the portico? As the bus sits idling in front of it, I study the façade, trying to place which window was his—a front-facing window, wasn't it?—but on which floor? Isn't that the one—second from the corner, on the third floor? I want to believe I've nailed it, but the rows of windows stare back at me, inscrutable, and suddenly I'm not sure.

Fugue: Blowing (hot and cold)

How I loved my clarinet! I loved the faint spicy smell of the grenadilla wood from Madagascar, I loved the word *grenadilla*, I loved the ebony-smooth surface of the dense black wood in which, in strong light, you could see glints of deep red-brown and hints of grain. I loved the feel of the metal rings under my fingers, the quiet clicking of the keys, their soft silver gleam against the blue plush lining of the alligator case where my instrument lay nestled, in sections, when it was not being played. After all this time, my hands still curve automatically around an invisible clarinet, remembering the correct position as if they held one only yesterday—the proper curve of the fingers, feel of the holes against the pads of the fingers, exact position of the hole's imprint on the pad of the finger, pressure of the thumb-rest on the joint of the thumb.

I remember the paraphernalia: the flat round tin of cork grease for the tenons, its sweetish waxy smell giving way to a rancid odour as it aged; my chamois swab on its weighted string—dropping the lead weight down the bell of the instrument held upside down after playing, drawing the chammy out dark with moisture; the fuzzy swab for anointing the inside of the shaft periodically with bore oil, to protect the wood against moisture and extremes of temperature. And quirky individual things: my inelegant solution to sore embouchure—the little squares of paper towel I would tear for myself and fold in four to place over my bottom front teeth, blunting their sharpness so I could extend my practice time (I could tear one to the exact size with my eyes shut)—always a couple of these little paper wads, dried to the shape of my teeth, in the side compartment of my clarinet case along with swab and reeds. For years after I stopped playing, my tongue could feel vestiges of the ridged callus on the inside of my lower lip, a callus whose thickness at any given moment told me how much I had been playing, how recently I had played, how much longer I might be good for today. When the ridge finally disappeared completely, I accepted that I was no longer a clarinetist, but even today my tongue knows where it used to be. The callus on my thumb, a fleshy bump on the side of the knuckle where the weight of the instrument rested, outlasted the one on my lip; sometimes I think I can still see a trace of it today. I played clarinet for ten years. Only ten years? It felt like so much longer.

Reeds. Ah, yes, remember reeds, the bane of those years. Rico reeds in high school, Vandoren reeds at Conservatoire, Réal reeds when my teacher decided Vandorens had gone downhill. Without a reed—a small wedge of tapered cane, an eighth of an inch thick at its thickest and the length of a thumb—a clarinet is mute: it's the vibration of the reed affixed to the mouthpiece that sets the column of air inside the shaft in motion, producing the sound. Reeds came in hardnesses measured from 1 or 1½, favoured for beginners, through number 3: "soft" reeds were easy to blow but harsh and honky, "hard" reeds required more breath but gave best tone and control. Reeds came packaged in little cardboard boxes of twenty, five rows separated by layers of tissue—a box was ridiculously expensive and might yield one or two good enough for performance, another three or four suitable for practice. Cracking open a new box to test reeds one by one; setting aside the occasional "yes," a few "maybes," while the pile of rejects grew and grew. A "yes" reed had to be cultivated and cared for to prolong its life—played enough to break it in, but never for long enough to get waterlogged; reserved for performance once it reached its prime responsiveness. And for all that, one's very best, cosseted concert reed could get a little nick at the paper-thin tip, or develop a fine split, and that was the end of it for performance purposes, maybe even for practice—lucky if it didn't happen the day of a concert. Hours consumed trying to find new reeds when my concert reed and best backup were past their prime: shaving hard reeds lightly with a razor blade, removing the tiniest powder of sawdust to make them easier to play; shaving off a fine layer of dirt to brighten the sound of an old reed gone dull. Going through rejects in hope that under different weather conditions. a few might prove salvageable. Adjusting

the metal ligature over and over to find the spot on the mouthpiece where a reed sounded best; wearing out the screws on
ligature after ligature doing this.

I did not love reeds. I envied flute players, brass players,
who never had to deal with this horrible adjunct to playing.
Reeds are why I quit playing clarinet. No, maybe that isn't fair.
Repertoire is why I quit playing clarinet. Nothing written for
the instrument before Mozart—nothing from the Baroque era,
my favourite period—no Bach. A dearth of great solo music; a
dearth even of great chamber works (though some transcend-
ent gems among the few).

But no, again. Reeds and repertoire may be why I never
went back to the clarinet, but they are not why I quit. I don't
think I even understood that I was quitting when I quit. There
was no decisive moment, just a long slow drift. There was a lot
of denial: my identity had been bound up with the instrument
for what was then almost half my life. I had a considerable
investment in this identity. I was on a track, and I continued
on it, albeit less and less happily, even as the magic of the early
years wore off and disillusionment set in, along with secret
doubts about the rosy future I'd painted for myself while still
in high school: graduate studies at the Paris Conservatoire, a
position as principal clarinet in a world-class orchestra, opportunities as soloist and chamber player. I could see it all so
clearly, but how did one actually get there?

In retrospect: I quit because I wasn't willing to sacrifice
all other interests for music, and found myself punished for
this in insidious ways. I quit because, having pleaded for and
been granted a single semester's leave from the *classe d'orchestre* at Conservatoire to attend a film seminar at McGill, I was
advised (only on my return) that in so doing, it was understood
I was ceding my long-held position as principal clarinet. (The
same individual who had granted me leave was the adjudicator,
later that year, for a failed exam at which I knew I had played
more than respectably—an exam I would have to repeat before

I could qualify to play my graduating Concours recital.) I quit because when I began playing union gigs with local orchestras, I was given to understand that if I turned one down, I risked not being asked again. I did not enjoy these gigs—usually a single performance in a second-rate hall, sometimes in an orchestra pit, after a single perfunctory rehearsal. There was a pecking order: no question of a rookie playing first chair. I sat in the pit dutifully counting out my 56 or 78 or 104 measures' rest to be sure of coming in on time with the other second-chair winds when, here and there, we got to play a few bars of descant or staccato offbeats. Backstage, the musicians played cards, bantered about sports and politics, gossiped about the local music scene. Was this the milieu in which I would be spending the rest of my life? Who would I talk to about the things that mattered to me—music not least? Nobody was talking about music.

I quit because my teacher, a consummate musician who by then had played first chair in the Montreal Symphony Orchestra for twenty-four years, was dismissed from his position in a purge of the wind section by a newly appointed conductor in a move that seemed at least partly political. That this could happen at his level was shocking to me; it felt like a warning. I was getting a whiff of the punitive atmosphere, intrigues, and cutthroat competitiveness of the professional music world.

I was also spending more and more time with poets and painters and theatre people, with amateur musicians and instrument-builders—bohemian friends and neighbours in the McGill Ghetto who not only seemed more interesting than my career-track music peers but seemed to be having a lot more fun. I was getting more serious about my writing. I dropped out of the master's program in philosophy in which, I realized, I had just been marking time; and when the West Coast called, I went.

My clarinet went with me because I could not have imagined leaving it behind. After finishing Conservatoire I played less and less, but the familiar ritual of unlatching the case, assembling the instrument, and launching into my habitual warm-ups had been part of my routine for so long, it seemed unimaginable that I could altogether abandon it. As I found out, I could, and without much of a pang. During a ten-month sojourn in the woods on Vancouver Island, I think I took my clarinet out of its case around five times. My embouchure lost its muscle tone. I lost my endurance and breath support. I knew what I had to do to get them back, but there was no motivation to do it. Instead I freelanced articles for the *Sooke Mirror*, reviewed books for the Victoria *Daily Colonist*, wrote five short stories, and worked on a manuscript that was to form the basis for my first poetry collection. And— with my then husband—hatched a plan to go back east, start a little magazine, buy a Platen letterpress and learn how to print. The transition from one life and identity into another was under way.

Some time after our return to Montreal, the MSO advertised an opening for second clarinet. Through the grapevine I heard they had received nearly three hundred inquiries from across North America and Europe, and had auditioned thirty players. The numbers were an eye-opener. *For second chair?* To give up all other interests to compete for a position of *second chair?* What on earth had I been thinking?

%

But to go backwards: How did I become a clarinetist in the first place? Strange to say, it might never have happened had I not been traumatized by sewing in seventh-grade home economics class. Our local high school offered four programs: Latin, Science, Instrumental Music, and Commerce. Latin and Science were university-track programs; Commerce was for kids who weren't college-bound; Instrumental Music was based around the high-school concert band during the heyday of such programs, before they were deemed "frills" and largely eliminated.

Science wasn't an option for me: I had no head for math. The Latin and Instrumental Music programs were similar, designed for students heading for Arts in university; each offered Latin plus one science. But in first year, the Instrumental Music program offered typing where the dread words "home economics" appeared on the Latin program. To my mind, this was sufficient reason to learn a second instrument. I had a head start: I could read music. And why not learn to type? I wanted to be a writer. My mother wondered about dividing my musical energies, but Mr. Cohen didn't think it a problem. I signed up for Instrumental Music. After some research on the instruments listed in the school's inventory, I chose clarinet because it seemed the most versatile, with a place in both band and orchestra, equally at home in classical, jazz, and folk traditions. In a concert band, clarinets were the melody instrument, equivalent to the violin section of an orchestra. All this sounded good. I had never seen an actual clarinet.

Our high-school music teacher and band leader, Cy Cooper, was reputed to be the best in the city: every year his bands, ensembles, and soloists took the lion's share of prizes in the interprovincial music festivals. In our first music period, he distributed to each of us a case containing our chosen instrument and showed us where to sit in the band formation. We opened the cases. Well-used instruments, no less wonderful for signs of tarnish and denting, winked up at their new owners from worn, patchy plush linings. My clarinet was an Olds Ambassador, the name embossed in the black wood in faded gold script lettering. I could hardly believe I was going to be allowed to take this home with me. We had first to be taught the names of the instrument parts (five sections, for a clarinet) and how to fit them together; then Mr. Cooper asked us to disassemble the sections and put them away except for the mouthpiece.

With these, he demonstrated how each instrument produced its sound. Brass players had to buzz their lips against a mouthpiece shaped like a cup; flutists had to rest their lower lip on the edge of the tone-hole and blow across it as if across the mouth of a bottle. Clarinetists and saxophone players first had to moisten a reed and attach it to the underside of the mouthpiece with a ligature, then blow into the mouthpiece with upper teeth resting on top and lower lip covering the bottom teeth, keeping the mouth tight all around to prevent air from escaping out the corners. Mr. Cooper used helpful comparisons: "Rest the reed on your lower lip and jut out your chin. Now bite down on the mouthpiece with your upper teeth as though you were biting into a chocolate bar. Think of your mouth as an elastic band around the mouthpiece—don't let the corners go slack." For the rest of the period, we were to practise making sounds on our mouthpieces.

An array of grunts, farts, and raspberries rose immediately from the brass section as lips buzzed against mouthpieces of trumpets, trombones, tubas, and French horns. There were more clarinets in the band than any other instrument, eight or ten of us trying clarinet mouthpieces. Assorted squeaks and squeals duly came out of one after another, but not mine; for the life of me I couldn't produce a sound. What was I doing wrong? It wasn't fair! I was the one with the musical background! Most of the class was packing to leave as Mr. Cooper strolled over to see if he could help. Since it was last period of the day, he said I could stay awhile and keep trying; he wasn't worried. But, "Are you sure you want to play clarinet?" he asked. "We have so many clarinets! Wouldn't you like to play something more unusual and challenging, like the oboe? I have an oboe no one in this class wanted." I shook my head, not trusting myself to speak. I wanted to play clarinet—the versatile instrument, the melody instrument! Minutes later I succeeded in evincing the feeblest of squeaks from my mouth-piece, and was dismissed with a kindly pat on the shoulder. But a fierce determination surged in me as I left that afternoon, clarinet case in hand. I vowed to myself that just as I was the last to make a sound today, I would be the first clarinet player in the class to acquire some real proficiency on the instrument.

Very quickly, the high-school auditorium became the centre of my life. The thrill of playing in a musical ensemble, of hearing how our individual parts blended into one huge tapestry of sound all around me, did not wear off. I went from being a grade-school student who wasn't above faking sick to miss school to a high-school student who sneaked out of the house before anyone could suspect I had a fever, not to miss a band practice. My progress was so rapid that I was soon playing in the intermediate and senior bands as well as our junior band. Practices were noon hours and after school; sometimes Mr. Cooper even scheduled morning "sectionals," coaching brass, woodwinds, or percussion separately for half an hour before classes began.

Under the stage were lockers containing gym equipment and four large metal trolleys that housed our instruments when they were not in use. First act of the school day was to stop by the auditorium to deposit them. If no sectional was scheduled, I liked to arrive early and practise there before class: the live acoustics made the tone of my clarinet so much fuller than at home, and it was a chance to show off my progress to Mr. Cooper, who presided over the auditorium like its resident genie. If he was not too beleaguered by students requesting new reeds or cork grease or adjustments to their instruments, he might stroll circuitously over in my direction and take a seat nearby, making me the focus of his attention. Nervous but gratified, I'd try to feign nonchalance as he sat, chair tilted back, handsome in his familiar brown tweed jacket, exuding an air of slight amusement and a faint essence of tobacco and aftershave. Sometimes he just listened and smiled. Sometimes

he offered a pointer, or asked me to repeat something I had
played, as if to see if I could pull it off a second time. He was
proficient on clarinet himself, as on all the band instruments,
but his own instrument was trumpet. Legend had it he had been
a prodigy but had ruined his embouchure playing in military
bands during the war—had torn a lip muscle and been forced to
quit playing professionally. He was charismatic: thronged by
his students, both male and female; covertly eyed by students
in other programs, watched by his fellow teachers—sometimes it seemed all eyes in the school were upon him. He was
demanding: girls who begged off band practice for noon-hour
volleyball, boys who signed up for sports teams, were given a
hard time. He expected our loyalty.

We played two major concerts a year: *The Song of Christmas,*
an annual extravaganza with choir, and a late spring program
that varied from year to year. We competed in the spring music
festival—local preliminaries and out-of-province finals. The
senior band kicked off every graduation ceremony with the
processional, *Sine Nomine,* and ended it with the anthem. We
had a concert uniform—a blazer in school colours, worn with
grey skirts or trousers and a white top. We felt important to
the school, as much as the sports teams, maybe more than the
sports teams. I loved everything about playing in the band.

Perhaps strangely, if I had to choose one memory to stand
for the way I experienced those years, it might be how the
auditorium *smelled* after a noon band practice, if one had to
go back for some forgotten item. There would be a particular
slightly sour, raunchy smell in the air—the smell of thirty or
forty adolescents' after-lunch breath blown hotly and lustily
through trumpets, trombones, French horns, clarinets, saxophones, flutes, oboes, bassoons, baritones, and tubas, to linger like an invisible cloud above the small puddles left on the
hardwood floor where the brass players "milked" their valves
to free their instruments of condensed breath and spit. It was
a smell that made me happy. It was metamorphosed salami

sandwiches, cheese sandwiches, chicken, egg, and tuna sandwiches, apples, chocolate milk, and soft drinks, blown through lengths of brass tube slightly green with bacteria, moulds, and corrosion, picking up along the way the edgy essence of warm metal and saliva. It was a collective waft of warm breath lately blown from young lungs, in a directed burst of pure, ardent yet insouciant energy, to raise a canopy of music—something miraculous and taken for granted. For perhaps a quarter of an hour after, it hung there on the air like the benign ghost of that miracle.

Far from dividing my musical energies, the effect of learning a new instrument was to expand and intensify my interest in music on all levels. Our home had a modest collection of classical recordings, my mother's from college, long silent in the hurly-burly of raising five kids. Here were symphonies by Beethoven, Tchaikovsky, Dvořák, Mendelssohn, and Schumann I could listen to, guided by her old hardback *Victor Book of the Symphony* which alerted me to the highlights of each symphonic movement: the main and secondary themes, the orchestration, the solo entries of wind instruments that occasionally, briefly, carried the melody over an orchestral background. I learned to recognize all the instruments, but mostly I waited for the clarinet solos, burning the sound into my ears—not the flat-toned quacking of novice high-school players but the exquisite tone of the instrument as it was meant to sound: limpid, luminous, *pear-shaped.* I would not be satisfied with less. A good reed was a reed with which I could get *that sound.* Other clarinetists in the class didn't agonize over reeds; they were satisfied to quack or honk out the right notes on any reed they could blow comfortably. Mr. Cooper noticed my fussiness and understood the reason for it. He graduated me to Number 2½ reeds, and soon after, to his limited supply of Vandorens, reserved for his more advanced players. He frequently had me play alone in class, holding up my tone quality as a model for the clarinet section.

Whether it was the inspirational effect of listening to symphonic recordings, the improvement in my sight reading thanks to band practice, or the heightened awareness of musical voices that came with playing in an ensemble, my piano playing also blossomed in my first year of high school. I'd had a small crisis the year before, a period when I wasn't practising much or regularly and my mother asked me to commit to an hour a day or give up the lessons that were a strain on our household budget. She relented when I wept at the thought of quitting, and let me continue even though my compliance remained spotty. But now everything was different. I fell in love with pieces well beyond my level that I heard older students playing, and begged Mr. Cohen to let me learn them. His usual response was to suggest we first work on some piece that could serve as a stepping-stone, preparing me for the technical challenges I would face. Motivated by the promise, I learned whatever he prescribed, and learned it quickly. Suddenly I was practising up to two hours of piano a day without noticing the time; this after practising clarinet for upwards of an hour on arriving home from school.

As the year progressed, Mr. Cooper began to talk about the Quebec Conservatoire; he thought I should apply. Admission was on a scholarship basis; if I got in, I would have free private lessons with the principal clarinetist in the Montreal Symphony and access to a full musical education free of charge. He offered to coach me for the audition in June, but better still would be to take a few private lessons with the teacher there: Ralph Masella would know best how to prepare me.

I'm sure my mother's heart sank at the thought of a second private music teacher, but she gamely set up a meeting with Rafael Masella. On a Saturday in early May, I left my piano lesson (at which I read through one of my coveted pieces, Chopin's Fantaisie-Impromptu, for the first time) and took two buses downtown to the McGill Conservatory, housed then in a rundown Victorian on McTavish Street. I waited,

as instructed, on a small bench in the entranceway, listening
to someone upstairs playing piano very badly, and in another
room, a shrill-voiced woman giving a singing lesson, until the
front door swung open and a short stout man with a thick black
moustache hurried in. With a nod to me and a brief "Come
on," he set off briskly down the hall and I followed him up a
leaning, damply creaking, carpeted staircase, through a warren
of rooms and passages, across a tile floor to a small airy studio containing a piano, table, music stand, and two chairs. He
offered me one, sat down on the other, and asked to have a look
at my Olds Ambassador. He examined the whole instrument
very carefully, pressing down each key, then looked up gravely
and said in a hurt tone, "But this does not play!"

"Most of the time it does," I said lamely. He shook his
head doubtfully and handed it back. "Well, let's hear you play
something. A scale—anything." I ran up and down the Bb concert scale. "Very good lip position," was all Mr. Masella had
to offer. He asked me to play three or four more scales, then to
sight-read an étude that was a little beyond my depth. "It's not
hopeless," was his verdict. (Did I detect the barest twinkle?)
"Not hopeless at all."

However ... I thought, smiling inwardly. And sure enough,
he went on to show me all the things I would have to correct. A
new way to hold my left hand, with the fingers curved instead
of straight; a new way to use certain keys, rotating the wrist so
that a knuckle could activate them with minimal finger movement; a new way to tongue detached notes. It was all about
economy of movement, something familiar to me from piano.
But the new hand position was daunting. I couldn't seem to
keep the holes covered if I curved my fingers; it was like learning to play all over again from scratch. "Don't worry," he said,
watching as I struggled to keep the pads of my fingers in contact with them. "You'll get used to it. Then you'll wonder how
you ever played with straight fingers." And he winked. When
discussion of his fee came up, he saw from my face that I didn't

think we could manage it and said he would work something out with my mother. But I would need a better instrument.

My grandparents came to the rescue, offering not only to pay for the six weeks of lessons but, wondrously, to buy me a clarinet. In this regard, unwittingly, I had chosen well: of all the band instruments, clarinets were the least expensive. (My grandfather was a cutter in a garment factory.) Towards the end of May, on another Saturday that began with a piano lesson (at which Mr. Cohen, deeply excited at my progress with the Fantaisie-Impromptu, promised I could learn the Rachmaninoff C sharp minor Prelude and maybe a concerto that summer), I floated down the stairs of the Chantilly to the car, where my mother was waiting to drive me downtown to Archambault, the city's principal music store. Five floors of instruments, accessories, and sheet music: wind instruments were on the third floor. After trying clarinets for close to an hour on the prompts of a helpful salesman, I chose a French-made Buffet 187, a middle-range professional model that was one of two or three Mr. Masella had recommended. Three weeks later, I played a successful audition on it and was accepted to the Conservatoire.

I did not know it yet, but I was now on a course that would govern the next ten years of my life.

V   INTERMEZZO: LISTENERS

FROM MY EMAIL FILES:

To: Alan Fraser
Sent: Friday, May 08, 2009

So I met with Phil at last. He didn't have much to say
about my playing—just listened. And then talked. Some
of what he was saying sounded familiar, some not, I'm
not sure how well I was understanding him. But he says
he'll do one session with me soon, then have Pamela work
with me until he has more time. The subject of a recital
didn't come up, and I certainly wasn't going to raise it. He
probably thinks I was nuts to propose such a thing—I'm
starting to think so too …

From: Alan Fraser
I think you should not take any negative impressions of
your meeting with Phil as a sign that you were crazy to
think of playing a recital. The paradox is, you have to be

your own person to be with him, you have to be your own person to be an artist, but the guru-disciple relationship by nature requires the disciple to give up her own will and allow the guru's will to be hers. There's a profound growth available in that process that is not achievable any other way, but ... It's a catch-22. An interesting question: is such a relationship appropriate so "late in life"?

From: Robyn Sarah
I never really thought of Phil as a guru but it's true his kind of teaching seems to require some surrender of will—I'm remembering this. But can you be your own person and give up your will at the same time? Your question, whether such a relationship is appropriate at my age, is interesting. A few months ago a photographer friend of ours visited from overseas, and we sat up late one night talking about his relationship with the photographer Robert Frank, a big influence who for the past fifteen years has been a sort of guru figure to him (he used that word). This has mostly taken the form of a correspondence they've maintained—J. working out his thoughts in handwritten letters that incorporate his own digital photographs and other visual material, both original and found. He will work sometimes for days on such a letter, writing two or more for every reply he gets. Lately most of his creative energy has been going into these letters. He says he considers this to be his current "work" as an artist and that it may even survive as such, since RF's correspondence will likely be published one day.

J. says writing these letters fulfills a need for him. He says as a visual artist who may go years between exhibitions, he needs to feel "someone's listening" in order to sustain his creative life. I said why does it have to be Robert Frank—he could write letters to us, or other friends. I thought he was too fixated on RF as a big-name

photographer, and that by cultivating this relationship
he might be failing himself—failing to develop his own
artistic path. I remember saying, "You're almost sixty,
you shouldn't need a guru at this age, you should BE
someone's guru at this age"—and thinking, even as I
said it, *Then why have I been toying with the idea of
re-establishing contact with Phil Cohen?* I knew it wasn't
just about improving my piano playing. It was about
putting myself into the hands of someone inspiring,
someone who seemed to know what mattered in art and
life. Maybe it doesn't have to do with age—maybe there
are stages in our life when we need a guru? Phil said
yesterday that every musician needs *feedback*, that even
famous concert artists arrange occasionally to be heard by
a mentor-figure. Which hearkens back to J.'s need to feel
"someone's listening." Phil was someone whose *listening*
I trusted.

I may be able to establish more of a relationship of
equals with Phil by talking to him about my work as a
poet—this seems to interest him. He asked whether I write
freely or whether there are a lot of drafts. Well, no serious
writer writes "freely," but writers have different processes,
and mine may be unusual: I begin with a few lines that I
hope may evolve into a poem, but each time something
doesn't sound right, I have to stop and find something that
does, or I can't go on. I scratch out the lines that aren't
working and try new ones, testing them by reading aloud
from the beginning, because I need to hear them in context
of what came before. For many years I even felt compelled
to physically recopy from the beginning with each new try
at a continuation. So my "drafts" are really one continuously evolving draft, with most of the revision happening as
I go along, and my ear driving the process.

And now it occurs to me that one of the things I've
wanted to overcome at the piano is a compulsion to stop

and self-correct, or even go back to the beginning, every
time I miss a note or play something that doesn't sound
the way I wanted it to. Could I be applying my writing
process—which happens privately, in stages, taking as
long as it needs to take—to musical performance, which
has to unfold continuously in real time?

Hmmm. This may be a revelation. Alan, thanks for
being my sounding board!

I'm struck, now, by that line. *Thank you for being my sounding board.* It amounts to *Thanks for listening*—words we say to
people who may have no better answer to our personal dilem-
mas and puzzlements than we do ourselves. People whose willingness to listen is all the answer we really need; people whose
listening helps us find our own answers, or helps us accept
that sometimes there is no answer. Clergymen. Therapists.
Teachers. Friends. Or strangers on a train.

VI   EMBARKATIONS

Prelude: Silent Glissandos

MY FIRST SESSION WITH PHIL, A SUNDAY MORNING IN May in Hingston Hall, is not unlike my first lesson with him at the age of eleven, in that I scarcely play a note. It's a mix of talk (him doing the talking) and exercises at the keyboard, mostly silent ones—exercises for tactility, balance, coordination of movement (hand, arm, body, head), and breath rhythm.

He asks me first to situate myself in relation to the piano— to find a seating position that allows me to move in any direction and reach any part of the keyboard without overextension or strain. "Three areas of stability: your seat, your feet on the floor, your hands on the keyboard. Find your centre of balance. Whatever part of the keyboard you are playing on, your movement and position should seek to recreate your centre of balance." Then he directs me through a series of exercises— warm-ups, he calls them—sliding up and down on the keyboard with both hands, starting from centre, parallel motion: palms and undersides of fingers in contact with the keys and moving lightly over them in a slow silent *glissando*, body leaning after the hands; foot swivelling on the heel so leg can

follow; head turning last as the hands reach the upper end of
the keyboard and reverse direction—as if the head movement
triggered the change of direction. Hands moving the other way
now, back through centre and down towards the bass end of
the keyboard—body following, pivot on heel, head last to turn,
then slow swivel of hands as I return to my primary centre of
balance. The piano keys just barely dip in rapid succession,
making the faintest clicking, like the sound of a thumb flipping
through a deck of cards.

"Remember to keep a steady, continuous breath rhythm."

After a few tries, I see it's a logical choreography, like the
swivel at the wrist when a violinist's bow reverses direction—a
fluid, rhythmic, continuous sequence of movements. It takes
concentration but feels natural; a false move is immediately
experienced as jarring.

"Now try doing the same thing, but in contrary motion."
He guides me: upper palms flat on the white keys, undersides
of fingers brushing the black keys, hands sliding along the surface of the keys, moving outward and away from each other
towards opposite ends of the keyboard, wrists rotating outward as the body leans slightly forward; hands then moving
back towards each other, slowly swivelling inward at the wrist
again like windshield wipers coming together in slow motion—
then crossing and uncrossing a couple of times, over and under,
before returning to centre as the body straightens and realigns.

"Good, that's it, you have the idea."

Do I? But what is *the idea? Why call this a warm-up? I'm
barely moving my fingers—how is this supposed to prepare them
to play?* Something tells me I shouldn't need to ask these questions running through my head like subtitles on a screen while
I repeat the motions. As a child, I didn't try to understand the
purpose of the strange "swimming exercises" he had me do at
my first lesson. Maybe that's why I *did* understand—even if
not in words? It was as if the movements themselves *were* the
purpose. Or they enacted it somehow.

Phil is watching me, but he's wearing sunglasses again, I can't see his eyes.

"You know what the challenge is, don't you, with the piano. To play a musical instrument with real facility, it has to be like part of your own body. When you sing, the music is coming directly from your body. With a wind instrument, your breath makes the sound and connects you physically with the instrument, makes it continuous with you. With a stringed instrument, you're holding it under your chin or against your body, you feel the wood vibrate, you feel the vibration of the string in your bowing hand—you're in contact with what makes the instrument sing. But with the piano you don't have that contact. When you press the keys, you're activating a mechanism to make the sound. It's a stringed instrument—strings are what make the sound—but you aren't bowing or plucking the strings. You're never in direct contact with what makes the sound, you're pressing keys that activate hammers to hit the strings. And as long as you think of playing piano as pressing keys, you're thinking of it as a percussion instrument. You're thinking *vertically*—one note and then the next, instead of a singing line." He demonstrates: a melody played as a series of individual notes struck from above, *plunk, plunk, plunk,* like a child's one-finger playing, or a mallet hitting xylophone keys.

"Vertical playing is percussive playing. So this becomes the problem: how do you turn a percussion instrument into a *singing* instrument? And how do you establish physical connection with an instrument you can't hold? An instrument that's also a huge, complex machine—I mean, look at this thing, it's nine feet long, you have to get up and take a walk to touch the other end of it, you can't see what's going on inside when you're playing. How do you make something of this size and complexity feel like an extension of your body?"

It isn't something I've ever asked myself. I look at him blankly, the sunglasses look back—behind them, is he waiting for an answer? But now I remember the intimacy of holding my clarinet—channelling my breath into it, feeling the reed vibrate against my lip. The protective curve of my hands loosely crad-ling the instrument when I wasn't playing, fingers poised lightly over the ring keys and open holes, thumb balancing the familiar weight so securely on the thumb-rest that I could effectively let go with all my other fingers and not drop it. The way the wooden shaft and the metal keys warmed to the touch as I played ...

"Here, give me your hand," says my teacher. He turns it palm upward and runs his thumb lightly over the upper third of the palm—the fleshy area just below the fingers and the hollow immediately below, between head line and heart line. "The palm of the hand, this area right here especially, is one of the most sensitive parts of the body. When you warm up this way—feeling the keys with your palms, moving laterally—you establish a tactile relationship with the piano. Physically, you signal yourself to experience the keyboard as a continuum, to feel the instrument's range as a continuum—not as a series of separate keys to strike. You give yourself the basis for a sing-ing line, for playing that's lyrical."

So strange to be sitting side by side at the keyboard again, hearing that utterly familiar voice by my right shoulder. It's as if no time at all has passed, except that I'm so much older, he's so much older. I feel like Rip Van Winkle. Was I asleep all this time? Where *have* I been?

And where am I now, and where are we going? I seem to be back at the very beginning—encountering the piano as if for the first time. How long will it take me to get from here to where I thought I was?

%

Phil has more to deliver during this session, more than I can assimilate at once; I can only scribble notes and hope that when I look at them at home I'll be able to unpack what I now understand only in theory and see how to apply it. There's more about sketching as a way of working with the score. There are new concepts: one is "expressively directed timing," which he says should govern everything I do at the keyboard; another is listening to an inner conductor, what he calls an "embodied" conductor, to keep myself focused on where the music is going. There's the principle of using parts of me that aren't actively engaged—the hand that isn't playing, for example, or my own voice, scat-singing—to guide myself rhythmically or to guide my movements: "Two fingers of one hand can tap out the rhythm on the back of the hand that's playing. Or you can scat the rhythm while you play it. One hand can guide the movement of the other, or remind the thumb not to stick up in the air by holding it down as you play. These are ways you can provide yourself with reinforcement even when you're alone."

Laying a hand lightly against the fallboard of the Falcone, he continues, "The modern piano has possibilities no earlier keyboard instrument could offer. Not only can it play multiple voices, but it gives the player access to seven full octaves, a full dynamic range, and multiple colours, multiple tonal possibilities. It's like having a whole orchestra at our disposal. Creativity at the piano comes from understanding the music orchestrally—hearing the voice lines as if they were different instruments, interacting, talking to one another. An orchestra has a conductor to cue the musicians on how and when to bring out their individual parts, but a pianist has to be conductor and player at the same time. You need to get yourself out of the way and find your 'self' as performer—it's about replacing self and the worries of self with an internal conductor you can listen to instead." And now his voice changes, shifts from authoritative to private, personal—a suddenly gentle voice, intimate, almost entreating: "When we're working creatively, we see the world in a different way. Expressing something creatively—bringing out something from inside—when we're doing this, we're in touch with what's real. This is when we're our real selves. The rest of life is something else."

I know this voice, the voice of my childhood piano lessons. And I know this truth: I have lived by it as a writer.
Momentarily, I'm flooded with that remembered sense of being
in touch with something age-old, precious, mysterious, and
profound, of being inducted into something secret and sacred.

Later, packing up to leave, we both pause again by the
framed photograph of Alfred Cortot with its handwritten
inscription, *"à ma chère élève et amie Yvonne Hubert en sou-
venir d'admiration pour son grand talent et de sincère affection."* How young Cortot looks in this picture! I wonder how
old his protégé was then. Phil says, "I remember when he died,
in the 1960s. Yvonne phoned to tell me. I'll never forget that
phone call, the way her voice sounded ... how devastated she
was ..." I feel the presence in the room of a chain of instruction—Cortot to Hubert to Cohen; it's as if for a moment Cortot
and Yvonne Hubert are in the room with us, embodied in Phil
briefly lost in reverie. I never met Yvonne Hubert; I never
heard Cortot play. But looking at the photograph, I think, *This
is a portrait of my great-grand-teacher.*

Phil phones the following evening. "I didn't want to go
away without making sure you understood everything." (He'll
only be gone for a week!) "Are you getting the picture? Is there
anything you're not clear on—anything I can help you with?"
Maybe more than anything else, it's this phone call that makes
me feel I've come home.

Fugue: Vous êtes convoqué(e)

Come with me now: round to the side entrance
and down the marble stairs,
past the Sunday dwarf who guards the *Vestiaire*,
to the basement hall with its faint smell
of a scooped-out pumpkin—quickly, come,

we are late, you see—already
the bows are sliding up and down
under the dim spotlights where smoke
from morning cigarettes collects to hang
like a blue island on the musty air ...

You can write your name in dust
on the wooden seats of the fold-down chairs
where the hinged cases lie open
like empty carapaces, lined in old plush
moth-eaten blue or threadbare red

blackened by tarnish from silver keys
or dandruffed by rosin. On the *scène*
the *chef d'orchestre*, haloed by wild hair,
bohemian in a new red flannel shirt
points at the brass with trembling stick,

and the bell of a French horn, raised on cue,
gleams a reply. One long golden note
hurts into being, drawn out pure till he
clips it off with a flick—then drops into a
mincing squat, hissing

Pianissimo!
(and beyond the heavy drapes, out
on the snowy street, making moan,
the hooded pigeons promenade
to a solemn bonging of bells.)

At the mercy of three city buses before the Métro was built, it
took me well over an hour to get from Montreal's west end to
the Conservatoire's main address a few blocks east of "The
Main," or Boulevard St-Laurent, the street that roughly divides

the city along linguistic lines. Leaving directly from school, as I did two or three afternoons a week, I'd hit the Atwater terminus downtown at rush hour and squeeze onto a jam-packed, overheated Number 15, hanging on to the overhead rail with one hand, gripping the handles of my homework-stuffed briefcase and clarinet case in the other, sometimes dozing off on my feet, head resting in the crook of my elbow—held upright only by the press of bodies around me, my fellow sardines. Past a certain point, French began to replace English as the language of most of the passengers, but in those days the drivers still sang out in both languages: "MIN' the doors, *attention 'portes! En arrière, s'il vous plaît*, step to the rear please, *y a place en arrière,* there is place enough at the back!" Suddenly I was in a different Montreal, one whose existence I had barely been aware of, living on the other side of the invisible wall that divides the proverbial Two Solitudes. And when I reached my destination, it was to take my place in an environment that was remarkably international: alongside Canadians of both the French and English persuasions, my teachers and fellow students were Italian, French-from-France, Viennese, Hungarian, Armenian, Romanian, Ukrainian, Russian, Japanese, Israeli, Lebanese, Moroccan—representing the cultural diversity of a city then still the most cosmopolitan in Canada. We communicated and were taught in a mix of French and English spoken with a variety of accents, but the common language was music.

Beginning from the second year I studied there, the Conservatoire was housed in the Show Mart Building or Palais du Commerce on Rue Berri, a low-lying, block-long structure that had served as Montreal's main exhibition hall since the early 1950s. For that whole year, the sidewalk that hugged its south side dropped away into a gargantuan excavation site, visible through windows cut in the board construction fence erected the length of the block. Far below, tiny workers in yellow hard hats milled around yellow machines with

caterpillar treads in the great muddy pit that would be the
Berri-de Montigny Métro station when the subway opened
in fall of 1966, in anticipation of the world's fair the following summer. In the meantime, I arrived at school on a sort of
trestle.

The Conservatoire moved to new quarters soon after I
left in the early seventies, and the Palais was razed in 2002
to make way for the Grande Bibliothèque Nationale that occupies the site today, but old photos of the Show Mart still flood
me with nostalgia. For a few years I was deeply happy there.
It was a make-do home for a music school. We had no auditorium, no cafeteria, no lounge. Our common room was the
Vestiaire by the elevator, a large cloakroom lined with metal
lockers. A row of windows, too high to look out of, admitted
shafts of afternoon sun in which a haze of cigarette smoke
lingered. At centre was a large oak conference table with two
long benches—a sort of island where you could socialize over
a coffee, read a newspaper, eat a hasty brown-bagged or take-
out supper between classes, or spread out Xeroxed pages of
sheet music to tape into folios. Our orchestra rehearsed a block
away, in the dusty basement auditorium of the Bibliothèque
Saint-Sulpice, or farther uptown facing Fletcher's Field in the
Pavillon Mont Royal, which had once housed the Jewish "Y"
and now belonged to the Université de Montréal. Most of our
concerts were at Plateau Hall in the Parc Lafontaine, where the
Montreal Symphony performed before Place des Arts was built.
All the rest—administration, private teaching, chamber music
rehearsals, classes in *solfège, dictée musicale,* and the advanced
theoretical subjects—happened in the Show Mart, whose upper
corridors traced a city-block-long rectangle around the high-
ceilinged show space. This was a world of its own.

I spent ten to twelve hours a week along those studio-
lined corridors whose wall panels were painted a dizzying
alternation of lime green and teal blue. Each studio had an
outer door padded in dark-red upholstery leather with bronze

studs, and an inner door of wood; in each, a small square window at eye level. Walking up and down in search of a practice
space between classes (*green … blue … green … blue …*) you
could glance into studio after studio through these double
windows: here a violin lesson in progress; there a cellist,
her wrist oscillating in slow vibrato; here a male singer belt-
ing out the chromatic scale on long vowels, up past the fifth
and down again, "*Ay-Oh-Ay-Oh-Ay-Oh-Ay-Oh—Ay-Oh-Ay-
Oh-Ay-Oh-Ay-Oh—Aay!*"—then starting anew a semitone
higher, in response to a plunked chord on the piano. Next
door a pianist thunders through scales in double octaves.
Then an empty studio—locked, alas. Another, one of the larger ones, unlocked—your heart leaps—but no, a peek inside
reveals waiting instruments balanced on open cases, chairs
in a semicircle: a chambre rehearsal in progress, members
on a short break. Here is a tall flautist, his music stand pre-
cariously extended to full height, bobbing and swaying to an
energetic étude; there, a *solfège* class beating time with their
right hands; here, a percussionist getting up a private racket
on cymbals and snares. In every box, the feel of solitary or
communal industry, of deep engagement.

The studios were soundproofed, but you could always hear
a faint cacophony in the corridor. Even at lessons, the tenor's
vigorous *Ay-Oh-Ay-Oh's* leaked through the wall from next
door. The outer doors had to be pulled hard to open, sucking
air as the plush edges yielded their seal; the inner doors were
lined with strong-smelling cork for further insulation. The
rooms were stuffy year-round and horribly overheated in winter: sweat ran when we played. The windows stuck. What tri-
umph to succeed in dislodging a frame, letting in a frigid blast
that mixed with the heat rising from the radiator-grill to make
the air shimmer above the sill: seen through this, the façades of
the derelict row-housing across Saint-Denis seemed to ripple
and dance.

Ralph Masella's studio was always blue with his Balkan Sobranie pipe smoke, whose aroma blended nicely with the cork smell. My lessons were at five in the evening, usually on Tuesdays, symphony night. The tower bell of the Église Saint-Jacques down the street would be bonging its solemn monotone as I assembled my clarinet. Beyond the window, the downtown sky displayed sunset colours above low rooflines, then turned twilight-blue while the city lit up. The window went black and mirrored me back to myself. As I warbled through my week's endless étude—working my way, over the years, through progressive levels of Labanchi, Périer, Blancou, Jeanjean, and the *Grands études concertants* of d'Elia—Mr. Masella would lean back in his chair and sometimes his eyes would drop shut, a slight twitch under the lids the only sign he was listening. I could feel his struggle to stay awake; he worked a long day. On symphony Tuesdays, with other Conservatoire teachers, in three hours he'd be on stage in the brand new concert hall at Place des Arts, playing first chair with the MSO.

%

My induction into this world in fall of 1964, at the age of not quite fourteen, was almost as unlikely as my learning to play clarinet in the first place. I had not been born into a family of musicians; my parents, though they appreciated classical music and owned a few cherished LPs, knew little about the music world. I had never been taken to a symphony concert or ballet. When I was small my mother would occasionally put a Beethoven symphony on the record player (she was particularly fond of the Seventh), but my reaction was usually to beg her to turn it off because the emotions it evoked in me were too overwhelming to be pleasant. My private piano lessons were regarded as recreational, my playing to be pursued for my own and perhaps others' occasional enjoyment—a potential social asset if I kept it up. When I signed on for music in high

school, my knowledge of the symphony orchestra was limited
to what I had gleaned from *The Golden Stamp Book of Musical
Instruments*, the same children's series from which I'd learned
to recognize and name dog breeds and bird species. Certainly
there were no expectations at home that I might end up in a
professional music school.

The same was true for most of the younger wind players at
Conservatoire, who came there (as I did) from the high-school
band programs that had begun to provide a feeder stream for
the first North American music institution of higher learning
to be entirely state-subsidized. The Conservatoire de musique
du Québec à Montréal was founded by the Quebec government
in 1943 in the tradition of European conservatories, and mod-
elled on the Conservatoire de Paris. It was the first of the network of nine regional conservatories in the province that would
constitute the Conservatoire de musique et d'art dramatique
du Québec (the theatre program was added a few years later).
That the instruction there was free (it is no longer) now seems
to me extraordinary; that the regional network meant rural
kids, too, could receive high-level music instruction without
having to move to the larger cities, at least as much so. Only in
retrospect do I understand how phenomenally lucky I was to
benefit from what I then took for granted and imagined to be
the norm: first the widespread existence of high-school band
programs, then the Conservatoire's full subsidy for advanced
studies on any instrument.

It was a serious school, and very French—the atmosphere
formal and unapologetically authoritarian, the curriculum
fixed. Everyone upon admission had to do one year of music
theory. After that came three years of compulsory ear training
in the form of *solfège* (sight singing) and music dictation, two
hours a week of each, leading to a "Certificate in Theoretical
Studies." Only then could one go on to the advanced theoretical subjects that were prerequisite for those who wished
to study musical composition or conducting. Participation in

ensembles—orchestra and chamber music—was assigned; by whom and on what basis remained mysterious.

Communications from *La Direction* arrived by mail each September, summoning us to register on a designated day and receive our course lists and schedules; similar mailings advised of mid-term and final exams in all of our subjects. We also received invitations and programs for upcoming concerts and theatrical productions by the students in *Arts dramatiques.* The notices were in French, sometimes with English translation verso; they all began "*Vous êtes convoqué(e)* ..." followed by the event, date, time, and place ("You are convoked ..." made me giggle, it sounded so pompous in English) and they ended with the formulaic "*Veuillez agréer, Mademoiselle* (or Monsieur), *l'expression de mes sentiments les plus distingués.*" So much grander than "Yours truly"!—if more flowery than the occasion seemed to warrant. There was something thrilling about these missives, even in their stilted English versions (*"You are convoked to an examination of solfège on the Tuesday, 4 March, in Room 301, at 2 h."*) They had class. I seem to recall they were printed on creamy, deckle-edged paper, but surely that was only the concert invitations.

One had the sense the school had been even more serious before the influx of high-school students from the band programs. The Conservatoire was conceived and designed to be a full-time music program, not an extracurricular one. There was a tacit expectation that if we did not withdraw from high school on acceptance, we should at least demonstrate our seriousness of intent by putting our musical studies first. An effort was made to schedule younger students' lessons, *solfège*, and dictation classes after school hours, but we were often "convoked" for exams in the middle of the school day and had either to skip school or request a change of time—requests generally granted, if frostily; one didn't want to ask too often.

Short of quitting high school, I did eventually have to request special accommodation there. Between daily practice on two instruments, Conservatoire class hours, and the endless time on public transit, there was no way I could get much schoolwork done in the evening, so I appealed to the principal for permission to spend one class period a day in the library, getting a start on homework. In view of my strong academic standing this was granted, but I didn't always spend those periods doing homework. The librarian, Mrs. Petrie, was too interesting. She was the niece of Group of Seven painter A.Y. Jackson, whom she called "Uncky Dunck," and she had stories about accompanying him, as cook, on one of his Baffin Island expeditions. She showed me the book that her sister wrote about this expedition, with reproductions of his paintings and sketches. She also liked to recommend reading to me. When I mentioned having loved the story "Miss Brill," which we'd read in English class, she led me to the appropriate shelf and put Katherine Mansfield's *Complete Short Stories* into my hands—a landmark moment for me as a writer—and with it, the Mansfield biography by Anthony Alpers. From the latter I learned that when Mansfield first sailed to London from her native New Zealand at fifteen—my own age at the time—it was with aspirations to become a professional cellist.

§

Solfège Des Solfèges. How would you even translate that? I'm looking at a three-inch-high stack of identically formatted pamphlets—a graded series edition, printed in France, with publisher's addresses in Paris and Brussels—pulled out of a dusty storage box of old sheet music. Fourteen soft-covered, dun-hued, staple-bound compilations of sight-singing exercises, accumulated in three years of ear training at Conservatoire. The long-forgotten names of compilers and composers—Lemoine, Danhauser, Lavignac, Gaevaert,

Samuel, Fétis. The blue-ink rubber stamp of *Ed Archambault Montreal* on cover or flyleaf, with the Canadian price: *75 cents*. How many domestic relocations must have I dragged these relics through, as life carried me farther and farther from the years when they had a place in it? Surely I never imagined I might practise these exercises again. But something about the covers with their classic letterpress design, some kind of European dignity, seemed to preclude throwing them away.

Thumbing through them now, I'm impressed. Was I really able to sight-sing in all those clefs? Not just treble and bass, but also alto and tenor, with the clef sign changing every few bars? I remember my horror at fifteen, a self-conscious age, on learning I was going to have to *sing*—sometimes alone, in front of teacher and class—using *do-re-mi* syllables while beating time with my right hand. How quickly the dreaded activity became merely tedious. We were five or six to a class, most older than I, but something about *solfège* made us regress. We yawned; we complained; we whispered, passed notes, cracked jokes to distract our teachers, who tolerated all amiably enough—but when called on to sing, together or separately, we sang.

Dictée musicale was too challenging to be tedious. By the second year, even the students blessed with perfect pitch, or next-best, "relative pitch," were kept on their toes. I had neither: I could not identify a note's exact pitch on hearing it, nor could I instantly identify the interval between two heard notes. In *dictée* class, we sat in rows at long study tables while the teacher played a short musical composition on the piano. Then he'd give us the key signature and time signature and play it again in four-bar segments, which we were expected to transcribe by ear onto music staves. He would repeat each segment three or four times to allow us to get it down, then call on someone to read out the notes they'd written, and someone else to read out the rhythm, correcting them where necessary. There was barely time to amend my copy or fill in blanks before he was on to the next segment. The musical selections were in four voices from the start, and progressed from simple chorale style (voices moving mostly in tandem) to more complex scoring with voices rhythmically independent. Harmonically, we could expect accidentals and at least one modulation before the return to starting key.

The quality of attention it took to hear each voice separately and get both notes and rhythm accurately on paper on three or four hearings wasn't easily mustered after an hour on public transit at the end of the school day. If you misjudged a musical interval in one of the voice lines, the error in pitch perpetuated itself in every note that followed, and by the time you recognized something was amiss, it could be hard to locate where you'd gone off. Backtracking to correct the faulty voice line meant missing the start of the next segment, but keeping pace with the dictation meant you had to leave that voice-part blank and try to pick it up again later on. I always began the two hours gamely enough: pencil sharpened and poised, at my elbow a packet of Scotch mints to suck on as an aid to concentration (by the end of two hours my tongue was raw). But no matter how hard I tried to keep pace, soon enough I'd find myself in a sweat, frantically erasing, rewriting, erasing again, copying from the boy next to me, leaving more and more blanks as I fell farther behind. My eraser wore holes in the page. Sometimes I'd simply give up and put my head down on the desk, waiting out the end of the exercise.

I could get away with this because our teacher, Gabriel Cusson, was blind. Behind his dark glasses, he was blessedly unaware of our struggles to keep up. *"Minute-là ..."*—as his fingers scanned a page of Braille notation—*"Bon! On continue."* Beaming, benevolent, he would proceed at his own pace, delivering the next four bars on the piano, sometimes humming along with them in his rich baritone to emphasize one voice or another. Dear Monsieur Cusson! For all my travails in his class, I remember him warmly. An organist and composer, he was our teacher for all three years of obligatory *dictée musicale.* He must then have been in his sixties, a tall gaunt man with an aristocratic face, an impressive mane of wavy silver hair, and a benign smile playing perpetually about his lips. There was something majestic about his measured stride down the hall, on the arm of a woman considerably his junior whom he referred to only as "Madame"—reaching ahead with his white cane, posture preternaturally erect, head held high, his expression alert and cordial. In the studio, Madame led him to his piano stool, helped him off with coat and scarf, and arranged his Braille sheets on the music desk. From the first roll call, he remembered our names, recognized our voices, and seemed to know more or less where we sat, addressing himself in the general direction of the student he was calling upon.

"*Bon!* Victor, what-*are* my notes?" "*Alors*, Martin, '*ave*-you my rhythm?" He'd wait, smiling seraphically like his angel namesake, and if one student had it wrong, he'd call on another, perpetually optimistic. I dreaded his, "Robyn! '*ave*-you my notes?" and the gently disappointed "*Non?*" before he moved on to somebody else. His faith in us was egalitarian and unfailing, if in my case unfounded. It wasn't his fault that he couldn't see me flailing in my piles of eraser crumbs. Still, for the duration of the class I tried to rise to that faith, even as I waited for the reprieve of his ritual parting words, "*Bon!* *Un*-til next week."

§

On a Saturday morning in September of my second year at Conservatoire—I was about to turn fifteen—having been "convoked" to the *classe d'orchestre*, I arrived much too early at the Bibliothèque Saint-Sulpice for my first practice. The heritage building on Saint-Denis was in a transitional phase at the time. Founded by Sulpician priests in 1917, it had housed the first French-language library in Canada, and it still housed a collection of books and archival material, though one that was no longer staffed or open to the public. The elegant Beaux-Arts façade had been maintained, but the shadowy interior had the air of a faded beauty—a little mysterious, a little melancholy, abandoned but clinging to the dignity of her past. I could hear a violin from somewhere below as I entered. A distinctive bouquet of mould enveloped me as I descended the side stairwell, following the sound.

The hall was dark and empty except for the lone violinist, who looked to be in his early twenties and was pacing up and down the length of the dim-lit stage, energetically bowing double-stops. Seeing that he had left his coat and open violin case on audience seating, I took my cue and assembled my clarinet, leaving my own coat and case on a seat. What now? Others began to trickle in, unhurriedly unlatching cases, applying rosin to bows, adjusting tuning pegs, blowing into mouthpieces. They called greetings to one another in French. Some lit cigarettes; some had brought coffee in take-out cups, croissants in paper bags—they all seemed so worldly, so at ease! I felt terribly young and English-Canadian and shy. No one greeted me (had I expected a welcoming committee?) and I saw no one I knew well enough to speak to at first. But gradually musicians with their instruments began to move towards the stage. Someone was up there distributing sheet music; the stage lights bloomed; the early bird violinist sat down in the concertmaster's chair, and others began to take their seats. The conductor had arrived.

Those of us new to the orchestra that year were called by name and directed to our places, beginning with a girl cellist who looked no more than twelve, so at least I wasn't the youngest. I was to play first clarinet. Making my way across the stage, I registered with excitement that the music on the stands was Beethoven—Symphony No. 4. It wasn't a symphony I knew, but this was serious music! And it was the real thing, a step up from abridged adaptations for school band. The second clarinetist was already seated; he motioned me to the chair beside him. There were only two of us, centre stage at the heart of the woodwind section.

The music in front of me looked nothing like a first clarinet part for band: I saw at once that instead of playing melody most of the time along with the other first clarinets in a band section, I would be sitting out long blocks of rests and playing sustained notes or offbeats for extended passages while the violins and other strings had the melody. But there were parts marked "Solo" where, as principal clarinet, I would be carrying the melody all alone for a few phrases or a few lines—exposed in a way that I never was in band. Help! I needed some time to learn the solos before we began rehearsing this! Around me, everyone was warming up, the distinctive cacophony of an orchestra settling down to business. The conductor, stocky and balding with a ring of dark hair circling his pate and two unruly tufts above his ears, tapped on the podium for silence, signalling the oboe player to sound the "A." The penetrating, drawn-out note was cue for the more purposeful din of tuning: open fifths on the strings wavering their way to correct pitch, wind players sounding and adjusting their A's (I unscrewed the barrel of my clarinet by a hair or two to bring mine down); little snatches of chromatic scale here and there from individuals still in warm-up mode. Tap-tap on the podium again, and as the last of the din tapered off to silence, a brusque "*Premier mouvement*" from the conductor. Without another word, he raised his baton.

What! We're starting now? There was an aspect of sink-or-swim to everything at Conservatoire, but never would I feel it the way I did that morning as the opening bars of Beethoven's Fourth rang out and the music moved inexorably towards my first solo.

※

For the next two years, and intermittently thereafter, I played first clarinet in the Conservatoire Orchestra. We learned two new concert programs each year, rehearsing three hours a week, generally on Saturdays, and up to seven hours on concert weekends—Saturday morning, Saturday afternoon, then Sunday morning at Plateau Hall for a Sunday evening performance. The first year, we repeated our first program on a mini-tour of rural Quebec, travelling by charter bus (merriment and hijinks en route) to play concerts at seminaries in Valleyfield, Sainte-Thérèse, and Sorel. We played wonderful repertoire: Beethoven's Second, Fourth, and Seventh symphonies, Gabriel Fauré's Pelléas et Mélisande, Schubert's Entr'actes from Rosamunde and his Unfinished Symphony, Debussy's Prélude à l'Après-midi d'un faune, Dvorak's Eighth Symphony, Brahms's First Symphony, Ravel's Mother Goose Suite. Young soloists, usually pianists, joined us on the programs, performing Mozart's Piano Concerto in D Minor, the rarely played Rimsky-Korsakov piano concerto, César Franck's Variations Symphoniques. I also participated in chamber music ensembles, rehearsing and performing repertoire for wind quintet and various combinations of winds, strings, and piano.

A wonderland had opened up to me, a many-roomed mansion I moved through for a few years in a blissful sort of waking dream. It had its constellation of familiar haunts. Outside of headquarters at the Show Mart, there were the halls where we rehearsed and performed. There was the new concert hall at Place des Arts where, as Conservatoire students, we were privileged with discount tickets to the season's series and the occasional complimentary pass to Nutcracker or other special programs. There was Geracimo's, on Sainte-Catherine Street around the corner from the Show Mart, the eatery of choice for a meal-break snatched between classes or rehearsals (two egg rolls and an orangeade, or a heated plate of *macaroni au four* were the only items on the menu I could afford on my high-school allowance unless I shared an order with friends: I tasted my first pizza at Geracimo's).

On the same block was Archambault's, where I bought sheet music, reeds, and other supplies; and tucked away in the alley behind Archambault's, in a low, garage-like building, there was Maurice Twigg's musical instrument repair shop, where Mr. Masella would send me when my clarinet needed adjustment. A jumbled, dim-lit, Ali Baba's cave of a shop—floor covered with instrument cases, instruments suspended from the ceiling: dented, tarnished French horns, silver and gold saxophones, clarinets of both wood and metal, trumpets, baritones, curious unidentifiable brass instruments, the odd forlorn-looking violin. All were dusty and some looked ancient, leading me to wonder. Were they really awaiting repair, or had they been abandoned here by their owners? Was the ceiling at Twigg's a sort of half-life for instruments retired from service? Nothing seemed to change at Twigg's: worktable always littered with dismantled key systems (how did he manage not to mix them up?), old keypads with the glue crumbling, snippets of cork, smudged carbons of receipts, reed boxes, glue and oil cans, work tools, full ashtrays, empty Pepsi bottles; the blowtorch with its forked flame; the silent grey machinery; walls plastered with faded, autographed photos of defunct big bands and combos, current jazz and rock groups, fingering charts, music ads. French-language radio playing incessant pop tunes; the phone on its swivel-stand ringing continually, Mr. Twigg's curt "*Ouai*" as he picked up. He would be sitting there on his high stool, holding a saxophone key over the blowtorch, carefully picking loose a pad as the dark glue beneath it turned to a smoking liquid—the saxophone lying on its side on the padded board in front of him, looking bare and helpless with most of its keys missing, like a patient on an operating table. The doors constantly swinging open to admit blasts of ice-cold wind and aging French-Canadian saxophonists, a steady stream of customers, Conservatoire students, old-time band members, rock group members, high-school band leaders—they all knew Maurice, they all had news to exchange. Maurice answering laconically, his hands still busy; the musicians taking a lively interest in one another. I'd wait my turn until he could check my clarinet for leaks, blowing a mouthful of smoke into each of the upper joints, holes stopped, bottom of the cylinder blocked with his palm; we'd watch for tiny wisps seeping out from beneath a key, an indication that the pad closing the hole had become warped from moisture and was no longer sealing evenly. If smoke could get out, so could air, making the instrument much more taxing to blow and dulling the tone. Once the leak was located, it was my clarinet's turn to lie on the board while he removed the key section in question with a twist or two of a miniature screwdriver, heated the problem key to melt the glue, extracted the old pad and replaced it with a new one. Another deft twist or two and the key was back in place, ready for a repeat of the smoke test to ensure the new pad was seated properly before the glue dried.

％

May 9, 1965. I'm the first member of the orchestra to arrive at Plateau Hall for our spring concert, debut of our second program of the year. This is a critical moment for me. After a shaky beginning I proved on tour I could master my nerves enough to play my solos without mishap, but that was the same old familiar program. Now I must show I can play other music on stage—new pieces, different challenges. I have spent the afternoon in a desperate hunt for a reed, after a miserable morning rehearsal wrestling with one that responded beautifully at my clarinet exam just two days ago but chose today of all days to begin suddenly choking up. A rehearsal at which the conductor repeatedly shouted at me in exasperation, *"Davantage! Davantage, la clarinette!* A little more!

Plus haute! Can you not play louder!" while the wretched reed defied my best efforts to comply, reducing me to quiet tears of frustration. And no luck finding a decent replacement until, in a last-ditch faint hope, just before putting away my clarinet to start getting ready for the evening, I took out my old worn-out "best reed" from last semester's concerts (kept more for sentimental reasons than as a reliable backup) and discovered that today for some reason—the eternal mystery of reeds!—it has gotten its voice back: a miracle. Hardly daring to believe it, I tried all my solos; they sounded wonderful.

The relief is immeasurable; I've arrived feeling serene. An exquisite spring evening: late sunlight on young leaves, long shadows of trees slanting across Parc Lafontaine's emerald expanses, a faint cinnamon fragrance drifting from poplars in bud; behind the hall, the park's ponds rippling and glinting, small boys still playing tag on the slopes and sailing toy boats, their distant voices ringing on the cool air. From the dazzle of the park into the dimness of the stately hall; then down a level to the basement room under the stage, which is soon a pandemonium of musicians warming up—violin bows colliding, light catching the gleam of trombone slides, oboes running up and down little chromatic fragments in their peculiarly nasal way, now and then a lull in the crazy web of sound, letting through three ethereal notes of a French horn, or the beady curved bouncing notes of a scale played staccato by the second clarinet. I can barely hear myself in the general hubbub, but I go through my own warm-up routine until the signal to head upstairs. In a strange half-daze I follow others onto the brilliantly lit stage, where all is as it should be, chairs in their places, the right music on the stand. The lights in the hall have dimmed; the hum of the audience fades to silence; we tune ... now all is quiet and expectant.

And another miracle: for the first time on stage with the orchestra I'm unaware of even a trace of nervousness. With the first simple, tender utterances of the strings in Schubert's

Rosamunde, I feel myself drawn into the music: seamlessly, scarcely aware of my moment of entry, I find myself singing out without fear, joyfully, carried by the flow. My solos soar spontaneous and unrestrained. Beautiful sounds are all around me and I'm entwined in them, I'm part of them—we're one!— the crazily sawing bows from downstairs are now moving in perfect sync; out of the corner of my eye I catch the gleam of a flute raised to pick up a phrase where I left off. The stage lights shimmer in the crystal mouthpiece of my clarinet and flash on the gold of the ligature as I wait out a few bars' rest, then I'm playing again, flooded with a strange, sweet exaltation and an unreasoning conviction that everyone else is feeling this, too— the knowledge that we're one, that we're part of one another, dependent on one another, moving together, moving in and out of one another, mystically connected. I have found a perfect happiness, unlike anything I've experienced before. And it doesn't abate when the music stops; with each new piece on the program it's as if the stage lights and the hush in the darkened hall were casting a spell, turning our conductor's baton into a wand to fuse us into one again.

What is this magic? This is love. Now the pianist makes his entry; under his fingers the piano speaks in a million voices, at one moment pearly, then cascading like water, now solemn and bell-like, now tender and earnest, and suddenly I'm in love with the pianist, then the horn merges unexpectedly with the piano, a burnished phrase that almost hurts the ear with its purity, and I'm in love with the horn player, it seems I'm falling in love simultaneously with all of my fellow musicians, whom I can't separate from the sound of their instruments, and I have barely registered this strange thought when I realize it doesn't stop there, it extends out beyond the footlights and embraces the anonymous, silent listeners on whose account we are here, a collective ear out there in the dark, I'm in love with them too, connected to them, they too are part of it, part of us, they are bound to one another and we are bound together by the music, by the listening that is part of the music, the listening that invests the music with its higher purpose ... *And I am going to be a musician: this is my destiny, this will be my work, someday I will play in an orchestra and be paid for it, what heaven! Who could want to do anything else for a living if they can do this?*

Oh—*child!*—I think now, knowing what I know about that world's realities. Yet I know the truth of what that girl felt, one enchanted evening in May. It is real too. I can't take it away from her.

What happened? How soon after being "convoked" did the honeymoon end? Was there a pivotal moment that I somehow failed to register, or a series of such moments? Was it just a long, gradual process of losing heart, an accruing of small disappointments that cumulatively tipped the balance? How can it be that by the time I played my two Concours recitals, six and seven years later almost to the day, I was so little invested in them that I have no recollection of playing the first one and only a vague memory of playing the second—the first going altogether unrecorded in my journal of the time, the second dismissed in half a sentence, a week after the fact, amid a summary of other events that week?

VII INTERMEZZO

(THREE SHORT PIECES)

1. *The Silver Thread*

SCENE: THE CHANTILLY, PHIL COHEN'S APARTMENT ON a Sunday afternoon in April 1966. It's my last year of high school, third year at Conservatoire. I'm not here for a piano lesson, though I'm still taking lessons. Today, uncharacteristically, I'm standing beside the Knabe with my clarinet. Sheldon and I are rehearsing for a performance together on CBC Radio, and Mr. Cohen is coaching us.

Time passes. Kids grow. The presumed rivalry that certain adults took it upon themselves to forestall by leaving me in the dark about my stepbrother's piano teacher—the betrayal I felt when I learned the truth—the residual unease in my relationship with Mr. Cohen after an awkward confrontation and inadequate stab at air-clearing: all this has receded into a past that already feels remote, though it can't have been much more than a year ago. We've moved on. Clarinet is now my primary instrument; I'm content to let Sheldon be the pianist. If I pursue a career in music, it won't be on piano; I'm not in competition with my stepbrother.

Is this collaboration Mr. Cohen's idea, a way of redressing a well-intentioned misstep that backfired? Or was it my own initiative? Mr. Masella has put me forward to perform on radio—a special program for young musicians called *Premiers Pas* (First Steps). I will need a pianist, and somehow it was decided it should be Sheldon.

At this moment I'm struggling with a passage where the clarinet has to make a leap to a sustained high note, quietly played. Coming in cold on a quiet high note, or rapidly changing registers to get to one, is among the hardest things to master on the instrument: if throat and embouchure aren't perfectly synchronized in making their adjustment, if the breath stream isn't sufficiently strong and steady, the note will break or be choked off or simply won't sound; but if the breath stream is too strong, the note can lurch out uncontrolled in a loud ugly blurt, or morph into a piercing squeak. I generally err on the side of not enough breath to avoid the risk of a blurt or squeak, but with too little air the risk is that it won't come out at all.

This passage will be my undoing, I fear. At my lesson earlier this week, Mr. Masella spent a long time on it with me, giving me tips on how to prepare mentally and physically for the leap. And I have been working on it every day since, with some improvement, but today as we repeat the passage, I either miss the high note or it cracks, three tries in four.

I cast a look at Mr. Cohen, apologetic about the retakes: "I've been practising this part all week. We worked on it at my lesson and it was getting better. But my reed keeps choking up and now I get tense every time I come to it."

He looks thoughtful. He's not a clarinet player. He has never played a clarinet. What does he know from reeds?

"What's going through your mind when you come to that part?" he asks, after a pause. "Are you thinking, *I'm not going to get the high note*?"

"Not at all! I'm thinking about the things Mr. Masella says I need to do to make sure I get it. And trying my best to do them."

"What does he say you should do?"

Exasperated, I recite: "Narrow your throat as if you were going to say the letter *E*, a long *E* sound. Increase the speed of your breath as you tighten your embouchure, but don't over-tighten. Say *Heeeeee* at the back of the throat as you increase the speed of the stream of air. But I'm doing all that. I do it every time and it isn't working. Maybe my reed is too soft ..."

"Forget the reed." He has sat up in his chair. "Do you know the exact way you want that high note to sound? Do you have the sound of it in your ear?"

"Yes."

"Okay, close your eyes and think of the sound you want for that note. Hear it in your head. Now, imagine if that note were something you could *see*. What would it look like if you could see it?"

My eyes are closed. I'm hearing the high D the way I want it to sound in this passage, a pure sound, drawn out taut yet delicate, gleaming. What would it look like?

"A silver thread."

"All right, good," says Mr. Cohen. "Let's try again from where we started before, only this time, as you approach the note, forget about your throat. Forget about your embouchure, forget about the stream of air. Don't *think*. Just visualize the note. *See the silver thread.*"

I look at him dubiously. Sheldon raises an eyebrow as we exchange glances. He waits for my cue and we launch back into the music. And here it comes now, my stumbling block. *How can this possibly work?* But I visualize a silver thread. And out comes a perfect high D—clear-toned, delicate yet rock-steady, dead on pitch.

This has to be a lucky accident.

"Try it again," says Mr. Cohen. We do, with the same result. And again. Same. Amazed laughter is bubbling up in me. *The magic!* It's preposterous that this works. Isn't it? And he doesn't even play the clarinet!

"Okay," Mr. Cohen says happily. "Play it again a couple of times to reinforce it. This is the time when we *should* play over and over. Not when we're screwing up, going at it again and again like it will fix itself on the next try if we just keep repeating—that's how we reinforce our mistakes. It's good to repeat something when you're getting it *right*, even if you're not sure how you're getting it. But don't overdo it. That's how you lose it."

I go home still incredulous, try visualizing the silver thread, and it still works. It works for a few days, every time or nearly. After that, not so reliably.

Maybe I overdid it. Maybe I stopped believing it could work.

2. Pianist Envy

A slip of a girl named Claudette Berthiaume was soloist with the Conservatoire Orchestra the fall that I began playing in it. She was sixteen, only a year older than I, and she performed the Mozart D minor Piano Concerto exquisitely. I had ample opportunity to listen to her in rehearsal, since the score did not include a clarinet part (Mozart was the first composer to introduce the clarinet into his orchestral writing, but the D minor Concerto is scored for a reduced ensemble, really a chamber orchestra). Sitting out the Concerto week after week, I fell in love with the piece that would later, thanks to the movie *Amadeus,* become much more widely known and loved, and I was soon badgering Mr. Cohen to let me learn it. As preparation, we worked on Mozart's Rondo in D and then on the A major Sonata with its ravishing theme-and-variations first

movement. But even as I dreamed of playing the concerto, I had
to accept that I would never have the chance to perform it with
an orchestra. I wasn't in the piano class at the Conservatoire
or at McGill; piano was my designated "second" instrument.
I had never performed or even played an audition on piano;
I had no Toronto Conservatory exam credits—where was my
opening to be considered as a potential piano soloist?

Our next two orchestral programs also featured pianists:
Ireneus Zuk playing the Rimsky-Korsakov Concerto, Louis-
Philippe Pelletier the Franck Variations Symphoniques. There
were clarinet parts in both of these scores, but I was riveted
on the piano whenever I wasn't playing—awed by the pianists, and envious of them. They were doing something so much
more complex, so much richer in layers and textures than a
featured soloist on clarinet could ever aspire to. And I knew
that as pianists they had a fathomless repertoire to explore:
masterworks representing every period in the history of
Western music from the Baroque on up. The solo and chamber
repertoire for clarinet was, as I was finding out, limited.

Ironically, it was around this time that I decided to pursue
a musical career on clarinet, though *decide* and *pursue* may be
the wrong words: strong currents were pushing me in that direction and I accepted it was where I was headed. Performing
on piano had never come up for discussion—at least, not with
me. I do hazily remember my mother telling me she had asked
Mr. Cohen, around the time I auditioned for Conservatoire,
whether he did not think a career on piano was an option for
me. According to her, he said, "It's a very hard life. There are
so many talented pianists ... it's brutally competitive ... you'd
have to take her out of school, she would have to work very
hard and give up her other interests to have a chance of suc-
ceeding. And then it's constant travel, constant stress. Is
that really a life you would want for your daughter? Do you
think she would want that life herself?" My mother, being my
mother, must have felt she had to run this by me before making

any assumptions. I remember being a little surprised they had discussed it at all, but I had no trouble agreeing with her that it wasn't where I wanted to go. At that moment in my life, leaving the high-school band and Mr. Cooper was unthinkable.

To the best of my memory, the Mozart D minor Concerto was the last piece I worked on with Mr. Cohen before my lapse at seventeen. We were just getting started on the third movement when he had a car accident and suffered a serious back injury; hospitalization and months of rehab followed. My lessons had already become irregular as I juggled first-year McGill with Conservatoire; there were frequent conflicts, and it was hard to find pianos to practise on while living in residence. I started out in the music faculty, which gave me access to practice studios in the old McGill Conservatory building on McTavish Street, but by December I was chafing at the limited curriculum of the undergraduate music program and had arranged a switch into Arts for the following year. None of this was going to get easier. In the meantime, piano lessons were suspended indefinitely and it was almost a relief.

I visited my teacher only once at the Montreal Convalescent Home, after he'd been there for some weeks. I found him in pyjamas, alone in an airy solarium at the end of the hall, going through his physiotherapy routine. Embarrassed to come upon him this way and feeling guilty about having waited so long to visit, I was at a loss for much to say; I think we both felt awkward. He demonstrated the exercises he was doing, some of which were of his own devising. He was determined to avoid surgery. "They want to operate. I said no. No way am I letting them in there to start messing around." Then he told me soberly that once he returned to work in the fall, he was going to have to cut back his teaching schedule, giving priority to students in the performance program at McGill. He couldn't promise to see me as reliably as before, but he would make an effort to fit me in wherever possible if I wanted to continue.

I read his *if* as an oblique goodbye and bowed to what seemed the inevitable. It made no sense for me to resume lessons on standby, knowing I could not keep up a regular practice schedule: I couldn't justify making the claim on his time. Arriving ill-prepared for lessons that were few and far between was too depressing; there had already been too many of those, and I knew it would be the rule, not the exception. The choices I had made weren't compatible with continuing to study with him—this was a truth I had to face. The hiatus since the accident made it easier to accept that piano lessons had come to an end, and when fall came, I never phoned in to schedule one.

%

A memory from around that same time, my first year at McGill. A night in early spring; I'm in a third floor studio on McTavish Street, disassembling my clarinet after a long practice session. The building is open every night until eleven: when I arrived, there were many students practising and a bunch as usual playing cards in the basement lounge with its mouldering sofas, coffee urn, and noisy mini fridge. But now it's late, it's past ten thirty; the studios have emptied, the hall lights are dimmed. Only one other soul seems still to be here, a pianist a few doors down. A wing of light from the half-open door falls aslant the hall carpet.

Tiptoeing past, I see it is Ireneus Zuk; I hadn't realized he was also studying at McGill. Absorbed in the music, he doesn't glance up. The stairs creak as I descend to the entranceway, where the silent janitor nods, seeing me out. It's a misty night and lightly raining; tree branches are newly beaded, a spray of them silhouetted against the single lit window on the third floor. Through the raised sash, the sound of the piano floats down to the street with a heightened clarity on the humid air.

What is it about a piano playing late at night in an empty house? Ireneus is playing the Bach F minor Prelude from Book

One of The Well-Tempered Clavier, and as I stand below in the rain, listening, I feel myself being drawn deep into its centre, enfolded in melancholy and mystery. He's playing it very well. He's all alone up there now, wrapped in a perfect solitude, unaware of a listener beneath the window. The music seems to me inexpressibly sad and maybe the most beautiful piece ever written. The slow, solemn melody with its ascending line and inexorable pacing, the measured trills, the echoes within its continually modulating, contrapuntal call-and-response, fill me with an indescribable yearning. *I want. I want.* What is it that I want?

I want to be the pianist playing that music, alone at night in a dark empty house. I want to *be the music.*

3. At the Ritz (December 1969)

Sheldon's Sarah Fisher recital. I am twenty; it has been three years since I stopped taking piano lessons. Sheldon is eighteen and making his formal debut. The concert room at the Ritz-Carleton Hotel is ablaze, resplendent with curtains, carpet, and chandeliers, the great floating oval of ceiling relief pristine white, like a sculptured cake of soap. Two years ago I made my own debut here, on clarinet. The boyfriend sitting beside me tonight wasn't there to hear me; we had yet to meet at the time. Was Sheldon there? After our anomalous CBC performance in high school, we went back to our separate lives as distant step-siblings. But my parents have come in from Ottawa for his debut, as they did for mine.

The audience this evening is fluttery: ladies in furs, young and middle-aged; a family group out of an Edwardian painting—little girl in white lace stockings, little boy in a red velvet vest, proud parents in formal dress; women holding their heads carefully lest part of the coiffure descend; nuns, in pairs or in small groups, with their own young piano students from the École Vincent-d'Indy. In the front row, several of Mr. Cohen's piano students—I recognize one I used to know, the only one my age—are trying to find a block of seats together. They chatter away, all girls, mostly in their teens. "Rebecca is playing that piece ..." "Oh! That's the one Rebecca is learning!" "This afternoon when I was over at Rebecca's ..." "Have you seen her? There she is! Rebecca! Rebecca! Over here ..." Their voices bounce back to where I'm sitting. Just a group of high-school girls, nothing in their manner or appearance to distinguish them from their peer group—girls who chew gum, giggle about crushes, talk endlessly on the telephone. Yet I feel they are the Initiate; they are Mr. Cohen's students. Year by year they are absorbing his way of seeing, the values he communicates; under their flighty exterior even now, I know they are wise in ways no one would guess to look at them.

Beside us is one empty seat I want to save for a friend who hasn't arrived yet, but when an imperious woman in a fur coat asks if she may take it, my boyfriend doesn't feel he can refuse. The woman subsides next to him. A hard elegance about her. Whiff of perfume as she slips the fur coat off her shoulders and over the back of the seat. Still on the lookout for our friend, I have barely noticed she is questioning my boyfriend, when from behind me, as if the only sound in the room, comes the voice of the little girl in the white stockings. "Daddy. There's Mr. Cohen."

Three years since I've seen him. He is there, standing by the stage door, looking out across the audience in a preoccupied way, searching for somebody. I think, *But he's shorter than I remembered. Did his head always sit on his shoulders that way? And his face—has it changed, or have I forgotten how he looked?* Slowly the features become familiar again, dear again—a face I saw every week from sixth grade through first year university, a face I grew up with. My piano teacher. Why am I sitting back here, away from his students? Why am I not one of them anymore?

He begins to walk out and up the aisle, still scanning the audience. Inside me, a feeling of astonishment and pain is growing, as if it is only now, seeing him again, that I realize what a terrible mistake I made. I want to establish contact— long for him to look at me, give some sign that he remembers me, that he understands it was a mistake ... . And now his eyes, travelling, do fall on me. Begin to pass elsewhere, then return, startled. I want to smile at him but instead my own eyes fill unexpectedly with tears. Can only plead mutely for *him* to smile, signal a greeting, acknowledge our long connection ... or do those years mean nothing much, now? He hesitates for a moment, then—incredibly—turns away and moves on, again scanning the rows of faces. He has recognized me and that is all.

I'm crying now, hardly trying to hide it. The tall woman is still talking to my boyfriend and I begin to realize she wants to ask me something.

"Are you a student of Mr. Cohen?"

"A former one." The words stick; I clear my throat.

"All those girls in front, are they his pupils?"

"Yes."

"But how is it they seem to know each other so well? Does Mr. Cohen enter them in music festivals together?"

"Not that I'm aware of." (*What does she want?*)

"How *do* they all know each other, then?"

I wonder the same myself, but don't say so. "Sometimes Mr. Cohen invites a group of pupils to listen to a rehearsal, if someone is preparing to perform."

"But do *all* his pupils know each other so well? My Lenore takes lessons with Mr. Cohen, but she only knows the ones before and after her lesson. So when I saw all these girls, I wondered! I thought they must play in festivals together—I was wondering why Lenore wasn't asked. But I guess Mr. Cohen won't take on a pupil who isn't quite talented to begin with?"

"I guess *not*," I say shortly, more than a little sharply.

She seems not to notice. "My Lenore wanted to come tonight, terribly, but she has her biology exam tomorrow. Is Sheldon in college, too? Yes? Taking what?"

"Arts, I think."

She is relieved. "Oh, well that's quite a bit less work than science, isn't it. Lenore is taking science and it's so heavy. That's why she couldn't come, she had to study for her exam."

%

Thankfully, the dimming of the lights. Voices subside. On stage, Sheldon nods to applause, sits, adjusts the piano stool, adjusts it again. His long silent communion with the piano says that he won't be rushed. Waiting until he *aches* to play, until he can't hold back any longer.

I understand.

His program isn't flashy. Two sonatas by Scarlatti, three Chopin mazurkas. Subtlety of his phrasing. Undercurrents brought out with tenderness.

I understand.

When he finishes, he bows stiffly, not a real bow but a slight bending forward of the shoulders, as though he might be about to puke off the edge of the stage.

I understand.

VIII   FLUCTUATIONS

Prelude: Resistance

WHO WAS IT WHO SAID "ALL BEGINNINGS ARE HARD"? A rabbinic maxim, handed down over centuries. Within a week of my first session with Phil, I found myself feeling blue without knowing why. Was it just that the initial high of my new start had worn off? Was it knowing that Phil would want me to drop old repertoire and work only on music I'd never learned before? I had begun a first new piece with Pamela—Liszt's Consolation #2—but it didn't console. Excitement about the piano had given way to uncertainty, ambivalence, vexation. In my journal I tried to make more sense of my discontent:

> *Perhaps it's doubt about the process of working on tiny segments of a piece, resisting my urge to play through things. Playing through is a huge emotional release for me—and it is after all my goal, to be able to do it reliably. Or is it just that I was on a plateau for three decades, and suddenly I've begun to experience musical ups and downs again?*

How could I have forgotten about ups and downs? A good practice session, a bad one; a good lesson, a bad lesson. Small breakthroughs and discoveries alternating with sudden impasses. Over the months that followed, journal entries narrate a turbulent re-entry:

JUNE 5, 2009

Phil wanted Pamela to audit a session with me so she could see how he wants me to be working, since he will only be able to see me from time to time. We met at her studio, the Westmount Piano Studio on Sherbrooke Street. When I arrived, Phil was talking about a concert he attended in Sicily, how there's an old tradition there of audience involvement—people applaud between movements, after or during virtuoso passages, they talk during the performance, even call out comments. We agreed this was healthier than standard North American concert etiquette, the extreme hush, the inhuman silence of the performer. Phil said in Sicily the performer addresses the audience at the outset, and sets the stage for the program with an informal improvisation in the style of the music to be played.

We worked on four lines of Liszt. On getting a real singing line; on avoiding unwanted accents. He is showing me how to work in a more directed way. To "sketch" based on the SOUND *I want in a given phrase, initially without worrying about fingerings or even which hand I'm playing it with. To do whatever it takes to get that sound in my ear first.*

JUNE 17, 2009

Two hours with Pamela on two pages of Liszt. It is so hard—to get and maintain the legato, to get the beauty of tone and smoothness of movement—to find ways to organize myself, and then to remember them every time.

It takes such total attention. At one point Pamela said, "Talk to me about what you've been doing in these two lines, what you're trying to get in them." I was surprised at how much I didn't want to "talk about." All I could give her was a blank look. To my relief she didn't press it: "Okay, you don't want to talk—so, SHOW *me what you're doing." Again I felt music is my embrace of a different kind of mind—a mind* EMPTIED *of words.*

JULY 3, 2009

Very discouraged after a long session at Hingston; came out feeling utterly drained and in the dark. We must have been at it for close to three hours. Phil doesn't seem to get tired at all; he seems to have no awareness of time passing. His focus is total and non-stop.

Later he phoned and said he needed to apologize for "losing my temper." He was referring to a moment when he said the things we were doing were all about simplifying, and I said, "Then why are you making it all so complicated?" I meant it teasingly, but he didn't pick that up. But if he was angry, I didn't pick up on that, either. On the phone he said there were lots of people who could help me enjoy playing more by giving me little tips, nicer fingerings, but that he wanted to work with me in a more serious way—towards being my own teacher and towards creative performance. He said he knows we're in a process that's uncomfortable for me.

I did feel a lot of anxiety today. Sometimes he would say "You've got it"—would even flash me that AHA! *glance that I remember from my early lessons—but I couldn't flash one back at him, because it wasn't an* AHA! *moment for me and I wasn't going to pretend. At one point I even felt tears sting my eyes as in childhood days. At home, I tried to summarize the session in my notebook so I would at least remember what we did:*

"Two tries at playing through the Liszt—broke down both times, the first after two pages, the second after nearly three. Then we worked. In the passage where the melody is split between hands in the tenor voice, Phil had me play melody alone, but all of it with one hand. Focus on awareness of where I'm going next. Focus on 'singing phrase, not single notes.' Then the bass notes—focus on hand being positioned for the note it will need to move to next. Then the next melody statement, split between the hands in octaves: focus on no unwanted accents or extraneous movements, focus on bringing out the melody, leaving out the bass notes at first. Then adding them, working on bass note triggering left-hand movement back upward to join the right hand again. Then back to the opening with its repeated notes—aiming for a different tone quality on the second note, fully integrating it into the ascending melodic line. Keeping the broken-chord ornaments relaxed and slow, hearing them as part of the melody. Then on using the right thumb as 'conductor'—having it slide along the keys after the other fingers, contribute its strength to weak fingers, nudge the playing fingers to help them shape a lyrical phrase, SIGNAL *them that it's a lyrical phrase."*

How am I supposed to remember all this while playing? Phil may not like the word "technique," but even he kept using it today. When he addresses a technical problem directly, it helps me. When he focuses on the musicality of the phrase, he's saying what I know but can't seem to DO consistently. The musicality of the phrase is never far away from my inner ear, but it is sometimes far away from my hand—for stupid, obvious reasons I've never even registered.

JULY 6, 2009

*Al Fraser is in Montreal for a special tai chi program
and came by this morning, wanting to hear me play. I
tried my best to demonstrate what Phil has been doing
with me at the piano, then played a couple of pages of
Liszt. When I described the radical uncertainty this
work has been creating in me, he said it sounds like
Phil is trying to bring me to a state that Buddhists call
"Beginner's Mind"—a washing away of all past associations, preconceptions, and habits, so nothing interferes
with a direct experience of the activity as if coming to it
for the first time.*

*In the evening, he came back in company of two
friends to play a run-through of the all-Chopin program he will soon be performing—a nocturne, three
mazurkas, two études including the Revolutionary; then
the four Ballades. Alan's playing is robust and public;
mine is delicate and intimate—my little piano could
not give him what he was asking of it. But I thought the
Ballades, which he has performed many times, came
across beautifully.*

*Afterwards we all had coffee and cake on the bal-
cony and talked until midnight. Al said that witness-
ing the transformation of my playing after just three
months back with Phil was a revelation—it made him
realize that in repudiating the neurotic aspect of his
student relationship with Phil, he lost sight of valuable
things he never properly tried to integrate with what he
has since learned with Kemal. And today he called to say
he'd spoken to Phil. He wants to work with Phil again!
So it seems we two have been catalysts for each other.*

JULY 24, 2009

*At the studio today, after we worked on the first sec-
tion of the Liszt, Phil took me through two short Chopin*

preludes, showing me how to read them based on hand placement and movement, on understanding the structure of the music and the voice leadings. At the end of the session he said he was pleased with how it went: "I hope you're able to tolerate some praise."

I don't know how to describe these sessions and their effect on me. There's the intensity of concentration, almost hypnotic. There's the suspension of judgment, a following along on faith. There's deep emotion in the way Phil's presence links me to my childhood, adolescence, early twenties. There are the things he says. Today it was about the truth: "The score is 'the truth,' but it isn't the WHOLE truth. There are secrets in the score, things that musical notation can only approximate. It's up to the performer to discover those secrets and bring them out."

AUGUST 4, 2009

Again at sea with Phil. It seems as if he's always changing what he wants me to do. And I'm chafing under the slowness of learning a piece in increments; I have a huge need to be PLAYING MUSIC, not dwelling endlessly on minutiae. Today he said it was important that I be "suspicious" when I think I've nailed something. That I should never get it in my head that there's only one way, or become too comfortable with any particular way of playing something. He says I should always be varying the way I work, to build the flexibility that makes it possible to perform without breaking down, or to recover seamlessly if I do.

He does give me a lot of what amounts to technical help. Transferring from one finger to another on a held note to maintain smoothness in a melody with leaps; reinforcing a weak finger by bunching it with another finger; sliding laterally along the keys to get to a new register, instead of lifting my hand and risking a missed leap; finessing repeated notes by riding the key back up before playing the note again—catching it with a different finger just before it comes flush with the other keys.

AUGUST 27, 2009

On the phone today Phil acknowledged that the things we've been doing are intended to prepare me for performance. He thinks within six months I should be able to play "for more than three people." I like the modesty of the approach. Right now, I can barely play for just him. He named a number—"around thirty"—and I asked, "Is there a difference between three and thirty, between thirty and more than that?" Yes, he said; there is. "And there's a difference between playing in somebody's living room and playing for what we might call CHAIRS IN A ROW."

AUGUST 29, 2009

Another DIFFICULT *session. I feel so stupid. I forget what I learn from one time to the next; I'm never sure I've understood what we're doing and why. Phil doesn't always articulate things well. I find myself closing my ears to what he's saying, and just imitating what he does when he demonstrates something—watching him like a hawk and listening with ferocious intensity to the piano. I come out exhausted and fall asleep repeatedly on the bus ride home. But he still says some iconic things. Today it was, "Try to play in such a way as to put the future always in your hands." (At once I thought, "Yes, and try to live that way too.") Then he digressed and started talking about glassblowers in Florence— how they write little notes on their creations, asking forbearance for the flaws: "Please forgive the mistakes. Understand that they are important." He keeps wanting*

*me to understand that mistakes are human and "a sign
of genius"—in the sense of spirit, I assume he means.
Human genius.*

*Al is in Montreal to give a Feldenkrais presentation for
piano students at McGill. Yesterday he phoned, per-
turbed by his first session with Phil. Apparently Phil
talked for a whole hour before they did any work, and Al
said he didn't come away with anything new. "I wanted
to understand what happened to me when I studied with
him twenty-five years ago, and now I think I do understand it. He seems to have to create this atmosphere of
mystification as a set-up for something that really* IS
*mystical and doesn't need the set-up. He gives you gold,
but it comes in this distorted package—you don't get
one without the other." Then he said he was seeing Phil
again today.*

*I asked, "Why are you going back again, if it was so
unsatisfying?"*

*He said, "Because he asked me." And then, in a dif-
ferent voice, "Because I love him."*
*—Late afternoon: an email from Al, a short message on
the fly, to say that today's session was "*MUCH *better!"
His excitement was palpable.*

*Unexpectedly today, Phil asked me to play the Liszt,
which we haven't worked on for a while, and suddenly
it was back to square one. I thought it sounded good, but
he told me I was hearing what I wanted to hear. It was
back to "preparedness," having my hand in position for
what's coming next: "The future creates the present."
It was about a* REAL *cantabile, a* REAL *legato. It was
about letting the music direct my movements—the*

SOUND *making the finger move. Sometimes I despair of ever being able to apply any of this in the way he intends it. The totality of focus required feels beyond me.*

On the way home I made a detour downtown to Archambault and bought the first piano sheet music I have bought for myself since I was twenty-three. The Bach-Busoni Chorale Preludes, Scarlatti Sonatas, Chopin Preludes. Came home and wondered aloud to D: Why am I doing this? What insanity propelled me into it? Isn't it much too late?

OCTOBER 25, 2009

Another hour with Phil today. He guided my reading through the E flat Bach-Busoni Chorale Prelude— Busoni's piano transcription of Bach's organ score, "Wachet auf, ruft uns die Stimme ..." ("Awake, the voice commands us"—"Wachet auf" for short). He's showing me how to "block" the music as a way of learning the notes—placing my hand over groups of notes, all the notes I can reach without having to shift position; then shifting the hand to the new position. Not PLAYING *the melody; just placing the hand over one block of it and then the next. I am just beginning to catch on—to recognize where the shift is, to think not according to the bar or even the phrase, but according to the shift. Phil says, "Don't think about fingerings, they're not important. Think about placement of the hand. I call it 'handing.'"*

I confessed to him that I'd come home Friday, tried the Liszt and it seemed to me I was already doing all the things he showed me. He said I was doing the things he showed me before—and that I was able to get some beautiful sounds—but now he's showing me different things. I told him I come home full of self-doubt, to the point of being afraid to play. He said, "Self-doubt is good." He doesn't let me get away with a thing. And part

*of me is still fighting this, while another part accepts I'm
now in the jaws of a process that is what I said I wanted.*

OCTOBER 31, 2009

*A long talk with Pamela at my lesson. I admitted to my
insecurities—how I'm never sure I understand what
Phil is after; how I come out feeling dumb and worry
I'm wasting his time. Then she said she could share
something: "I had a session with him recently myself,
and I also came out feeling dumb. I realized I was slipping back into old habits. I thought I was doing what he
showed me, but I wasn't actually doing it." She encour-
aged me to hang in with the process: "You can't expect
all these things to sink in right away—it takes time."
I talked to her about my past with Phil, his formative influence on me. I quoted the most recent thing he
said that I had to write down: "The future creates the
present." She asked if he had shared this wonderful
quote from Louis Pasteur: "Chance favours the prepared mind."*

*I've been trying to work as he showed me on two new
pieces, the Bach-Busoni and Scarlatti A major Sonata
(K208), but already it's falling apart. I get the hang of
blocking for a couple of lines, then it breaks down. And
if that's how I'm supposed to be working—well, I'm
finished in ten minutes. I can't get in touch with the
music that way. Yet I'm afraid to go back to what I do
intuitively, I've lost confidence in my "natural" way of
learning a new piece.*

NOVEMBER 3, 2009

*Al is in Canada again, this time to visit a dying friend.
He's staying with us tonight. He showed me videos of
his last session with Phil, and I tried to show him some
of what I've been doing. I'm finally understanding that*

nothing Phil shows me is meant to be more than a temporary way of working a passage—I'm not meant to go home and "install" it. As Al put it: "What he's doing is showing you different possibilities and training your LISTENING *as you engage with each of them. If you do four bars of Liszt, take home what you did in those four bars and see how you can transpose it to another passage. Try to recreate the process Phil showed you in those four bars, the way of thinking about the music. See if you can integrate it as a tool." But he also says I should ignore the restraints. "Go ahead and play through a whole piece when you feel like it, play your old repertoire. Do what you need to do to find your joy in playing again." Yes!*

DECEMBER 18, 2009

Worked on the Scarlatti A major with Pamela, reading a couple of bars at a time, hands separately then together, looking at the voice leading, looking at the shape of the phrase, finding ways to prepare my hand for what was coming next. And then we got in a long discussion about my resistance to working this way. Pamela argues for an intimate acquaintance with the score, for practice based on an intellectual understanding of the music's inner workings. She says I have a magical approach to music—that I think things happen by themselves, I don't claim ownership of what I'm doing. But what makes me resist claiming ownership? Am I addicted to the not-knowing, state-of-grace feeling that it is NOT *coming from me? Or am I just being lazy? From the beginning Phil has maintained that his beloved sketching should be fun, that it shouldn't feel like work, but work is what it feels like to me. And the precision of movement Pamela is advocating seems to take away my instinctive (if unreliable) fluidity, replacing it with a*

hyper-conscious hyper-perfectionism—the exact oppos-
ite of "getting myself out of the way." I couldn't seem to
get across that this isn't some sentimental scruple, it's a
real grief I'm feeling. The closest I could get was to say
that I lose my love for the music working this way—that
the heart goes out of it. Pamela was quiet for a moment.
Then she looked at me seriously and said, "I think you
should write that down. Go home and write something
about it."

Fugue: Transitions

Until 1967—year of my Sarah Fischer debut recital, Canada's
centennial year, and the year Montreal hosted the World Fair—
it seemed I could do no wrong at Conservatoire. That was the
year of my successful audition for the *Matinée Symphonique*
series, with a callback to repeat the program a few days later
in La Grande Salle at Place des Arts as one of sixteen finalists.
Within days of being notified that I was one of the winners, I
played my final technique exam, at which the sole adjudicator, acting director Fernand Graton, invited me to participate
in a choir he was assembling to take to Israel that summer to
represent French Canada in an international choral festival.
Wondrous things just kept happening, and I had no reason to
believe this would not continue. But by 1968, the year that
began with my *Matinée Symphonique* concert, a tide had
already begun to turn.

I was halfway through my fifth year at Conservatoire, third
year in the BA program at McGill, honouring in philosophy.
It was the year I failed my clarinet exam and the spring that
Franz-Paul Decker, newly appointed conductor of the Montreal
Symphony, issued notices of dismissal to fourteen wind players—my teacher and four of his brothers among them. The
purge included all the first-chair players with the exception of
the principal oboist. No reason was given to the musicians;

press reports claimed it was done "for the good of the ensemble," but rumours flew that the Board of Directors was behind it, using the new conductor to get rid of certain orchestra members who had been acting as spokesmen and coming into conflict with them over business and contract matters. In the midst of it all, I was offered my own first professional engagement, a replacement contract to play second clarinet with the MSO in a weekend concert. The phone call came from Rodolfo Masella, first chair bassoonist who had also just been dismissed; he too taught at the Conservatoire. He said the more rumpus we students could create on behalf of the fired musicians, the better. There was a flurry of rallying to the cause—petitions, letters to the editor (one particularly eloquent one in the *Montreal Star* from Melvin Berman, the first chair oboist spared the axe). But to no avail. The rumpus died down, and after the year's notice period had elapsed, new wind players were hired.

The failed clarinet exam that May, coming just three months after my solo debut and coinciding closely with breaking news of the MSO firings, was totally unexpected and a shock. I knew I had played well. I was nailed for hesitancy, a couple of false starts—assigned a grade just two points short of a pass. "Don't let it bother you" was Mr. Masella's advice. "They did the same to me when I first went to Paris. They ranked me eleventh in a class of twelve—and I thought I had played well." In retrospect, I can see he was giving me a message about how "they" do things in the classical music world, but at the time, it didn't mitigate the slight. The reassurance that I could repeat the exam at mid-term and not have to lose a year was not much comfort.

Back in January, as twice before, I had auditioned for the National Youth Orchestra, a hand-picked ensemble from across Canada that rehearsed an intensive summer program and took it on cross-country tour. Getting a third refusal that spring was demoralizing, and this year, for the first time, two of my close friends did make the cut, deepening the smart of rejection.

Franz-Paul Decker was conducting the NYO that summer, an awkward situation for those whose teachers he had just fired: this helped somewhat to assuage my disappointment, but I had to make a conscious effort not to dwell on feeling left behind by my musical peers. (Only recently, on reconnecting with a couple of friends from my Conservatoire years, did I gain a new perspective when one of them wrote, "I thought it very unfair that you never made the NYO. The adjudicators for clarinet were from Toronto and they gave priority to their own students. All the clarinetists, both years that I played, were from Toronto, except one from Calgary who was studying in Toronto." I wish she had told me as much at the time!)

I chose to stay in Montreal that summer, for the first time since my family's move to Ottawa when I was still in high school. Taking a temporary job as typist to pay my rent and save money for the school year, I moved from my dorm room in Royal Victoria College to a furnished room on Aylmer Street in the McGill Ghetto, a neighbourhood of rundown greystones converted to rooming houses and populated by a mix of students, summer visitors, American draft dodgers, artists, hippies, and transients. To further save on rent so I could get a proper apartment when classes resumed, I shared my tiny single with a friend from high school, escaping her parents' staid Montreal West home for the adventure of living downtown. Space was at a premium with two of us in a room not much larger than my residence cubicle, yet containing a fridge, stove, and sink. I brought in a borrowed army cot to sleep on so Janet could have the studio bed. The broom-closet-sized closet was barely wide enough to fit a handful of clothes hangers—three "office temp" outfits apiece for our weekday working hours— and could not accommodate our musical instruments (Janet played French horn); we had to stow them under the army cot, pulling the bedspread down to the floor so the cases couldn't be seen through our ground-floor window giving on a back alley. I remember Janet's dad showing up without notice one evening and quietly installing an improvised metal grill over that window, an old piece of chain-link fencing he had cut to size—doubtless more out of concern for our safety than that of the instruments, though he did not say so.

Neither of us did much practising that summer, one of the hottest in years. By the time we got home from work, the little room was a sauna; we'd peel off nylons and damp dresses, change into bathing suits, and pass out briefly on our beds before cooking supper (hamburgers, chili, or Kraft Dinner), then eat and wash up, throw on T-shirts and shorts over the bathing suits, spray Raid to keep the roaches down and head out into the evening, rarely returning before midnight, when the air had cooled enough to get a breeze in the window and air out the lingering smells of frying and insecticide.

The night city was our playground, the vacated McGill Campus an enchanted garden in its midst, with hippie minstrels strumming guitars in the grass and tootling on recorders in trees, the flares of cigarettes and joints like stars come down to earth, sweet burning-leaf whiffs of marijuana drifting from little groups scattered about the green. It may sound strange to say but that summer of '68—a stinking hot summer of working nine-to-five as a typist and coming home to a roach-infested room with shared bath—still stands out in memory as one of the happiest of my life. It was that heady first taste of real independence; it was the colourful people we met sitting on the stoops and balconies, fire escapes and rooftops of the McGill Ghetto during long, charmed twilights and weekend afternoons; and it was the times—the Sixties in full swing. We had a record player. (Not a stereo; a record player.) We had a few records. In the tiny rectangle of available floor space, we danced on the spot to The Beatles' *Revolver*; we sang with Simon and Garfunkel, discovered Orff's Carmina Burana, learned the Latin lyrics off the liner notes and sang along with the composer's spirited modern settings of troubadour songs. At the end of the summer Janet bought Leonard

Cohen's recently released first album. We listened to it over and over in the apartment we'd rented for the school year, in a soulless high-rise across the street—sitting on the floor, on the beige wall-to-wall broadloom, because we couldn't afford to buy living room furniture. Never mind. We had our own bathroom! And no roaches! And the view out the front window, the romantic façade of our old rooming house, was picturesque.

That fall, briefly, my batteries as a musician were recharged when the Conservatoire Orchestra rehearsed intensively under Pierre Dervaux, a conductor who worked "a magic, if an iron-handed magic" with our ensemble, as I put it in a letter to my mother. I had been demoted to second chair after my ill-advised semester's leave from orchestra, but Victor Sawa, the ambitious young Japanese Canadian clarinetist who replaced me, magnanimously offered me first chair for one piece on the program, Ravel's "Mother Goose" Suite, saying Brahms's First was enough for him. Our performance won seven rounds of applause and an enthusiastic review in *La Presse*, but what mattered more to me was that for the first time in a year, I was completely swept away by the music, in love with it again, "bursting with happiness the whole time we were on stage," I wrote in the same letter. The doubts and discontents that had begun to cloud my musical horizon went into abeyance as I re-experienced love of music for its own sake and something akin to the ecstatic feelings I'd had when ensemble playing was new to me. Sadly, Dervaux didn't stay; his successor was considerably less inspiring, and my rekindled excitement wore off as I resigned myself to the position of second chair.

%

Early in the winter semester of '69, in the weekly conference for one of my philosophy courses, an intense-looking young man sitting across from me entered the conversation for the first time with an allusion to the organ fugues of Buxtehude, dropping the name as if it were a household word. I assumed he must be in the Bachelor of Music program, taking philosophy as an academic elective, but when I asked, he said he was in Arts. How had he heard of the seventeenth-century Danish-German composer, outside the context of a course in music history? He confessed to a passion for organ music and a long-standing dream of becoming an organ builder. He had never studied music formally, but was an amateur classical guitarist, self-taught. His interests were eclectic; he told me he and his twin brother had spent one high-school summer co-writing and illustrating a history of Rome. The brother, whom I was soon to meet, was a poet, also of eclectic interests, and formidably well-read.

They were American. "Navy brats" born in Johnstown, Pennsylvania, James and Fred Louder had come to McGill via Newfoundland, where they'd finished high school on the US naval base in Argentia. A pre-graduation class trip to Montreal had persuaded them this was where they wanted to go to university, and here they were, loping around campus and the ghetto in their navy duffel coats—keen-eyed, heads craned forward as if sniffing out the air, hungry for books and people and ideas and whatever the city had to offer. They always had books under their arms and stuffed in their pockets; it seemed there was not a topic on which they were not knowledgeable (Janet once called them "a walking encyclopedia, Volume One and Volume Two"). They were identical twins; it was a few weeks before I could unerringly tell them apart. An incipient romance with the first soon morphed into a contretemps worthy of a Shakespearean comedy; seventeen months later, I married the second. (An early gift from Fred, inscribed to me "in interest and affection," was a Modern Library edition of Katherine Mansfield's *A Garden Party*, prompting me to take the Alpers biography of Mansfield out of the library and read it again. A detail I had not remembered: Mansfield's first love was a musician with a twin brother, and she eventually transferred her affection to the second twin. However, she married neither of them and moved on.)

That spring I requested a semester's deferment of my clarinet exam, granted on the basis of a letter from McGill Health Services attesting that I was under too much stress to play it on schedule. Juggling Honours Philosophy with Conservatoire had become more than I could handle; I was disastrously behind on all my term papers as we headed into the Arts exam period. If not the cause, my emotional life at the time was no help, with my first serious boyfriend considering taking a leave from McGill to accompany his family on a two-year posting to Iceland, and Janet deciding precipitously to move in with her own boyfriend, leaving me scrambling to find a replacement roommate for the large, scarily expensive apartment on which we'd just signed a year's lease with a third girl. In the end Fred decided to stay in Montreal, a roommate turned up just in time to pay the first month's rent on the new apartment, and I was lucky enough to be hired to play in the Expo Band from June through August, a dream job compared to office work: two rehearsals a week and concerts every Sunday, noon and evening, on the site of Expo 67, which was being maintained as a permanent summer fairground.

One evening towards the end of May, I was arrested by the sound of a piano drifting out of a basement window on Prince Arthur Street. Someone was playing Bach's Italian Concerto extremely well. The unknown pianist followed this up with Ravel's *Sonatine*, and another piece that I didn't recognize that also sounded like Ravel. There was something familiar about the playing, something in the tone colourings and phrasing that felt like home. I sat on the window ledge listening for about half an hour before getting up the nerve to knock on the upper pane.

The music continued briefly, then stopped, and a lively, almost elfin face appeared at the window, smiling up through the screen; I could see inside just far enough to discern that it belonged to a small, slightly built but energetic-looking young man in faded jeans and sandals.

"I just wanted to thank you for the concert. I've been here for a while. Did you study at the Conservatoire with Yvonne Hubert, by any chance?"

He shook his head. "No, I didn't grow up here. I'm from the States."

"Did you study with someone who studied with Cortot?"

This elicited a quick glance of surprise. I couldn't explain my hunch, but I was right: he had studied two years at the École Normale in Paris under a disciple of Cortot.

"Would you mind if I came in and listened?"

"Not at all! Would you like to come through the door or through the window?"

"The window might be nice."

Kneeling up on a sofa below the sill, he removed the screen; I swung my legs inside, kicked off my shoes, and slid barefoot after them onto the slipcover to find myself in a spacious, carpeted basement apartment. Thus I met Robert Sigmund Jr.— twenty-two years old, draft dodger, BA from the University of Pennsylvania, resident of Montreal for five months, jobless, planless, and down to his last seventy-eight cents. Bob told me he was looking for work, and apart from that, living day to day pursuing his deeper interests: music (piano and classical guitar) and linguistics—he'd chosen Montreal as his destination in Canada so he could keep up his French. We parted friends, and within a day he had met Fred and James and invited us all over for a shared piano and guitar recital. A week later, he found work in a record store downtown, where he met Véronique Robert, a beautiful young classical guitarist also just hired there. They were both shortly fired for repeatedly putting classical music on the store's sound system instead of the latest Beatles release; unfazed, they found new jobs together at Berlitz down the street, Bob teaching English, Véronique French. She soon moved in with him.

Classical guitarists were popping up everywhere like spring flowers. Suddenly I was surrounded by them. Fred had a guitar of his own and could also play, though by tacit agreement he took a back seat to James, who had the more serious musical aspirations. By the end of that summer, even I had a nylon-stringed guitar, bought on impulse for twenty-five dollars from a young man hawking it on campus; it had a too-high bridge and an impossibly stiff action, but I managed to learn a couple of Elizabethan dances on it. The pioneering work of Segovia, his revered recordings of music for guitar (some of it inspired by him and written for him), and of great music he transcribed for the instrument, had given rise to what amounted to a movement, if not a cult. A new generation of classical guitarists had begun recording: Julian Bream, Oscar Ghiglia, John Williams, Christopher Parkening. Concurrently there was a flowering of interest in "old music"—more and more groups devoted to reviving medieval and Renaissance repertoire, played on authentic period instruments. New releases on Nonesuch and other labels were bringing this music to life in imaginative, spirited performances. The lute and the harpsichord were making a comeback. A new demand was driving a wave of instrument-building: some guitar makers began building lutes on the side; companies like Zuckermann and Hubbard designed and produced build-it-yourself harpsichord kits with precut pieces. Bob Sigmund already had his eye on these. He wanted a harpsichord, and it seemed the most affordable way to get one might be to build it.

Musically, that summer of '69, I belonged to two worlds. The world of professional musicians by day: the Expo Band under Michel Perrault coalesced quickly into a tight ensemble, spirited and well-disciplined. We played band transcriptions of orchestral works—challenging repertoire for clarinets taking the place of violins. After two summers as an office temp, it felt like a coup to be paid to play music. But it was still a job: it was somewhere I had to be, three days a week, more than somewhere I wanted to be. During rehearsal breaks and the long dead time between our Sunday noon and evening concerts, I held aloof socially, preferring to retire with a book to a corner of the cool cement-floored room under the outdoor stage, where our instrument cases kept company with shadflies and daddy-long-legs under a bare light bulb. The continuous semi-boisterous banter of my fellow musicians irritated me—a mindless discharging of surplus energy, with digressions into local musical politics or shoptalk about mouthpieces, reeds, ligatures. It wasn't communication so much as a kind of environmental noise or bee-hum. Relieved when it receded as small groups headed off across the fairground in search of ice cream and other diversions, I read Durrell's *Alexandria Quartet* under the stage that summer.

Nights were a different story. Evening after evening, a group of us gathered in Bob Sigmund's apartment to make music in various combinations and to listen to music. It was the first time I had been among serious music lovers outside of music school: people with other jobs, other interests, no musical program to adhere to—just coming together to share a common passion. For the first time, too, I had a pianist I could work with—not a paid accompanist brought in for a one-rehearsal audition or exam, but an engaged and ongoing collaborator. Bob had decided to lay classical guitar aside to concentrate on piano for the summer, and he was interested in exploring repertoire for clarinet and piano. We read through many pieces and rehearsed two or three in more depth, among them Debussy's haunting Première Rhapsodie.

The word "amateur" had dabbler associations that in no way fit this world I had dropped into when I slid off Bob's windowsill, landing in the basement apartment that became our central. I preferred to think of it as a world of "free" musicians, almost a secret society. In its embrace I found a new freedom, a joyous versatility as I switched back and forth from clarinet to piano to recorder over the course of an evening's demands. Typically Bob and I would kick things off with a piece for clarinet and piano; then we'd take turns playing piano; then James would give a solo recital on guitar. After that, Bob would play a long, taxing work on piano, the highlight of the evening. Then coffee in the cozy kitchenette, under posters of Dégas and Toulouse-Lautrec, one wall above the counter papered with wine-bottle labels Bob had soaked off and collected during his two years in Paris. Then maybe some guitar and recorder with James—sometimes a Handel sonata, sometimes his own transcription of a medieval dance, or some free improvisation in medieval style—after which Bob might regale us with a bit of boogie-woogie on piano. Past eleven, when the piano had to be silent, Véronique would take over, giving us a contrasting interpretation of a guitar piece James had played earlier.

We were musicians and we were listeners—some only listeners, but the best kind of listeners. Two of our regulars, Fred and Eliza, were serious poets, sufficiently knowledgeable about music to provide intelligent feedback. (Eliza, James's new girlfriend, was a diminutive but spirited waif from Victoria who had moved to Montreal in search of literary community, after some months' correspondence with Fred.) Towards two in the morning, instruments were laid aside and we took up pens. Bob would put on tapes from his extensive library, often guitar or lute suites, sometimes jazz. The scribblers among us (myself included) worked on poems or wrote in journals while the guitarists hand-copied pieces they had heard each other play and wanted to learn. Sometimes, collectively, they transcribed new pieces off recordings, Bob lifting and dropping the stereo needle phrase by phrase: what motivation, what patience! I was impressed that Fred and James, who had no formal music training, could do what I had struggled to master in three years of *dictée musicale*.

Things wound down slowly as the night waned. By three we were usually listening to jazz, Bob's choices (Coltrane's *Ballads*, Modern Jazz Quartet, Bill Evans, Thelonious Monk), while a breeze came up, wafting off the south face of Mount Royal—summer breeze of nascent day blowing in through the screen (ever since, mellow jazz has evoked the smell of that breeze for me). We lay around on the carpet, on cushions, on the wide ledge of the recessed window, talking now a little dreamily, drifting in and out of sleep—quiet talk about music and art and books, about ourselves and our lives and life in general—until the sky began to lighten and the first birds were sounding tentative chirrups. That was the signal to break it up, strap sandals back on and go out into the street to see the sunrise before heading home to sleep.

Precious, unforgettable nights. And a breath of fresh air, like that pre-dawn jazz breeze, to my music-schooled soul. Here nothing was strenuous. The various unhappinesses that had crept into my life as a musician were altogether absent from this world, where music was a simple joy to be shared, not a job to be done, a test to be passed, or an arena of conquest. Maybe I didn't have to be a professional to share music with others in a meaningful way—the thought at least became thinkable. Weren't people like these my *real* people?

And what about my own first passion? I had neglected it these many years—had written so little since high school: a few short stories, a handful of poems I suspected weren't very good. Seeing Fred and Eliza exchanging new poems, reading them aloud, critiquing each other's drafts, was a wake-up call. What was I waiting for? In a letter to my mother dated June 18, 1969, I announced a new commitment: "I made a serious decision this week. I am going to be a writer."

IX INTERMEZZO:

KNOWING THE SCORE

"GO HOME AND WRITE SOMETHING ABOUT IT," SAID
Pamela as I struggled to explain what I was balking at, six or
seven months into my new start at piano. Probably not a bad
thing to say to a writer. I went home and tried. This is what I
wrote:

%

"Is it true that the consistency I want in my playing is something I can only get by becoming a lot more conscious of what's
going on in the score, a lot more intentional in my physical
organization based on that knowledge? Why does the conscious focus on structure take the heart out of learning a new
piece for me? In high school, I accused my English teachers
of spoiling poems by making us analyze them formally. I just
wanted to experience the poem as a whole—to let myself be
moved by the synthesis of its sounds, images, and word associations. If I liked a poem, I wanted to learn it by heart (people
often use this expression to mean 'by rote,' but I really mean
by *heart*: not just being able to recite the words from memory,

but internalizing the *feelings* they communicate). It's the same with a piece of music: I want to plunge in cold and learn the notes quickly, even if roughly, so I can experience what the whole piece is saying, what it *means* emotionally, before I look at how it's constructed. I bring each section up to tempo before I'm fully ready, because that's how I find the movements and fingerings that make it *possible* to play at tempo. But there are always some passages that defeat me, places where I'm winging it, or faking it. These are the black holes I will later have to relearn if I want to be able to play without risking derailment every time I come to them.

Still, there's a rapture associated with this unconscious learning process that I seem to be hooked on—the magical feeling of sometimes being able to play very well, without knowing how I'm doing it—as if the music is playing itself, just using me as a conduit. But of course this is unreliable. And even when it does happen, it is coupled with the awareness that I may lose it at any moment: a stumble, even a single missed note, can bring it to a crashing halt.

When Pamela says I'm unwilling to claim ownership of what I'm doing at the piano, she means I want to think of it as a matter of lucky accident or grace when I play well, rather than conscious application of what I know. But I have a fear that if I know too much about what I'm doing, something will be lost. I think this is behind my resistance to a more solidly based, deliberate way of working, though I recognize (how can I not?) the good sense of it.

I'm reminded of a passage from Mark Twain's *Life on the Mississippi* that I used to use in the classroom during my teaching years. Twain's subject was steamboating—the challenges of piloting a craft down twelve hundred miles of river. He compared the face of the river to a 'wonderful book ... not a book to be read once and thrown aside, for it had a new story to tell every day'—but a book written in a language that first had to be learned:

Now when I had mastered the language of this water
and had come to know every trifling feature that
bordered the great river as familiarly as I knew the
letters of the alphabet, I had made a valuable acquisition. But I had lost something, too. I had lost something which could never be restored to me while I
lived. All the grace, the beauty, the poetry, had gone
out of the majestic river! I still keep in mind a certain
wonderful sunset which I witnessed when steamboating was new to me. A broad expanse of the river was
turned to blood; in the middle distance the red hue
brightened into gold, through which a solitary log
came floating, black and conspicuous; in one place a
long, slanting mark lay sparkling upon the water; in
another the surface was broken by boiling, tumbling
rings, that were as many-tinted as an opal; where the
ruddy flush was faintest, was a smooth spot that was
covered with graceful circles and radiating lines, ever
so delicately traced (...)

I stood like one bewitched (...) But as I have
said, a day came when I began to cease from noting
the glories and the charms which the moon and the
sun and the twilight wrought upon the river's face;
another day came when I ceased altogether to note
them. Then, if that sunset scene had been repeated,
I should have looked upon it without rapture, and
should have commented upon it, inwardly, after this
fashion: This sun means that we are going to have
wind tomorrow; that floating log means that the river
is rising, small thanks to it; that slanting mark on
the water refers to a bluff reef which is going to kill
somebody's steamboat one of these nights, if it keeps
on stretching out like that; those tumbling "boils"
show a dissolving bar and a changing channel there;
the lines and circles in the slick water over yonder are

a warning that that troublesome place is shoaling up
dangerously (...)
　　No, the romance and the beauty were all gone
from the river. All the value any feature of it had for
me now was the amount of usefulness it could furnish
toward compassing the safe piloting of a steamboat.

There's something here I recognize in my gut. To borrow
Twain's imagery, I'm willing to risk my steamboat in order
not to lose my feelings for the poetry of the river. I don't want
to *pilot* my steamboat—I want it to pilot itself. Or: I want to
be pilot and passenger simultaneously. I don't want to have
to give up being the wonderstruck passenger in order to be
the pilot.

But that's only part of the story. Recently, talking to a friend
who teaches high-school English, I mentioned that when teachers used to ask us to write an outline before we wrote our essay,
and to hand it in for part of our mark, I always had to write the
outline *after* I'd written the essay. I couldn't write an outline
first to save my life. My friend found nothing unusual in this. She
said in her experience there are two types of student writer—
the one who writes the outline first, and the one who writes the
essay first: "The ones who write the essay first are the ones who
trust the writing to show them what they have to say."

That has always been the case for me: my approach to a
topic is to start "thinking aloud" on paper, not in note form but
in full sentences, feeling my way towards some sort of truth.
Occasional key words, jotted in the margin as they occur to
me, are as close to an outline as I ever get. Along the way, I
may move paragraphs around, again by instinct—"this thought
seems to go with that one"—but only after I've finished can I
go back and analyze my structural moves. They aren't always
conventional, but they're always discernible. And often they're
musical: I use theme-and-variations a lot, I use contrapuntal
lines of thought, I use refrain.

Another association comes to mind. For a couple of years in the 1990s I took tai chi classes with an older Vietnamese couple who worked in tandem but in contrasting ways, two groups going on simultaneously in the same studio. Mr. Pham went through the movements with great fluidity, never pausing, so you couldn't tell where one movement ended and the next began. From him we got a feel for the rhythmic continuity and flow of a sequence. He didn't explain very much, just had us mirror his movements. When he spoke, it was about spiritual aspects of tai chi: the opposing forces, up-down, empty-full, moving through centre, in-out breath rhythm. His corrections were minimal, just minor adjustments to help us keep our balance. On the other side of the room, Mrs. Pham would be demonstrating the movements in a totally different way: breaking them down into micro-segments, very precise, pausing during and between them so you could see clearly what she was doing, exactly how one movement led into the next. When she spoke, it was about arms and shoulders, hips, knees, feet. And she would go around correcting people's posture, stance, and movement, down to a hair.

Beginners were always sent to Mr. Pham, and I always had to start learning a new part of a sequence with him, because I needed to experience it first as a continuous whole. Later, when I had a rough idea of how it went and where I was having trouble, I would cross the room to watch Mrs. Pham, relearning the trouble spots as separate movements. I wasn't interested in what Mrs. Pham was doing until then. Breaking it down only became meaningful once I had physically felt my way through whatever it was that she was breaking down.

All this may shed some light on my current impasse at the piano. There seem to be two things going on. One is a mystical attachment to the idea of "not-knowing," maybe a romanticization of it. This I can probably get over. But the other—having to write the essay before the outline, needing to work with Mr. Pham before Mrs. Pham—would seem to be my learning process. My inclination is to work *backwards*: I need to experience the whole as something *known*, physically and emotionally, before I can appreciate the parts.

I know from teaching literature myself that analysis doesn't have to kill appreciation, on the contrary can enhance it if approached in the right way. And I know that the practice of any art requires both conscious and unconscious process. But this is where I'm stuck. The passage from Mark Twain illustrates what I fear: that in gaining conscious knowledge I will lose the rapture of experiencing the music unmediated. And I'm up against a long-entrenched learning process that doesn't want to proceed methodically step by step; it wants to find its way by feel."

%

When I shared what I had written with Al Fraser, it elicited this thoughtful response:

> "I too wanted to play from instinct. But, having come to Phil as an adult, I had bad technical habits and was sometimes painfully aware that unless my physical capability developed big time, I hadn't a hope of realizing my musical ideas with my hands. Hence my struggle first with Phil's input and then with Kemal's. I played better during the period when Kemal worked intensively with me, but even then I was dimly aware that my good musicianship was a veneer sounding well over some unresolved physical issues.
>
> "Phil's input since I've come back finally makes it clear how to solve the physical problem. But one problem still remains: *listening*. And to me this is the crux of your dilemma. This is a lifelong problem for everybody, not just you and me. We all suffer from habits of listening. We assume something is sounding a certain way when it is actually far from the case.

"Something else: Kemal tells me that as he matures,
his imagination is always farther out ahead of the level of
his execution. His physical ability is constantly increas-
ing because his imagination is constantly making more
extreme demands on it. Paradoxically, as he gets better
and better he actually manifests a *smaller* percentage of
what he imagines the score to contain and communicate!
I believe the genius of Horowitz lay in his having the rare
gift to make his inner musical imagination fully manifest
in physical reality, actually vibrating in sound."

Instinct. Imagination. Physical execution. Listening. And
intellect: knowing the score. They all come into play—into
playing. I'm coming to see that good musicianship is a nego-
tiation between different parts of the self—finding one's own
way to bring them into balance.

X   REVELATIONS

Prelude: Parisian Laundry

MY SIXTIETH CAME AND WENT. HAD I HONESTLY
imagined I might mark it by playing a piano recital on my
birthday? By the time things got off the ground in the form
of a first lesson with Pamela, I was already four months into
the year I'd first envisaged for the project, and the pieces I
had thought I might play in a recital had been mothballed.
The Idea wasn't dead, exactly, but mentally I had long since
deferred the recital to my sixty-fifth. On a deeper level I understood it was no longer about a recital. I had become a music
student again. I was doing the undramatic; it was ongoing,
and that was okay.

Only months into my new musical commitment, I was
offered a contract to start a poetry line for a small-press publisher in Toronto, working from Montreal. It was a position I
had myself proposed, wearied by the constant hustle for small
freelance contracts, daily outreach that could eat up as much
time unpaid as the contracts themselves. Three small-press
publishers failed even to acknowledge my proposal. The fourth,
improbably, said, "Let's talk," which we did, off and on for a

year, before he decided to go ahead. I signed on immediately and gratefully for a three-year trial with Cormorant Books, and soon found myself in deep. Accepting what I thought would be a half-time job, I saw that if I did not monitor my hours carefully, I could find myself working full-time and overtime, with nothing left over for my own writing—let alone music. Gone were the two-hour blocks I had been managing to find for the piano a few times a week while juggling smaller, short-term editing contracts.

I began to work in a different way: taking short breaks from the editing and spending them at the piano, going back and forth all day between two types of keyboard. An hour at the computer, fifteen or twenty minutes at the piano. Two hours or longer at the computer, half an hour to forty minutes at the piano. The breaks weren't scheduled; I took them when I got tired or felt I had reached a good stopping point. Sometimes, at the end of a day, I might manage a supplementary half-hour or longer at the piano; other times, under pressure of deadlines, I might get in only three or four ten-minute "piano breaks" all day. I didn't clock my breaks strictly or keep track of totals, but for the most part my practising became discontinuous.

Strangely enough this change seemed not to affect my progress. The much shorter but more frequent practice sessions served to concentrate my energy very effectively on particular problems; by necessity I had to focus on smaller segments of the music. Moreover, when I next tried a full run-through, the work I had done in these short bursts seemed to integrate itself as effectively as if I had hammered away at the passages in a longer session. On weekends I tried to reserve a block of time to play through my entire recent repertoire, to remind myself of what needed attention in each piece and as a means of keeping them all under my fingers.

Phil, at first dismayed to learn of new demands on my time, soon acknowledged that I had discovered or invented a very good way to work. And one old friend got quite excited when I described it to her. A lapsed musician who still had some years to go before she could retire from a career in language education, she exclaimed, "I could get back into playing my flute if I did it that way! It's trying to schedule an hour or two a day as a block that always defeats me!"

Perhaps being forced into this modus operandi is what broke the impasse I'd described to Pamela; perhaps it was the cathartic effect of writing about it, and the insights that emerged. For whatever reason, things were beginning to move again for me musically. Playing through the Liszt in the months that followed our conversation, I recognized how I kept going layers deeper with this piece. I was hearing more acutely and becoming much more demanding of myself. I finally understood the totality of awareness required to bring a piece of music to life and keep it alive—to *sustain* the aliveness, not let it lapse into a mindless, automatic imitation of itself.

I was just now, after a whole year, beginning to be able to play better for Pamela. "It's like there's a block between me and the way I play at home, when I play for a teacher," I wrote in my journal that second spring. "I don't let myself go for broke, I don't tap into the tonal possibilities of her piano, I play on the surface of the keys, timorous, decorous. It's as if I feel that to play the way I do at home would be—what? unearned? shameless? showing off? It's a false modesty. The opposite of Parade of the Elephants. It's not letting the elephants loose."

We were working now on the Bach-Busoni, "Wachet auf." Pamela was pleased with how it was going. She was planning a June recital for her students—kids and adults together—and suggested I participate, but it was scheduled the day after a poetry conference I would be attending in Pennsylvania. I didn't feel up to a first public performance without a few days to prepare, but I was gratified to be asked; timing aside, I did feel ready for this next step.

You could say the project was still on target, if a month or two behind schedule. Okay, not a full recital. But a move

towards performance had begun. And in the end I did take part,
though I hadn't planned to. On the last full day of the poetry
conference, I managed to get access to practice studios in the
deserted music building on campus and to spend a couple of
hours in the morning, and again in the afternoon, practising
on a Steinway upright—on several of them, in fact. Going
from studio to studio, each piano seemed to have something
wrong with it—a sticking key, a broken string, a wobbly pedal,
a whole octave lacking in resonance: off-season music school
instruments, awaiting pre-September tune-up. The one I settled on had the best sound, but a smeary pedal that squeaked.
No matter. I felt so much more grounded rehearsing "Wachet
Auf" than I had felt the past few days at conference activities.
The solitude, the disciplined focus, the clarity of purpose—all
were a balm.

Back home I called Pamela and told her I looked forward
to hearing her students' recital, but didn't feel sufficiently prepared to take part.

"Really not?" She sounded as if she couldn't imagine
why. "Well, it's up to you, but why not leave it open? You can
decide at the last minute—it's no problem to fit you in." She
had invited eighteen students to play, each to bring one guest
if they wished, together making an audience of around thirty.
She had rented a space—the Parisian Laundry on Rue Notre-
Dame, an old laundry converted to an art space. It was like
a big warehouse with a Steinway baby grand in it—no stage;
moveable benches and chairs arranged in an L for participants
and guests. What Phil had called "chairs in a row."

I arrived guestless and deliberately empty-handed that
June evening in 2010. Bringing a score would have felt too
much like a commitment. My interest was in hearing and
observing how others did this. When I came in, people were
milling around, greeting friends, socializing as they eyed the
spread of fruit, crackers, and cheese laid out for afterwards.
Late sunlight streamed in the windows. Amid a hum of chatter,

each arriving student was invited to try the piano, and when Pamela beckoned me to do the same, I sat down without hesitation—the chance to play on a grand, any grand, was still irresistible for me. This one felt forgiving and sounded good as I tried a few chords, then a run-through of "Wachet auf."

Was I being silly not to play? Wasn't this the perfect situation for getting my feet wet? For a moment I wavered. Then suddenly I noticed Phil just inside the door—it hadn't occurred to me he might be coming. *Well, that settles that.* I certainly wasn't going to play publicly in front of him—not my first time! But he came over to greet me and it turned out he'd arrived earlier, while I was at the piano, and had heard the whole piece. "It's sounding pretty good," he remarked affably. "Maybe I shouldn't say that!" He seemed in great good humour.

Pamela was making the rounds with a notepad, letting performers know their place in the lineup. All at once, having Phil there felt like support rather than pressure. His relaxed, casual words had seemed to take it for granted I would be playing and to believe I could do it. And really, why shouldn't I play? Pamela, unsurprised by my change of heart, did a little juggling of the list and wrote in my name, fourth or fifth from the end.

With at least a dozen participants ahead of me, it was going to be a long wait—ample time to get good and nervous. This didn't happen. I wasn't even thinking about playing; I was too curious and interested to hear the others. A handful of kids began the program, followed by adult beginners, each announcing their selection; all had obviously done this before. Most played classical pieces; a few played arrangements of popular songs. Two or three had to stop close to the beginning and start again, but all then managed to get through their selections and comport themselves with aplomb, resuming their seats in the audience with smiles of relief. Even a couple of the more advanced students had small memory lapses or false starts; this was reassuring. And when my turn came to play, still I wasn't nervous. I did get a little rattled at the first muffed note—not a wrong note, just one that didn't sound fully, but it was an important note, the beginning of a melody restatement. I felt a sharp disappointment at the spoiled entry, knowing I couldn't go back and play it again. *Keep going. Don't let it throw you.* I made it through to the final cadence with just two more fluffs of the same sort, not as prominent. Bizarrely, it was only after I had taken my seat again that I started shaking and felt my heart hammering—as if it had taken till then for my nerves to catch up with me!

Through a sort of haze I listened to the last few participants. They were the most advanced students; some played more than one selection. Two played pieces I had worked on with Phil in my teens—Chopin's first Impromptu and Debussy's exquisite little Prelude, *La fille aux cheveux de lin* (The Girl with the Flaxen Hair). Dimly I recognized that my insecurity about performing was way out of proportion to my level of achievement. It was hard to believe that nothing major had gone wrong; even more, that it felt so normal to play piano in a quasi-formal performance situation for the first time since my fiasco in fourth grade. Already I was looking forward to doing it again and doing better: not just getting through my chosen piece without having to stop, but playing it *beautifully* from start to finish. And here came a new moment of truth. *How could I ever have thought I'd be satisfied to play one recital?*

A recital could never be an end; it would be a beginning. If I played a bad recital, I would want to play a good one. If I played a good recital I would aspire to play a better one. Just as I was always refining and perfecting a new piece of music, it would be about refining and perfecting my public performance, my handling of a program. And then a new program. It would be about developing performance skills. Mastering nerves. Learning to get past disappointment at my misses and absorb the lessons they might furnish. It would be another bottomless process, just as learning to prepare a piece was a bottomless process. The goal I had initially set myself made no sense for someone who was still a musician at heart; was I to reach the level of being able to play a full recital on piano and *stop* there? But to embark on the second bottomless process made no sense for a sixty-year-old writer who still had to work at other things to make ends meet. A writer who still wanted to write! *This feels familiar; haven't I been here before?* Could I replace literary editing with busking, I wondered fleetingly—then remembered pianos aren't portable. How had I beguiled myself into this bad joke?

%

The writer, meanwhile, had been busy. Back in April, after a drought of more than a year, a poem had waylaid me. A poem about aging. In essence it was a lament for the past, a paean to lost pleasures of childhood, to endless summers once taken for granted—summers that seemed to have ended. From the start it felt freer and more open-ended than anything I'd written before, and over the next three months, by fits and starts, it developed into an extended, continuous composition in nine parts. The individually-titled sections were like musical movements, each picking up on lines, phrases, and thematic strands introduced earlier, building cumulatively on repetition with variation. I completed the last "movement" a few days after playing in Pamela's recital, and named the poem "My Shoes Are Killing Me." It would be central to my next poetry collection, to be published five years later.

Phil phoned the day I finished the poem. It was the first time we'd spoken since the recital. He said I had done more than just get through my piece; he thought I had played pretty well, and he hoped to give me some time later in the week. During the school year, our sessions had depended on availability of the studio; he had to work around his partner Anna's teaching schedule in the department and the practice schedules of her students. But over the summer it would be easier for him to arrange time. For now, he offered a few words about performance in general: "Never let what you're doing with a piece become reflexive. Reflex is unreliable."

I mulled this over. Wouldn't you think reflex would be what *was* reliable? If we cannot rely on a reflex, something we do automatically, then what *can* we rely on? Then he said something else that gave me pause: "When you're performing, even if you don't feel calm, play the part. Act as if you are calm. Performance is an act. You're assuming a role on stage—you're communicating the music the way an actor communicates a role."

I had never thought of musical performance as a form of acting. I had recognized, during my years at the front of a college classroom, that *teaching* was a form of acting—that to keep the attention of the class and manage time effectively, I had to assume a sort of stage persona: projecting and pacing my voice differently, keeping my face animated, never allowing my attention to lapse or wander, always remaining aware of a structure to the class period within which, allowing for some improvisation, a prepared package of information had to be delivered. When I began giving poetry readings in my late twenties, my teaching experience took the terror out of this other form of being on stage. Yet in all my years at Conservatoire, I had never considered musical performance in this light.

%

The Girl with the Flaxen Hair was haunting me. A piece I first learned at sixteen, it was one I hadn't revived in close to two decades. Hearing it at Pamela's recital made me want to play it again: just two pages in length, it would not take long to relearn. But where was my sheet music? I turned the piano bench inside out, finally gave up and began reconstructing it by ear and from memory—aural memory aided by muscle memory. The artless, insouciant melody, enhanced by Debussy's then-revolutionary harmonies—the overtones that bloomed from his layered, shifting chords—had always conjured for me a vivid picture of the piece's subject. I saw *La fille* as if in a film clip—saw her standing on the side of a hill, knee-deep in long grasses bent by wind, a tartan skirt blowing against her legs. A girl no longer a child but not yet a woman, gazing at the vista, her long fair hair sometimes blowing across her face like a veil as cloud shadows swept the ground and afternoon sun played fitfully over the landscape. I saw her from afar but also seemed to embody her, for I could feel the wind lift her hair, hear it hum around her ears; I breathed hints of wildflower fragrance, sensed the presence of sheep nearby, unseen.

Biographer Oscar Thompson called Debussy "the poet of mists and fountains, clouds and rain; of dusk and of glints of sunlight through the leaves ..." On a musical path of his own even during his student years, the composer allied himself with the Symbolist poets and Impressionist painters, becoming the father of Impressionism as a musical movement. The poetic titles of his compositions (*Reflets dans l'eau*, *Jardins sous la pluie*, *Des pas sur la neige*, *La Cathédrale engloutie* ...) suggest both visual images and hints of narrative: Reflections in the Water, Gardens under the Rain, Footprints in the Snow, The Engulfed Cathedral. While it's rare for music to evoke visual images for me, the music of Debussy often does, even without verbal prompts.

Yet rather the opposite happened on first encounter. In sixth grade our teacher once played a recording of Debussy's Afternoon of a Faun as inspiration for our weekly art lesson, instructing us to put our heads down on our desks, close our eyes for a few minutes, and then paint what we saw. I saw nothing. Mesmerized by the music, I did not lift my head or open my eyes until it was over, and then resurfaced as if coming up from under water. Around me, classmates were putting final touches on colourful paintings. I ended the art lesson with a blank sheet of paper and the name Debussy engraved in my mind as a code word for enchantment.

⁂

The future creates the present. The future causes *the present. Know where you're going—know where the music is going. Music is movement.* These were Phil's watchwords as we began working together on a more regular basis that summer. And as always, I found myself hearing them not just as musical counsel but as life directives. Here a little struggle began. *Isn't it counterintuitive to say the future creates the present? Isn't it the past that creates the present? We can plan a path, we can have intentions, but do they really define where we are now? Is it even desirable for our intentions to govern the present? Yes, it is good to live directionally, but what about "living in the moment"? Isn't that also desirable? How does one live with intentionality, but still live in the present?*

By mindfulness, I answered myself. *But what is mind?*

Waiting at the bus stop with Phil after one of those early sessions, I remarked, "I've been remembering all the pieces I learned with you as a kid, but I can't remember how I learned them. Pieces that would take me forever to learn now. The whole Pathétique—I was fourteen."

"I know you were," he said. "And you could play. But there was no consistency."

Why was that, I had time to wonder on the long ride home. Was it because I was doing too many other things—an unreadiness to commit myself to any single one? Was it being divided between clarinet and piano? Was it emotional turbulence? A lack of discipline? Nobody standing over me with a stick? *Am I still that way?* I recognized my tendency to bounce between pursuits. Excitement about one thing always had the effect of rekindling my interest in another. Engaging deeply in one activity seemed to trigger a wish, almost a compulsion, to jump up from it and do something else, almost as though I feared entrapment. Was this just restlessness, a form of escapism? Or did the activities serve to revitalize each other?

Whatever our pursuits and passions, the rest of life encroaches on them with its own exigencies: social obligations, family dynamics, health issues, work crises. That summer, family worries and money worries were rumbling under me. Usually I was able to shelve them for the duration of a session with Phil, but one July afternoon I arrived feeling distraught, unable to concentrate. When I confessed this, Phil dropped any sort of program for the session and said, "Why don't you just play a little—no expectations. Play anything you feel like."

I had wanted to work on a Chopin étude that day (the F minor, Op. 10 No. 9), but for some reason my hands launched almost inadvertently into *La Fille aux cheveux de lin*, which I had continued to reconstruct at home until I'd recovered it in full. Phil, I could tell, was surprised. He sat back, he listened, he was very interested. He didn't seem displeased that I was playing old repertoire.

"Did you bring the score?" he asked when I had finished.

I said, "I couldn't find it—I haven't looked at it in a very long time, at least twenty years. But ever since hearing it at Pamela's recital I've been wanting to play this again. I learned it when I was in high school, remember? I've relearned it by ear just from hearing it again once—I don't know what it means that I was able to do that."

He sat up on hearing this. "It means you learned it *very well*."

Seizing courage, I began without a word to play Debussy's Première Arabesque, which I'd first learned around the same time. Unlike *La fille*, I had kept this one up as a favourite since my late twenties. And again Phil was startled; he leaned back in his seat, his face deeply alert. After a couple of pages I stopped and waited. I sensed wheels turning.

"The continuity is excellent, why did you stop?"

"I can go on if you want."

He said, "It's a revelation for me to hear you play these pieces. You're playing them without the score and without any of the technical issues you've had with new repertoire ... I must say I'm tempted ..."

"Phil, it's all still there. Every piece we ever worked on is still in my hands and my ears and my body, it's just dormant. You gave me a grounding I never lost. I can get things back very quickly when I want to relearn them, no matter how long it's been since I've played them."

He was still thinking. Fingers of one hand playing a four-note figure on the back of the other. "It's very tempting ... you have a freedom and expressivity in these that I haven't seen with new pieces we've worked on. I see that you play with more variability when you're not hampered by looking at the music or thinking about it. I'm thinking we can come at some of the things I've been wanting to get across by working with music already in your hands. We can start without the score and *then* look at the music, and I can show you new things in it."

"That makes sense to me," I said immediately. "I think I learn backwards."

A beat's pause. Then Phil said quietly, as if something had just fallen into place for him, "Of course you do. You're a poet. All poets learn backwards."

※

Having permission to play my old repertoire felt like being let out of a straitjacket. It had taken over a year, but here I was, where I had hoped to begin when I first picked up the phone to call my teacher. Only not exactly: I was somewhere better. I had all the refinements of the year's work with Pamela, and Phil's mind-bending input. An August journal entry attests to this:

Something new is happening at the piano. I've been working on the two Debussy pieces and on Chopin's

Fantaisie-Impromptu, mostly doing clean-up, but it feels effortless, freely inventive and pleasurable. I have tools I didn't have before, there's much less hit-and-miss. I'm hearing things I never fully heard before in pieces I thought I knew inside out. Phil said something this week that hit home: he said "playing around" with the music allows you to get to know it much better, makes it yours; that practising creatively involves reinventing bits of the music—PLAYING WITH the score instead of playing the score. And always doing it in new ways. I now see what he means by reflexive: how, if I try to retrain myself to do just one small thing differently, the rest of the passage goes haywire. That's the sign that my knowledge of the passage isn't real knowledge at all. But I'm finally seeing I can acquire real knowledge, and that it's not even so hard to do.

For the rest of that summer we worked on music I'd played before. Phil recognized the way I always had to go back when we isolated a passage to work on, approaching it from an earlier point so I could feel where the music was coming from. But I had no corresponding awareness of where the music was *going to*, nor did I feel a need to think about it. "The future creates the present" was still a conundrum to me. "Know where the music is going" had the ring of sound advice, but it didn't come naturally, even with music long familiar under my hands.

It was Phil's reminder of my first calling, coming just as I had begun writing poems again, that furnished some insight into why this might be so. While composing poetry, I had that same need to backtrack, to let the momentum of what had come before carry me forward. But I never knew where the poem was going to take me next. I forged the future out of the present by trial and error, leaving myself open to the unexpected—taking as my watchword Robert Frost's "No surprise for the writer, no surprise for the reader." My poems were not premeditated.

Could it be, I wondered again, that my writer's process was governing how I played music? Awareness of what lay ahead, as I played, was vague: a sense of moving trustfully into uncharted waters, waiting to be surprised by what came next. Was it any wonder this made my playing unreliable?

Fugue: The Glass Axe

In life, "what came next"—going back, now, to the fall of 1969—was a digression. Yet I look back on it as not only noteworthy in itself but more significant musically than anything else I was to experience during a year of musical disappointments. Not everyone, in the course of a lifetime, gets a chance to help build a harpsichord. That fall found six of us suddenly involved in the project of building one, unsupervised, in a basement bachelor apartment on Prince Arthur Street—the same six who had spent the summer nights making music in that apartment.

Bob Sigmund had a contagious capacity for joyful engagement, a sense of drama that invested everything he did with celebratory energy—whether it was playing a new piece of music, reading aloud from a favourite book, cooking a meal, eating a meal, doing a jigsaw puzzle, building a bookshelf, playing Frisbee, hanging a month's worth of laundry on makeshift indoor clotheslines. Even the most mundane activity assumed a kind of glamour once he decided to make it the order of the day. There was nothing mundane about building a harpsichord, but for five of us it had not exactly been on the agenda. The unplanned takeover of our month of November was precipitated by the Sigmund contagion effect, after a wedding gift from Véronique's family enabled the newlyweds, married that October, to order a Zuckermann kit harpsichord. "My axe," Bob called it, endearingly, in jazzman's lingo, when the first of two immense packing crates arrived on October 30. This one contained the case; the next would contain the mechanism.

It was a foregone conclusion we were all to take part in the building.

We assembled the inner case in a night, wielding screw-drivers and nail files while a reel-to-reel of Bach cantatas ran itself through twice and the *Harvard Lampoon* parody of *Time* magazine made the rounds of the room. Then a long hiatus while we waited for the "guts of the axe" to arrive, which they did nearly two weeks later, in a crate labelled "Glass - Handle With Care." (There are no glass harpsichord parts; the word was clearly added to ensure fail-safe respect from shippers. But we dubbed the instrument the Glass Axe.) Now there were drawings to pore over, instructions to read, parts and materials to identify, sort, and separate. No glass and no feathers: traditionally, harpsichord strings were plucked by goose quills inserted in the jacks that correspond to piano hammers, but in modern instruments of the time, the plectra and sometimes the jacks themselves were made of a special hard plastic called Delrin.

At no point were we building from scratch. The panels of the case were precut; the wooden keys and other parts of the mechanism also came ready-made for assembly. But there was plenty to keep us busy. In my journal, days after the second shipment arrived, I proudly listed the tasks in which I had taken part so far: "Screwing the inner case together, gluing cherry-wood surface on keys, clamping with elastics, cutting cherry-wood to size with coping saw, filing keys down, marking keys for insertion of lead weights, cutting key felts, lacquering soundboard, gluing in soundboard. Now bridge-pins are being inserted. Tomorrow we start work on the jacks ... It's a break from intellectuality, this patient, wearying labour with our hands—scarcely any conversation, the only relief being music, guitar or piano, as one or another of us takes a break to play a little; coffee to keep us going into the night. I feel so lucky to be taking part. I begin to understand the harpsichord, its workings and its problems; by the time we're done, I will feel my acquaintance with the instrument to be intimate."

A week later my hands were covered with sores; everyone sported workplace injuries. Fred was the only real casualty; a slipped screwdriver cut one finger nearly to the bone and he had to make a visit to Emergency. The team forged gamely on, converging daily in Bob's apartment-turned-*atelier* for a few afternoon or evening hours of communal work. On November 23 I wrote, "The jacks are proving tedious. Endpins, adjustment screws, tongue felts, damper felts, springs, and leads. The girls do the springs and leads, crouching around the fondu like witches round a cauldron, heating screwdrivers to melt the plastic. Much swearing, many minor cuts and burns. Meanwhile the men are stringing the axe! Twangs and oaths ..." On November 25, the four-foot stop was working and Bob played us a set of variations by Giles Farnaby on the song "Lothe to Depart," from the *Fitzwilliam Virginal Book*. By the 27th, both the four-foot and eight-foot stops were working, but with the final positioning of the outer cabinet and jack-rail, a lot of the keys stopped functioning; this would have to be corrected gradually by individual adjustments. Then the jacks would have to be "voiced" for evenness of timbre and volume throughout the instrument's range. That night, the task was just putting on the outer case—the final phase of actual construction. At 3:30 a.m. on November 28th, the lid of the axe was hinged. It was the last step. The six of us joined hands spontaneously and dropped to our knees around the instrument in a moment of reverent joy! There was champagne to celebrate, and a tape of Scarlatti's harpsichord music to listen to as we sat gazing at the fruit of our labour: the Glass Axe, strung and waiting, lamplight glowing on the warm rose of the cherry-wood keys.

Only after the sawdust had settled did the implications of Bob's new axe begin to dawn on me. Bob being Bob, it was inevitable he would throw himself wholeheartedly into the next project: exploring a huge new repertoire of early keyboard music. He was soon in love with the harpsichord. No more long nights of Ravel at the piano: no more *Jeux d'eau, Sonatine, Gaspard de la nuit*; no more Prokofiev Preludes. When we assembled for an evening's music-making, the dark old Lindsay upright stood silent while Bob shared the latest harpsichord pieces he had learned: works by Couperin, Rameau, and names less familiar—a different sound, a different aesthetic, a new world of music to discover. Even the familiar Bach pieces he had played so often for us on piano were transformed on harpsichord. To hear each new piece played live, on the instrument we had helped build, was a gift. But there was no repertoire for clarinet and harpsichord: in the harpsichord's heyday the clarinet had not yet evolved from its much more limited predecessor, the chalumeau. From time to time, when guests were over, Bob and I still played some of the repertoire for clarinet and piano we had rehearsed in the summer—the Five Bagatelles by Gerald Finzi, the Debussy Rhapsodie, a movement of the first Brahms sonata—but his motivation to work on them further or to learn new repertoire ebbed. I had lost my pianist.

%

That year, 1969-70, was supposed to be my last at Conservatoire. I was supposed to repeat my failed Supérieure II exam in February and play my Concours graduation recital in the spring; programs were already under discussion. I was supposed to do this while completing my final undergraduate year at McGill, in an honours program in philosophy that required me to write a thesis-in-miniature for which I had submitted as topic "A comparison of the doctrines of negative theology as propounded by Moses Maimonides and Thomas Aquinas within their respective faith traditions." Perhaps I had bitten off a bit more than I could chew. One thing I was *not* supposed to do that year was to help build a harpsichord, but it is the thing that shone brightest afterwards in memory. To participate in the making of a musical instrument was at once humbling and exalting; to partake in such a hands-on way in the musical revival then in progress, the reclaiming of Renaissance period instruments and repertoire, felt like a privilege.

At Conservatoire it turned out to be a year of "supposed to's" that never panned out. I was supposed to play a full recital in the fall which, for reasons I don't recall, never happened. I was supposed to play the Brahms Clarinet Trio in the spring with an excellent cellist and pianist, coached in Otto Joachim's chamber music class, but after a few exhilarating sessions the cellist had a serious dispute with her teacher and withdrew from the Conservatoire. They reconciled a week later and I was overjoyed to see her back, but just as we were to resume rehearsing, our pianist was diagnosed with mononucleosis. It was too late in the semester to find a replacement. In the end all I succeeded in accomplishing that year was to repeat my Supérieure II exam, for the same adjudicator who had failed me the previous year and who now deliberately kept me hanging, declining to let me know if I'd passed. I begged an assistant teacher to see if he could find out for me; he came back with a report that I had "passed, but with some difficulty," and that he had been explicitly instructed *not to tell me.* By early spring, mired in medieval philosophy and existential angst—not to mention marriage plans for that summer, fast-tracked by a year on account of Fred's legal status (or rather lack of it) in Canada—it became clear I would have to defer my Concours until the following year.

Sheldon had played his Sarah Fischer debut recital that December. Shaken by seeing Mr. Cohen again after three years, across a distance that seemed unbreachable, I was overwhelmed by feelings I could hardly name. How had I ever let the piano lessons go, how had I left my teacher? I noted the event briefly in my journal, promising myself to come back to it, but nearly two months passed before I could bring myself to write about that evening.

※

Perhaps it was just as well that I should have to return to Conservatoire in the fall. Had I graduated on schedule, I would have missed out on meeting my next pianist, thanks to whom—for a while—I was able to find some joy in playing my clarinet again.

I had spent the summer depressed, having graduated from McGill with first-class honours in philosophy, accepted a teaching assistantship I didn't really want, and enrolled for a master's degree in which I had no interest. It was all my mother could do to persuade me to attend my own convocation. Finally freed from the year's school pressures and knowing I had an income lined up for fall, I took the summer off. I wanted desperately to be writing, but I wasn't writing. Day after day I sat at my corner desk in the furnished two-room apartment Fred and I had leased when we combined households, and wrestled with a mind unaccountably gone blank, silent, empty. I wasn't practising clarinet much, either; the desire to play was gone, leaving only guilt to prod me to it on occasion. A greyness hung over everything—a disenchantment with the city I loved, with the McGill Ghetto (now threatened with demolition by a developer), with our little apartment that already felt claustrophobic. September loomed, with registration dates for both schools already marked on the calendar: in no time the gates would clang shut on me for another academic year—the thought made me frantic.

At the start of October we moved again, this time to a three-room unfurnished, in hope that a change of scene and the diversion of setting up house in our own style would boost my spirits. One cheering thing happened as soon as we were installed: Bob, who had moved with Véronique to an apartment building just across the street from ours, offered to loan us the Lindsay. He wasn't playing piano much anymore, and he was going to need space to begin building his next harpsichord. For the first time since high school, I had a piano under my own roof again, an unasked-for gift that went some way towards sweetening the days.

A young pianist, Marcel Lachance, was soloist that fall with the Conservatoire Orchestra in which, for the moment, I was back in first chair. It is indicative of my state of mind— still benumbed from the summer and alienated from everything I had signed on to do that year—that I don't remember anything on the concert program, not even which piano concerto we played (it may have been the Emperor), but I do remember being impressed and moved by Marcel's playing. He was a protégé of one of the more respected teachers and apparently bound for a major career. Not quite twenty at the time, though he seemed older, he cut a dramatic figure in the school hallways: tall and lean, with wild dark hair, a mobile face, and eyes of such a dark brown they appeared black, though in conversation they could open wide and flash with excitement like a child's. He had an aura of singularity about him, as though he had dropped into the Show Mart's upper corridors from the sky, or from another planet.

We toured our program to a nearby town towards the end of October. Getting on the bus with the rest of the orchestra, I was taken by surprise when Marcel, who had been sitting up front with the conductor, excused himself to take the seat beside me, commending me on my clarinet playing. We had not spoken before. That he had noticed my solos at all, let alone that he would single them out from the weave of the orchestration as praiseworthy, buoyed me a little. I was interested to learn that he lived not far from me in the McGill Ghetto: he had taken room and board, for the school year, in the home of a middle-aged matron who owned a grand piano. Later that week, while I was practising at Conservatoire, he knocked at the pane on my studio door and stepped inside to ask if I had change for a dollar. Framed in the doorway, in a huge black army-navy greatcoat and dark glasses, he looked like a man on a mission. I counted the quarters into his hand and picked up my clarinet again, but halfway out the door he turned back. Maybe, he suggested, we could try working together a bit sometime? He had heard me playing the first Brahms sonata; it was a piece he'd like to learn—did I have a pianist?

Now I did.

We had an immediate musical rapport. Having someone to work with catapulted me back to life overnight. Colour surged back into the city like a flood tide; my residual depression lifted like fog burning off and morphed into a state of euphoria and high energy. Suddenly I was practising clarinet four or five hours a day, spurred by a renewed sense of musical purpose; Conservatoire again felt like a place where I belonged, where I was known, where I knew who I was. On my way there to practise or rehearse, the familiar handle of the clarinet case in my hand was a ballast I clasped gratefully, *keep a grip on this, don't lose it, never lose it again!*

I saw Marcel as a providential messenger, sent to lead me back to the solid ground I'd turned away from, the *home* of music. Working on the Brahms with him at the Steinway in his landlady's peaceful, elegantly furnished parlour—such a contrast to Bob Sigmund's bohemian rooms—I found a dedication I now realized had been wanting, that blissful summer-before-last. Marcel was demanding of himself, and of me, in a way that hadn't happened at Bob's, where the idea was to get the notes of a piece down quickly so we could perform a creditable run-through for the pleasure of friends—then on to the next. For all of us it was an informal, exploratory sharing of repertoire, performing as soon as we had worked up a fluent reading, taking it no further. There was spirit, camaraderie, and happy exchange, but the deeper seriousness wasn't there—the willingness to devote hours to a passage in order to get it *right*, the unwillingness to settle for less. The seriousness I remembered from my years with Mr. Cohen.

I expressed these observations to a friend from high school and Conservatoire who had recently moved to the McGill

Ghetto, fresh from a summer session at the Aspen Institute. A clarinetist herself, she described how the teacher there had taken her back to the beginning with her technique, made her realize how much further it could be refined. "He had us doing those five-note exercises up and down across the break, like Cooper did with us in first-year high school. He wanted us to get the shift to the upper register perfectly smooth. Not what we normally think of as smooth—he meant to the point where your ear can't tell there's a break at all." Yet she thought I shouldn't be so swift to dismiss the seriousness of my musician friends in the ghetto. She spoke of hearing James play: "I knew then he had genius. He played—how can I describe it? Not perfectly—there were wrong notes, accidents—but he played *truly*. It was music. It's a very rare quality. He made each piece sound as if it had never been played before."

Her words brought back what I had valued about those evenings. Maybe this wasn't so simple. To play *truly*—wasn't *that* serious? I grappled with the question:

Maybe there are two ways to be serious about music— an internal way and an external way. The seriousness I say was lacking that summer was the external—the patience, the ACTIVE *patience, the rigour of working in depth. The internal seriousness—truth, emotion, love—was there in abundance. At Conservatoire many musicians have the external seriousness but are not true to music, and I think this is what I've wanted to flee from, believing it was to blame for their sterility. It isn't. But when the external seriousness becomes success-oriented—and in professional music, it has to be—it can overwhelm the inner. Musicians lose their innocence. They lose the joy and wonderment and become driven by ambition; they compete, compare, obsess about technique and get doctrinaire about different schools of playing. James is an* INNOCENT *musician. But I see now*

that the two kinds of seriousness must be ONE WHOLE
STATE OF BEING *to make a musician in the fullest
sense. Genius lies in the inner seriousness but fulfills
itself in the outer.*

In Marcel I thought I had found a musician who had both
kinds of seriousness, but maybe it was easy for him. He seemed
to have none of the financial worries, the frequent changes of
lodging and roommates and plans, that characterized the lives
of most young people I knew in the ghetto. There was no day
job to cut into his practice hours; he lived a sheltered existence that furnished every comfort and convenience to facili-
tate his work. I had only glimpses of this life. His meals were
cooked for him, linens provided by his landlady in the huge
house where he was free to come and go and bring guests as he
pleased. He had a girlfriend he treated with a kind of courtly
reserve; sometimes I would meet her, leaving, when I arrived
to rehearse with him at eleven on a Sunday ("We were up until
three in the morning listening to Wagner," he explained once,
apologizing for being less centred than usual). He told me his
piano teacher was seeing him almost daily that year: "He gives
me a minimum of five lessons a week. Sometimes one every
day, sometimes twice a day! We work for a few hours, then
we go out and he buys me supper, we eat together and talk. He
buys me a cigar, we have a cognac. Then back to work."

I was envious. I wanted that kind of intensity in my life,
music as a raison d'être. I had swung into overdrive in my
re-embrace of it, riding waves of exaltation that could flip
without warning into agitation: fear of losing the focus I had
recovered, impatience with everything that took me away from
it (marking papers at McGill, meeting with my thesis advisor,
keeping the house clean and the fridge stocked, putting meals
on the table). Would I be able to rise to Marcel's high standards? When I wasn't practising, I was consumed with nervous
energy, a constant inner trembling, as if the ground under my

feet was the lower deck of a ship with the engine room beneath. Every day I seemed to wake earlier, filled with excitement, eager to start working, but the day was never long enough to give me the time I felt I needed.

A November journal entry suggests my new collaborator sensed something was off-kilter, and called me on it, soon into our work together:

> *Marcel put me to shame yesterday. After we worked he talked to me, calmly but firmly, for some time; I could only listen meekly. He had one question: "Are you ready to be responsible?" A word that had not even entered my mind through this whole return! And how right he is. What kind of responsibility am I showing when from nervous excitement I forget to eat, stay up late because I'm too overwound to sleep, practise with a passion but distractedly, overworking my embouchure, letting my tempos run wild just to feel my fingers fly? Living at a fever pitch, driving myself, fearing that what I've found will get away again. "If you're afraid of losing it," he told me, "then you haven't got it. When you have it, it's there, it's in your hands, and if you let go for a minute, it's still there, and you know it will still be there." He said, "The excitement you're feeling is deceptive, it's dangerous to your own purposes. People confuse passion with nervousness. Passion is not nervous." He said, "Learn to think simply, immediately. Don't worry about finding time to work. It doesn't take so much time. When you want to work, sit down and work. If you have to stop, then stop—don't get frantic. Be calm and responsible—then you will be a feeling musician, a happy musician. Why make it so difficult?"*

Marcel Lachance was not his real name. I knew him for less than a year. We played the Brahms together in recital that

February, in what I remember as my best public performance on clarinet, but my memories of him are tinged with strangeness. Were it not for a scattering of mentions on yellowed journal pages, I might think I had made him up or dreamed him. He showed up at a confused time in my life; it was also, as I register now from the dates, a confusing time in Quebec. We met at the height of the October Crisis, the month a secessionist organization kidnapped two public officials in Montreal and murdered one of them a week later, in apparent retaliation for Prime Minister Pierre Trudeau's invoking of the War Measures Act. The murder shocked Quebecers of all political persuasions. By mid-month the Canadian Army had been called in to support local police; Quebec was under martial law. As we rehearsed Brahms through November, hundreds of arrests were taking place; Véronique's father, a left-wing lawyer with separatist sympathies, was held incommunicado for three days. How strange that my journal records nothing of this. Was I unable to process it in my wrought-up state? I remember the daily unfolding of the drama in the news, the atmosphere of unreality in the city. And I wonder if the inner trembling I recall might have had something to do with the larger picture.

Apparently it was a confused time in Marcel's life, too, for at the end of that school year he stunned me by announcing he was giving up music as a career, leaving his teacher. I was to see him only once more, after the summer, when I dropped off some borrowed sheet music at an address he gave me on the phone. He was sharing an apartment with another young man he introduced briefly—tall and lean like himself, francophone, not very communicative, or perhaps he didn't speak much English (Marcel's English was excellent and it was the language in which he always addressed me). Their apartment was in a fashionable building in lower Westmount, far from the McGill Ghetto. They were studying theatre together, he told me. I remember the walls of the living room were painted black.

※

But back to November of 1970. For all I fretted about finding enough time for the clarinet, my journal hints of more
going on: "I wake when it is still dark out and drink my coffee, torn between two desires—to write, to play the piano."
(*What?*) The Lindsay was now in our living room. Sheldon's
debut the previous December had set something in motion
in my head. Marcel was preparing to perform Beethoven's A
flat major Sonata (Op. 26); hearing him rehearse, I fell in love
with the piece, in particular the perpetual-motion fourth movement, and longed to learn it. Only a week after that eloquent
lecture on responsibility, heart hammering as I dialed, I made
the phone call I must have been edging towards for close to
a year—a simple three-minute call for which I asked Fred to
leave the apartment. I had to be alone in the house to take this
step.

Mr. Cohen was surprised to hear from me, but his voice
betrayed no displeasure. When I said, "I have to come back,"
he laughed.

"You have to come back? To what, though?"

I said, "I have a piano now, and I can't keep my hands off
it."

"Maybe it's frustration."

"No, seriously. I don't know how I ever quit."

"Well, you sort of forced yourself. Robyn, it's lovely of you
to call," he said warmly. "Let me phone you later on in the
week, and we'll get together on it."

I put down the receiver and sobbed aloud, feeling like the
Prodigal Son. A deep sense of gratefulness, of peace, of homecoming, enfolded me. It was like the resolution of a chord that
had been left hanging for four years.

CODA: SOMETHING WAS ENDING

MY LONGED-FOR RETURN TO THE PIANO AND TO MY teacher was not a real return. Spanning barely three years, it was interrupted repeatedly as the lessons, for one reason or another, lapsed for weeks or months at a time. These were hodgepodge years. Fred and I worked one summer as musicians and stagehands in a theatre troupe, a government-funded project for students and unemployed youth, bringing productions to local hospitals. Fred went on to more theatre and other community projects; I played my Concours recital and repeated it the following year in hope of achieving a better standing. I struggled off and on with two successive proposals for a philosophy master's thesis it gradually became clear I wasn't going to write. A week before the second Concours, we moved out of the McGill Ghetto, across Mount Royal Park to the immigrant neighbourhood of Mile End, and soon after I was hired to teach humanities and music at the newly opened Champlain Regional College.

Mr. Cohen was in full career stride when I came back to him. Engaged to set up a music division at the expanding Sir George Williams College, he was full of ideas and excitement, teaching most of the courses himself and putting untraditional subjects like ethnomusicology on the curriculum, building a library of field recordings for use in class. This was a whole new frontier for the recording industry: music traditions of non-Western cultures, remote communities and subcultures, recorded on site. Fred enrolled in this course as an adult student, and I secured permission to audit it with Bob Sigmund. As had been the case with "old music" a few years earlier, we found the exposure to world musics a revelation.

My piano lessons, which resumed as smoothly as if they had never stopped, were usually in the evening, in a grand old mansion on Bishop Street acquired to house the new division. With the old, remembered intensity—the same moments of lift, amazed discovery, comic relief, and deepened musical insight—we worked on the Beethoven sonata I had earmarked to learn (Op. 26 in A flat major), and then on another Beethoven sonata, the E major Op. 14, No.1 (Phil's idea). I learned Schumann's *Aufschwung* ("Soaring") from the Fantasy Pieces; I began learning Chopin's second Scherzo, Prokofiev's Sarcasms, and the Bach Second Partita. I never asked myself what I was doing taking piano lessons again; it wasn't goal-directed. Perhaps that was what made it easy for me to let other things take over my time, disrupting continuity as I repeatedly deferred lessons rather than show up unprepared.

Sheldon had by now moved out of home at his mother's to an apartment of his own. My return to Mr. Cohen brought us into closer contact, and for a while we got together regularly at his place or mine to explore repertoire for clarinet and piano. We understood each other well musically, and now, as young adults, we got to know each other better on other levels; I felt as though I had a new brother. We performed twice at soirées in the private home of one of Mr. Cohen's former students, and we recorded again for CBC Radio. With soprano Céline Dussault, soon to receive international acclaim as the first vocalist to win the newly created Stepping Stones competition, we rehearsed Schubert's ravishing trio "Shepherd on the Rock," and recorded that, too, for CBC, though I don't believe it was ever broadcast.

Happy music-making, all of this. But deep inside, I knew I was disengaging from music. On the eve of our move from the McGill Ghetto, I wrote, "This is so much more than a move for me. A phase of my life is coming to a close. I've hit a dead end. All year my musical work has been thwarted. One recital cancelled because of a public service strike, another because of a strike at CBC. I have lost three pianists—Bob to the harpsichord, Marcel to the theatre, and now Sheldon, because there isn't enough serious repertoire for clarinet to motivate him to go on working with me. He would rather work with a violinist or singer, and who can blame him? It's time for me to pack it in with this stale love affair that never really had any good moments."

Reading this now, I protest: *of course there were good moments!* But I can also feel the constriction in my throat, the ache of loss that led me to that morose exaggeration. I remember how, once I did stop playing, I couldn't listen to classical music for years. I stayed away from concerts, avoided friends from Conservatoire. The stereo sat silent. If the radio ambushed me with a favourite symphony, especially one I once played in, I had to turn it off; the same with a piano piece—it made me too sad. Not until after I had children, and had a piano at home again, did this begin to change, though I never re-established much of a listening habit.

It was not only disenchantment with my musical situation that led to the break. Other interests beckoned. My first poems began to appear in literary magazines. Vacation trips to Vancouver Island put the west coast on our map and drew us into the counterculture ethos of the decade: talk of homesteading, utopian communities, spiritual retreats. Postcards from absent friends extolled the romance of mobility, the mystique of the woods, the mountains, the sea. Canada was a big country. Did we really want to live our lives in a city? Two years after the move to Mile End, we gave up the lease on our sunny, spacious corner flat and headed west on an open ticket to find out. I had resigned my teaching post, giving up credits towards seniority; if we came back, I would have to reapply from scratch.

In retrospect, at least for me, it was more about cutting ties with a life I could no longer see a way to continue than it was about a serious wish to relocate. We were back in Montreal before a full year was out, but by then I was in a different place myself.

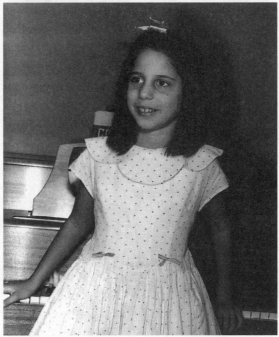

The author, age eight, with Mason & Risch.

January 31, 1968: backstage after MSO Matinee Symphonique concert at the Capitol Theatre (Photo: *The Ottawa Journal*)

Entr'acte

CIRCULAR: A PAUSE
TO TAKE STOCK

JANUARY, 2017. AT MY REQUEST, LONG-TIME FRIEND and music lover Barbara Scales has read my manuscript-in-progress—the hundred-odd pages I've managed to complete so far. Barbara has been an enthusiastic supporter of my return to the piano and is excited that I'm writing a book about it. I don't think she understands why it is taking so long. I realized, early on, that this was not a book that could be written quickly; it was a book I would have to *live* for a while first, if I wanted to say anything meaningful about what I was doing. And this in turn has meant watching my original idea change shape in response to lived realities. The book I am now writing is no longer the book I first envisaged. But the thing is finally off the ground, and I need to know how it sits with someone who has a serious interest in music without being a musician herself.

Barbara reads my finished chapters on a plane, which is where she does most of her reading. Back on the ground herself, a couple of weeks later, she thanks me for sharing them. "This is all quite wonderful and so insightful," she says. A tiny pause, and then: "But it seems to be more about *you* than it is about music. And isn't it rather circular?"

Her response throws me. This is a personal story; how can it *not* be about me? I was hoping to learn whether the shifting time frames were confusing, whether the musical discussion was accessible to a non-musician. Somewhat testily, I ask, "What is it exactly that you're looking for? I don't understand—what do you want to know about music?"

"I don't know—I guess I wanted to know what *you* think it is. I'd like to know what it is.What *is* music?" Her bright, expectant face, and the guilelessness with which she poses this huge question soften me into smiling.

Barbara Scales is an arts manager. She has worked with musicians for three decades. She books their tours, promotes their recordings, connects them with people she thinks they should know, listens to their woes, celebrates their wins, attends their concerts whenever she can. She's asking *me* what music is? I have played music for most of my life and have never given much thought to what it is. But now the question hangs in the air for me to consider.

The classic bare-bones definition, "organized sound," already touches on so many bodies and sub-bodies of knowledge it's dizzying to contemplate. Science of sound, mathematics of sound. Patterns of pitch and rhythm on which melodies are based; the beautiful textures created when multiple voice lines interact. Ranges of the human voice, timbres of different instruments—*All the instruments of joy / that skillful numbers can employ!* And that is just getting started. What about the evolution of *musics*, plural, in different parts of the world—the cultural contexts from which different forms of musical expression arise? What about the purposes for which different kinds of music are created? And if there's no one there to hear it, is it music? Is music, perhaps, the relation between organized sound and one who perceives it—a listener? Is music an interaction? A symbiosis? The ear hears the sounds, the body responds, the brain responds, emotions are stirred—even babies *in utero* exhibit a response to music; so do animals and, some claim, plants. Scientists are interested in how and why music does what it does to us, why music in one form or another seems to be universal to human cultures, why its origins seem closely associated with the religious or spiritual life of a culture. They are interested in the fact that music is able to reach the dying, the brain-damaged and brain-disordered (sometimes the *only* thing that can reach them). Why are stutterers cured of their stutter when they sing? Why do very young babies—what Phil Cohen calls "diaper dancers"—move their bodies rhythmically when they hear music, dancing on the spot with visible delight even before they can walk?

All these things are worth writing books about. Books have been written about them and will continue to be—books Barbara reads avidly; books I nose around in but rarely feel compelled to finish. What I feel compelled to do when I read about music is to put down the book and go practise. Whatever else it may be, for me as for any "practising" musician, music is a discipline. Its demands are implacable: neglect it and it abandons you. Yet this discipline need be no onus; pursued in the right spirit, it proves to be its own reward—a joy unequalled and ongoing, one that fuses mind, body, and emotions, bringing balance, stability, and grace into daily life. It's a metaphor with infinite applications, a form of meditation, a template for living, a source of serial enlightenment. Or so I have found it to be.

But isn't it rather circular?

Nearly two years into my new start at piano, I wrote, "The music-related journal excerpts that I've transcribed to computer are giving me pause. I see I've been making *the same* discoveries over and over again! It *feels* like progress, yet it appears I'm treading the same ground in circles, like Pooh and Piglet tramping round and round a spinney of larch trees, getting all excited by their own footprints in the snow. How am I to make a book of this? It's like a film loop!" Yet my intuition told me there must be a reason for it—or *reason to it*. And what I've been realizing as I try to recreate musical experience in writing is that the study of music *is* circular.

In many ways, music itself is circular. The tonal organization of Western music is based on the "circle of fifths" that I discovered at the age of eight, surprising my teacher Lorna. Reprise is built into the structure of music: the repeated phrase, pattern of a rhythm, chorus of a song, the melody that recapitulates, the return to the key the piece began in. Our ear learns to wait for these returns. As listeners, we have favourite songs, favourite pieces we want to hear over and over. We listen willingly to music that isn't familiar, but we don't tire of our old favourites, the ones we can sing or hum along with. Every repetition deepens our connection to them.

The musician, too, comes back again and again to a piece, going over the same ground but deepening it. This is true of the first stage of learning the music—getting the notes down to achieve a basic fluency—and equally true of preparing for performance (the French word for rehearsal is *répétition*). One goes back to the beginning to enhance that basic reading and create a moving experience for the listener. The same is true of reviving a piece that has lapsed from repertoire: one comes back to the score with a different perspective, seeing untried possibilities, giving the music a new reading. The circle is being traced deeper and deeper. And so with learning an instrument: one is always discovering new solutions, refining basic principles of technique, applying them more effectively, making more stringent demands on oneself.

When Phil Cohen told me as a child of eleven that every time I sat down at the piano, I should begin by saying "I know nothing," I now understand he was opening the door to this process. Even if it seems we are having "the same" revelations, the important thing is that we keep experiencing them as revelations. In fact they are *not* the same, because *we* are not the same. We embrace them as newly exciting, *momentous*, because we come to them at a different moment. We bring a new self to them, the awareness that comes of having lived a little longer—whether a day, a year, or a decade—integrating experience we didn't have before. But this renewal of excitement comes only if we begin from a place of not-knowing. If we begin from what we think we know, we lose that new self and the radical openness that allows us to refresh and deepen knowledge. Creatively, it is our willingness to be surprised—even by the same thing that surprised us yesterday—that gives us what we need to transmit surprise to others.

TOP: With Al Fraser at the Falcone; BOTTOM: With Phil Cohen and Alan Fraser (photos: Daniela Muhling, February 2012).

TOP: Youngest and oldest participant, Adamant Music School, summer of 2012. BOTTOM: With Franklin Larey, Coordinator. Adamant Music School, summer of 2012.

Governor General's Awards gala, December 2, 2015: playing Glenn
Gould's piano in Rideau Hall

PART TWO:

FOLLOWING THE MUSIC

I   INTENTIONALITY

FEBRUARY 1, 2011. MONDAY MORNING IN THE WEST-mount Studio, sun pouring into the piano room. Nearly two years since the afternoon I first rang Pamela's doorbell. These days I have a weekly slot with her here. We're winding up a good lesson on the Fantaisie-Impromptu; she's pleased with my new pedalling and phrasing in the slow movement. Earlier she asked to hear the Liszt, which I hadn't played for her in a year, and she seems satisfied with how it is evolving. We end with a full run-through of the Scarlatti sonata I've been learning (A major, K208), which I now have from memory. I think it sounds beautiful on the studio piano—playing on a grand piano is still enough of a novelty that the unaccustomed richness of tone can give me grand illusions about how well I'm playing—but she's not so happy with this one. She says, "You aren't following through on your own musical ideas. You start with what seems like a good idea and then drift away from it or do something else, without a thought-out transition. For me, as listener—I need more *direction* than you're giving me. I need for you to be *taking me somewhere*."

Is she saying I need to have a premeditated interpretation, a thought-out path through the whole piece? Wouldn't that activate the worst of my perfectionist tendencies? But she says, "Even if you don't think out the path in advance, you need to be able to do it on the spot. You need always to be *following a line* in the music, with an unbroken focus."

I take this home as my week's meditation. I think about "taking a listener somewhere." It connects with my thoughts about Mark Twain on the river—the realization that a part of me wants to be the passenger, not the pilot, while I'm playing music. And it connects with the difficulty I've been having comprehending Phil's "The future creates the present." I enter a piece of music as a dreamer. I *feel my way through it* instead of directing myself.

Synchronicity is at work: it seems no accident that this same week a friend and fellow poet emails me a quotation he came across that he thinks may be of interest. It's by the American poet Katie Ford, from an essay called "Writing About the City: New Orleans, Destruction, and the Duty of the Poet." The title would have led me to expect a manifesto about the poet's duty to address events and issues of the day, to be topical and political—an idea that has always made me uneasy because of the various kinds of posturing it can prompt. But Ford was writing as someone who actually lived in New Orleans before and after Hurricane Katrina, and the quotation was not about political imperatives but creative ones:

> The willfulness of the poet who begins with a subject
> in mind will be felt all over a page, pushing the poem
> into the desired subject, even as the poem wants to
> stray and find its own way. 'Like a piece of ice on a
> hot stove the poem must ride on its own melting,'
> Robert Frost said. It is the melting that is the poem's
> will, its organic and secretive path. Whichever way
> the ice melts, it is not so much a matter of a poet's

choice as it is the demands of the imagination and
countless factors of emotion, psychology, music,
literary influence, and, perhaps above all, confusion
that melt the ice.

"Our task is blind, we find our way by feel," Ford goes on
in the essay. The duty of the poet, she says, is to the poem, and
not to a subject. The poem's real subject is to be revealed in a
compositional process that destroys our preconceptions, stock
assumptions, shallow first thoughts and "hurried answers."

Yes, yes, yes, yes, I say. This is my experience as a poet and
this is what I too believe. When I write a poem, it's the poem
that takes *me* somewhere, not vice versa. Who was it who said
"How can I know what I think till I see what I say?" *All poets
learn backwards.* As a poet, I find out what I had to say only
after I've said it. Even on those rare occasions when I start out
with some notion of where I'd like a poem to end up—a notion
I may scrap en route—I never know how I'm going to get there.
I don't know the *path*; I have to discover it as I go along. And
in the same way, when I'm playing a piece of music, I want to
feel it is taking *me* somewhere, instead of taking charge so I
can take a listener somewhere. But there's a critical difference.
As a poet I have the luxury of solitude and unlimited time to
discover the path before any "listener" will experience what
I'm creating. As a performer, I do not have that luxury.

The impulse running its course:
carried, like a leaf on air,
through air, to rest—not just
the motion, but the path it makes
no leaf will make again—to this
I give what self I can,
what sight, what will.
Or winter warmed: a smell,
fresh, tremulous, and sweet,

we say is spring, that breathes
from heaps of shrinking snow
gone lacy in the sun—or steams
from rivulets that run
in all directions, out from under these.

This poem, tellingly named "Carried," was sparked by watching the trajectory of an autumn leaf falling from the tree outside my study window. The path from branch to ground was not a straight line but a choreography of response to givens: shape of the leaf, vagaries of the air. It seemed to embody a personal directive, both for how I wanted to write and for how I wanted to live my life: something about *finding the path while on the path.* Or maybe *finding the path by making the path.* What is the path of an air current? What is the path of snow melting? There's an element of the random in both. An air current in my life brought me back to studying piano. I am following it—going where it takes me, which is not where I first thought it would.

In musical performance, how do I reconcile the listener's need for direction with my own need for spontaneity, for impulsivity—my need to follow the "organic and secretive path" of an impulse running its course? This is not just my challenge; it is the challenge of creative performance and of art in general. On another level it's the challenge of life itself—at least of living creatively. What do we do with the unexpected, with chance, with accident, in our lives? Can we digress from our intentions without losing the path? I think what Pamela must mean is that in order to be able to let go of conscious control, I must first have established it. If I want to experience the freedom of letting the music carry me even as I play it, if I want to enable chance and impulsivity without risking a crash, I have to have a rock-solid knowledge of the score and a sort of default path mastered in advance. Knowledge of the score *is* my default path. "Let the music be your conductor," is how Phil puts it. "Follow the music."

II   FLASHBACK:

AN AIR CURRENT

YOU COULD SAY THE "AIR CURRENT" THAT BROUGHT ME back to studying piano came out of the bell of my clarinet. It came from following an impulse, taking a chance, letting myself be carried by someone else's idea—"carried" (also by air, and roughly a thousand miles) to blow a few minutes' breath into a wind instrument I had long since given up playing. A caprice. A digression—but one that was to prove a stepping-stone back to a lost path.

※

February, 2006. My old friend Eli Herscovitch won't get off it. Musician par excellence on several instruments, founding member of Canada's first Klezmer band, irrepressible comedian and storyteller, survivor of brain surgery, he's on the phone to me from his home in Winnipeg with his latest idea: we should team up and do a performance in Winnipeg. Alternating sets of poetry and music. The theme: Montreal. The city where we both grew up, meeting in the community of artists, writers, actors, and musicians that shifted its base to Mile End when developers moved in on the McGill Ghetto. We would recreate the spirit of Mile End when it was still a mix of ethnic communities and a growing number of students, artists, and counterculture types who somehow were able to share space peaceably in a neighbourhood known for its high population density. We could call it "A Taste of Montreal." He can get an eight-piece band together, he says. He has music he has worked on with his friend, Winnipeg composer Sid Robinovitch—pieces based on his Montreal memories, a narrative structure to hang them on: my poems will fit with it perfectly.

"You know how many ex-Montrealers there are, here in Winnipeg? All homesick. They'll come. We can even have a slide show—I'll put together some of Richard's photographs from the seventies ..." He's talking about Richard Tarlo, with whom he shared a flat for a few student years, a gifted amateur photographer who studied piano with Phil Cohen and was my son's first piano teacher. Richard who died of a heart attack in his early forties; whose photo archive ended up in Eli's hands.

Eli and his wife moved west when we were all in our late twenties, before Mile End began its own process of gentrification. The Montreal he remembers with undying nostalgia is, if not gone, greatly diminished, but enough of it remains to appease his hunger for bagels baked in a wood oven and reunions with old friends when he returns periodically to visit. In his head the old neighbourhood lives on, along with our younger selves: the mostly self-taught kid who got a chance to jam with Sonny Terry and Brownie McGhee when they visited his high school; the twenty-something girl clarinet player he later asked to coach him on the classical audition pieces he had to learn for admission to the Music Faculty at McGill.

"You can bring your clarinet," he says now, still spinning out his vision for a shared event. "We can play a classical number together, too—something as a bridge between sets."

"Eli, I haven't performed on clarinet for more than thirty years! I don't play at all anymore. I have no endurance, my embouchure's jelly—the last time I tried to get it back was seven years ago. After two months I could still barely get through a five-minute piece."

"You'll do it. I know you can do it. We can prepare something really short, a classical arrangement. Really—we just prepare it, and you can decide, even on the spur of the moment. If you don't want to play, I'll have a backup musical number. Just *bring the clarinet.*"

"Who's going to pay for this? I can apply to a literary program for the poetry part, but I can't ask for funding for even one musician, let alone an eight-piece band ..."

"We'll find, we'll find! I know some sources I can look into."

Eli is nothing if not persuasive. A week later a package plops through my mail slot: an arrangement, for flute, clarinet, and piano, of Gabriel Fauré's famous Sicilienne, and a CD called *Breaktime with Eli*, featuring several of his collaborations with Robinovitch. He hasn't found funding for the musicians yet, but he has lined up two venues that can give us consecutive dates. He has suggestions: we could introduce my first poetry set with a poem to be read as voiceover for a musical excerpt—then, to introduce his longer music set, we could play the Sicilienne. My second poetry set could end with a different poem as voiceover for the same music we began with, bringing things full circle.

We're soon working out a program, timing poems and musical numbers. The Sicilienne is three minutes. It will take two weeks of daily practise for me to regain the endurance to play for three minutes, and how can we rehearse this, with me in Montreal and him in Winnipeg? With option to bail firmly in mind, I open my dusty clarinet case, grease up the corks, spend a few days playing long notes to build embouchure. Then we rehearse flute and clarinet parts over long distance—two phones on speaker. We won't get to rehearse with piano until I'm in Winnipeg, but Eli says Gary's a pro, he could play it cold on stage if he had to. *Well. It's only three minutes*, I tell myself. *How much can really go wrong in three minutes?*

Meanwhile my application for funding is approved. Eli isn't as successful. The eight-piece band will simply have to be reduced. It's now down to Gary, Eli's keyboardist. Eli will alternate instruments: he's equally proficient on clarinet, saxophones, flute, harmonica—too bad he can't play them all at the same time. (Recently I found an old email from Eli in which he said he had thought of a new joke: "Some people find it very funny, some don't get it. *How many jazz musicians does it take to drive a taxi? Answer: Just ONE!* p.s. if you don't get it, try substituting something else, like poet, for jazz musician.")

My flight to Winnipeg lands just past eight on the night before our first performance, a lunch-hour gig at the Millennium Library. Eli meets me at the airport. He has arranged for Gary to rehearse with us at the house tonight, but Gary has another rehearsal and can't come before ten. I fret that we're cutting things a bit close—is this it, or will we get to run through it again in the morning? Relax, says Eli. Have something to eat. There are pickles in the fridge, there's rye bread, cheese, take what you want. Gary's reliable. He'll get here when he gets here.

And he does, at ten on the nose. The Sicilienne proves no problem; we run through it twice for tempo and balance, my embouchure holds, my tone is surprisingly good. The challenge, unexpectedly, is synchronizing my poems to the musical passage we've chosen to begin and end our program. Practising at home with the CD, I've paced my reading to musical cues that tell me when to start, when to pause, and when to re-enter so poem and music finish together. But when Eli and Gary begin playing, the cues I'm listening for aren't there! It hadn't occurred to me that as a jazz and Klezmer performer, Eli would

regard the score as a basis for improvisation, varying it freely
on the spot.

"Eli, can't you guys play it the way it is on the CD?"
They're flummoxed. The piece was recorded more than once;
Eli doesn't remember which performance was on the CD
he sent me and isn't sure he has another copy. Luckily I've
brought mine. They listen as I read my opening and closing
poems with the music, then mark their scores with the cues
I've depended on and some key words to cue themselves. We
rehearse a couple of times and call it a night.

※

No one but Eli could have gotten me on stage with my clarinet again after thirty-five years, even for three minutes.
Assembling my old Buffet in the library auditorium next morning, eyeing the dull tarnish on its once-silver keys, I can't
even remember my last public performance. Am I out of my
mind to think I can still do this—on two weeks' practice and a
single rehearsal?

There's a lectern for my reading over to one side of the
stage; Eli has all his instruments set up stage centre, on stands
of the sort jazz players use. A little forest of instruments: alto
sax, soprano sax, tenor sax, flute, and clarinet.

"What do I do with mine? Stick it under the lectern?"

"Don't be silly, I brought an extra stand for you. Here, put
it beside mine." I've never used a stand, but I set my clarinet
on the peg, reflecting that if I decide to bail, at least nobody
will know that one of the clarinets was mine and that I was
supposed to play it.

Eli is thinking aloud. "What's your last poem in the set?
After you finish, I'll take the mic and ad-lib a little spiel about
all the musicians on our block, back in the day—the way a few
would get together in someone's living room and read through
some Bach or Mozart, and people walking by would stop under

the window to listen. Then I'll say something like—*We'll give you a taste of that now ... how about it, Robyn, we'll jam a classical number for old times' sake*—that's your cue to walk over to centre stage and pick up your clarinet."

He makes it sound so easy. "What if I chicken out?"

"You can signal me before I start talking—just shake your head. But you won't chicken out. You'll play—you'll play."

People are beginning to arrive. The slide show—Richard Tarlo's photographs of Mile End in the seventies, set to "Pause" and displayed as thumbnails on the big screen up front—has already served to "out" some former Montrealers. They're doing that Montreal thing now, trading of memories, names, schools, neighbourhoods, people they might know in common. By the time we begin our program, the atmosphere is almost familial. The opening voiceover, "Rue Jeanne Mance," goes off perfectly; the poems that follow, depicting Montreal scenes and seasons, get a warm response. When the time comes for me to change hats and *jam a classical number*, I cross the stage with a laughing caveat: "This is entirely Eli's idea—I haven't performed on clarinet for thirty years. I take no responsibility for what's about to happen."

Famous last words. I pick up my clarinet from the stand where I've left it and—surprise—the whole stand comes with it. The bell of the instrument is stuck on the peg, the stand dangling from it. "Oops," I say to faint titters, putting the stand back on the floor so I can hold it down with one hand and tug at the clarinet with the other. But the clarinet won't budge.

"What the—? Eli, can you help me? It's stuck." The audience thinks this is part of the show; they're laughing out loud now. Eli holds the base of the stand firmly on the floor and I tug at the instrument again using both hands. This time the newly-greased tenon connecting upper and lower joints slides smoothly out of its socket and I find myself holding half a clarinet—the other half left behind, still jammed on the peg. I don't have to ham it up; the look on my face (source of renewed hilarity) is unfeigned. Eventually, with some jiggling and twisting, Eli succeeds in getting the bell unstuck. He picks up his flute and signals Gary to give us a chord to tune to; we each blow a note and we're right on pitch, first shot. "How about that?" says my old friend to the audience. "We've been perfectly in tune for thirty years."

Next surprise: the sound of my clarinet soars out into the hall as though I had never stopped playing—the tone robust, intonation dead-on, breath steady. And I'm *not afraid*. It's exhilarating to be playing music with others, on a stage, with listeners. Nothing feels at stake here; I'm just having fun. I know this throwback to my glory days on clarinet is a Cinderella moment: if the piece were even a minute longer, my embouchure would slacken, air leaking out the corners of my mouth as a warning that my bottom lip was about to give out. But something is stirring in me—a recognition that old performance terrors and bad associations may be far enough behind me now to have lost their grip. That somehow, perhaps I could find my way to a fresh start in music. That I would like to have music in my life again on an *ongoing* basis.

A bigger surprise is in store when we repeat our program next day at the University of Winnipeg. It comes before we begin, while Gary and Eli are setting up on stage to do sound checks. They're tinkering with wires and screwdrivers; it's taking a long time. At loose ends, I wander backstage to the dimlit green room and try a few chords on an old upright piano pushed against the far wall. It's in tune. Dragging over a scuffed wooden chair, I start playing the first movement of Beethoven's Pathétique Sonata, the piece I've been reviving by fits and starts over the past year—at some point becoming aware that someone has come in and is standing a few feet away, listening. Out of the corner of my eye I can see it's a man, maybe a sound technician. I manage to keep going to the end of the movement before turning to acknowledge him.

"Eli didn't tell me you were a concert pianist," he says then, and I realize this must be Harry Strub, artistic director of the university's concert series, who booked this event as he has many of Eli's performances over the years. I laugh, embarrassed, but he's regarding me steadily. "You play that very well. I could book you to do a recital here next year, if you're interested." Surely he's joking. I explain I'm a closet amateur, just trying to keep up a bit of repertoire as time allows, and we chat for a few minutes before Gary appears, summoning me to test the mic. Later Eli tells me Harry was genuinely impressed. "He was surprised to hear you never performed on piano. He says you've inspired him to start playing again himself."

Although it would be another three years before I hit "Send" on an email to my old piano teacher, a seed was planted in Winnipeg that week. It was probably too late to get my chops back as a wind player. But if the fear was gone—maybe I could actually perform on piano?

III BEYOND THE RATIONAL

SYNCHRONICITY, DEFINED AS "MEANINGFUL COINCI-
dence," is a phenomenon most people have experienced,
whether or not it's a word they recognize. Example: a woman
newly pregnant suddenly finds herself running into pregnant
women wherever she goes. She may find it meaningful, but
there's nothing uncanny about it: pregnant women are always
among us, she just has more reason to notice them now. Or
suppose someone strongly recommends a book to you—an
obscure book, something you'd have to hunt down in a used
bookstore or get in a library. A day or two later, you notice
your seatmate on the subway is reading that very book. This
too may not be as much of a coincidence as it seems: perhaps
the book was mentioned recently by some media personality, prompting both individuals to seek it out. This kind of
"meaningful coincidence" can be explained away, or at least
explained.

Other kinds are less easily fathomed. Once, in a filing cabinet drawer, I found an old wind-up wristwatch that had gone
missing a decade earlier. It began ticking when I wound it up.
Checking the correct time so I could reset it, I was stunned

to see there was no need: I had found and rewound the watch at the exact minute and hour when it stopped. (What are the odds?) Another example: while reading a story by Saul Bellow called "The Gonzaga Manuscripts," I scanned my bookshelf in search of something else by Bellow. In the process my eye fell on a book I had never read and had forgotten about, a critique of the poetry of Margaret Avison, written by a distant acquaintance who had sent it to me years earlier. Some impulse prompted me to take it off the shelf; later that day, I picked it up and opened it at random. There on the page was a quote from "The Gonzaga Manuscripts."

What to make of these unlikelier coincidences I don't venture to speculate. What I do know is that creative people of all sorts tend to be highly attuned to synchronicity in their lives. Ever on the lookout for material that may prove relevant to a current project, they pay close attention to their daily givens, and when we're looking for meaning in the seeming random, we often find it. (Ah! *Chance favours the prepared mind.*)

Synchronicity kicked in for me, in the form of piano-significant givens, almost from the moment I plucked up courage to contact Phil Cohen again. Just hours after the intrepid email left my outbox, I attended a book launch where I knew nobody but the author, who was thronged by family and friends when I arrived. Filling a plate with crackers and cheese, I listened to an exchange between two women around my age, standing nearby. The first was saying, "Right now I'm writing for a non-profit, but actually I'm a retired social worker. And you?" The second replied, "I'm a pianist." Perhaps if I had not *just* decided to study piano again, her statement wouldn't have caught my attention at all; it wasn't as if she had said, "I'm an astronaut" or "I'm a secret agent." But at that particular moment, in a room full of strangers, at an event that had nothing to do with music, it felt like a covert nod from the stars.

In direct proportion to my renewed focus on the piano, pianists began to appear in my life; pianos appeared, with invitations to play them; opportunities to perform presented themselves. Presumably they were always there, but now I saw them. I didn't have to go looking—they came to me, and often by improbable routes.

%

There was nothing probable about how my husband David and I met Clive B. And if even half of what he gave us to know about himself was true, there was nothing probable about the man himself. Stories tumbled from Clive. A classical violinist, then dancer, turned engineer: hired out of school by the company that built the Baltimore Aquarium—hired for his expertise on saltwater fish; he had briefly owned a pet store that specialized in them. Stricken with a rare form of cancer before he turned thirty; told he had four months to live; still alive at fifty and running his own construction company. Designer of his loft apartment down by the canal, in a renovated commercial building converted to condos. Amateur jazz pianist and drummer, collector of musical instruments, and owner of two concert grand pianos—one an 1891 Steinway that he bought from an old church in Virginia, brought to Montreal to be rebuilt, and eventually shipped to Steinway in New York to replace a warped soundboard; the other, a Bösendorfer that had belonged to Oscar Peterson. He had not meant to acquire two concert grands, he explained; he bought the Bösendorfer intending to sell it when work on the Steinway was completed, but in the meantime he became attached to it and had ended up keeping both.

This was not someone you would expect to meet where we met him: in a small heritage Orthodox synagogue, blowing the shofar to usher in the Jewish New Year, fall of 2010.

A new face in the small, very mixed inner-city congregation, he blew the ram's horn like a virtuoso: perfectly timed blasts, perfectly inflected; robust volume, steady pitch, the final long note drawn out pure and unwavering for longer than should have been humanly possible. He blew shofar like it was a musical instrument. (Not everyone was happy about this. The synagogue's overseer remarked privately to me, when I shared the thought, that sounding the shofar was not meant to be a musical performance—it was a call to attention, intended to focus hearers on matters of the soul, not to impress them with the skill of the shofar blower. I saw his point, but we had suffered through enough inept shofar-blowing over the years not to welcome a regular who could be relied on to deliver the prescribed series of sounds faultlessly on first try.)

Soft-spoken, tall and thin, always elegantly dressed for holiday services but apt to show up to the occasional supper-hour program straight from a job site, in work jeans, fleece vest, and construction boots, Clive seemed interested in my own musical story. I sensed some regret about his abandonment of the violin. As a jazz pianist he was self-taught. "I know it looks crazy, having two concert grands when I'm not a professional and have so little time to play," he admitted. "They do get played, though. I have friends over regularly on Sundays to play the pianos—some of my jazz pals, some local musicians I know." *Dare I ask*, I wondered.

"Do you play classical too?"

"Not really. I did as a kid. There's only one piece I still sometimes play—a piece I really love. Debussy's Première Arabesque." Out of the entire piano repertoire, he had named the piece I'd performed just that week in a pre-Christmas mini-recital of Pamela's students at the Westmount Studio.

"I don't believe it!" I exclaimed. "That's what I'm working on right now. I first learned it when I was fifteen. It's the piece I kept up the longest after I quit lessons." Then (deep breath, for this had to be a sign): "Maybe I could come over and try your pianos sometime?"

"With pleasure. Any time you want."

※

Clive's pianos, on the main floor of his sparely furnished condo, were at one end of the huge room, nestled back-to-back so two pianists could face each other across the width of the unit. In the centre an open staircase ascended to the second level. At the other end was a living area with open kitchen, dining table, leather sofa, and tall windows overlooking the canal. A drum set and various wind instruments on stands occupied the middle ground, ranged along the wall.

But the pianos. Curve echoing curve. Long, sleek, black, and gleaming, like a pair of racehorses. "Be my guest," said Clive, gesturing towards them after showing us around. The Steinway's lid and music rack had been removed. "Do you want me to put back the music rack?" I didn't. I hadn't brought any sheet music with me on this first visit. Our host, probably sensing some shyness about playing in front of him, occupied himself making tea for David, whose plan for the afternoon was to start working on a composite photographic portrait of Clive in his home with some of his instruments. Far across the room, the two of them were soon engrossed in conversation about architecture and photography.

Decades of living in triplex row-housing—old flats with shared walls, narrow rear courtyards with five other living units in earshot of open windows—had conditioned me to floor the soft pedal and keep it down when I played piano at home. I wasn't used to big sound. Even the Falcone, situated as it was in a small, low-ceilinged studio, was no preparation for the volume of a nine-foot, hundred-year-old duplex-scale Steinway with the lid removed, in an uncarpeted room with a twenty-foot ceiling. The bass was overwhelming. Down went the soft pedal as I moved tentatively around on the keyboard, getting the feel of the heavy Steinway action, trying openings of a few pieces in different registers. When I felt ready, I played through the Arabesque. The long sustain in the treble was intoxicating, the chordal textures vibrant; I sensed a colour range I had barely begun to draw on.

"Beautiful," Clive called from across the room. "Now get your foot off the una corda. You're leaning back from the piano like you're scared of the sound. You're choking it off with the pedal. These are concert pianos, they're meant to be played in a hall, the sound is meant to *fill* a hall. They want to be played robustly. Especially the Steinway. You want to bang the hell out of it to get it to sound. You have to *bang*."

I winced at the word—Phil's biggest no-no, his single *absolute* no-no. "Clive, I was taught never to bang. That you can get volume without banging. That it's bad for the piano."

"Well, just get your left foot off the pedal and play with full volume. Lean *into* the sound, not away from it."

Trying different pieces, I felt the challenges this piano posed to my usual way of playing them, heard how it changed them. Forgoing the una corda was easier said than done; my foot crept back automatically, until I hit on the solution of wedging it underneath the pedal to remind it to stay on the floor. I saw Clive was right; I had been holding back from the sound instead of giving myself to it. Then, a little way into Chopin's Fantaisie-Impromptu, something almost shocking happened. In a sudden, seamless shift, like the moment an airplane leaves the ground, I felt the piano become continuous with me—as if until then I had been "playing piano" but I hadn't been playing *that* piano. Now I *was* playing it, and it didn't sound like me playing at all.

"Ah! Now I'm hearing something," Clive called. I thought, *This is what a concert piano is—it can turn you into a concert pianist.* It was exhilarating, like the discovery of a new self.

But the marvellous resonance lasted only a few minutes. The harder I tried to get it back, the more it eluded me: thereafter, piece after piece that I tried just sounded dead.

"Clive, what happened? How did I get that sound? How did I lose it? It's like I was on a horse that threw me."

"Take a break," he suggested. "Why don't you try the other piano?" Standing up a little creakily, I moved to the Bösendorfer with its light action and crisper sound, and a feature new to me, unique to Bösendorfer: a longer keyboard, nine extra notes in the bass, the additional keys all black so as not to visually disorient the player. (What did one *do* with nine extra bass notes?) The Bösendorfer was easier to play, more forgiving, but I soon switched back: having once tuned in to the Steinway's full magic, even so briefly, all I wanted was to experience it again before we had to leave. It didn't happen that afternoon. There were flashes—enough to keep me trying for another hour—but I couldn't sustain it.

"Don't be discouraged," Clive said as we were getting ready to go. "Playing on a concert grand isn't something you grasp overnight. It's not easy, playing that Steinway. If you had a week with it, you would start to be able to play it. The way you're sounding on it now isn't a measure of your capability, I can tell." Seeing us out the door, he added, "It's astonishing you can play as well as you do, coming back to it so late. If you hadn't quit, I have no doubt you could have been an amazing pianist. You're welcome to come play here anytime. I'm away a lot—I don't have to be here for you to come, I can give you a key. Just say the word." So it was that at the end of 2010, access to not one but two concert grand pianos fell into my lap.

※

David had left a little recording device running inside the Steinway all afternoon. I woke the next morning to hear it playing back on his computer. From the bed, parts of it sounded good, but listening close up was worse than disappointing. While I knew I hadn't been playing my best, even the better takes had things in them that made me cringe. Unwanted accents. Note-to-note verticality instead of a moving line. I had imagined I was getting close to where I wanted to be, at least with some pieces; now I could see what a long way I had to go.

"My playing *lurches*," I lamented in my journal. "It isn't controlled. Sometimes I achieve a beautiful tone, beautiful phrasing. But at best it's the playing of a gifted amateur; it lacks discipline and consistency. Even the driest, most mechanical piano playing by young concert artists I hear on the radio, playing that leaves me cold, has a fluidity and polish I'm nowhere near to manifesting." What I was hearing, mostly, was inadvertent emphasis on notes that didn't need to be emphasized, interrupting the flow of the melodic line—especially, a tendency to land heavily on the last note of a phrase. How embarrassing that I hadn't been hearing these clunky phrase endings when I played.

Happier surprises were, fortunately, around the corner. Just before my initial encounter with Clive's Steinway, Phil had phoned to offer me a session, our first since summer's end; he hoped he could also see me a few times over winter break, when the Falcone would again be readily available. His new priority was "singing tone." He wanted me to work on just a phrase or two at a time, one hand, melody line only, listening intently to the connections between notes—hearing the way what he called the "decay" of one sound blended into the start of the next. I was just beginning to understand that singing tone was not so much about sounding the note as it was about timing the release of the key in moving to the next note.

One day I discovered that after a few minutes of working this way, if I digressed from the exercise to play through some other piece, the whole quality of my sound seemed to have changed. There was an enhanced resonance, as though I had brought Clive's twenty-foot ceiling home with me. Stranger still, I found myself recovering large segments of pieces I hadn't played for years, even without looking at the music. The Mozart A major Sonata, K331. The Beethoven E major, Op.14, No.1. The promise inherent in this new sound somehow brought them back to me, or me to them. Elated, I phoned Phil and tried to describe what was happening. Was I only imagining the change in sound? He seemed to know exactly what I was talking about.

"Terrific, that's terrific, dear. I'm so happy for you. No, you're not imagining it," he said. "This is what I've been waiting for. It's good that you're playing on different pianos, it's even good that you're being thrown off. You'll get it and lose it, but don't worry. You'll get it again."

At our subsequent sessions, the focus was still on tactility—staying low to the key, sliding my thumb along the surface so I could feel every note while getting from one place to another. On one occasion we spent more than half an hour on a single shift in the Debussy, the choreography involved in repositioning my hand for the phrase to come. Always it took me an unconscionably long time to see *why* we were doing what we were doing, but as before, incrementally, without fully understanding, I found myself beginning to apply the principles we were working with. My skepticism was breaking down. Again Phil insisted on the importance of testing and knowing what I was doing *by touch,* using the tool of having one hand test or guide the other—"I know you think it's stupid."

"I don't think it's stupid," I said. "I just can't seem to do it. The hand that's supposed to be guiding is never really doing that—it's just taking a ride on the hand that's playing."

"In a way, yes. That's okay. Just think of the guiding hand as *being there* with the hand that's playing. They're there *together.* Working this way will give you the solidity to allow for some risk, some spontaneous creativity in performance.

The way you're playing now, there's too much risk; it's almost all risk. It's inevitable that at some point you'll lose it."

I became willing again to try some of his suggestions I had rejected earlier—to put aside my doubts and just go through the motions, without expectations. (It now occurred to me that "going through the motions" might have been the point all along.) But it was hard not to be discouraged at the way seeming breakthroughs in my playing could go out the window, leaving me with nothing but my lately-acquired, hard-won continuity.

Nothing but? "Even a couple of months ago, continuity in itself contented me," I wrote in my journal. "It was, after all, supposedly my goal—just to be able to get through pieces without having to stop. But now simple continuity seems a dubious achievement. I want so much more! I want the aliveness of tone, the beauty of phrasing, the focused intentionality. I no longer have much interest in performing—I'm not ready—though Phil says I should be playing for people whenever I can, as long as it's for 'friendly' listeners. I feel I'm at the beginning again—a beginning on a higher level, but no less a beginning for that; it's clear that everything I've done so far, with Phil and with Pamela and on my own, has been to bring me to this beginning. It's a familiar road I'm on—a hilly one, and no destination, just a joyous and very demanding process. It is now unthinkable that I should not continue this pursuit for the rest of my life."

I brought the little recording device to our next session and recorded a run-through of the Liszt Consolation before we began taking it apart to work on. At home I listened to it and was appalled. Then I listened to more of the recording from Clive's. Early on, both Al and Phil had told me I was hearing what I *wanted* in my playing and not what I was actually delivering. They could discern my intentions, but they also heard where my execution fell short. While I didn't doubt them, it was one thing to hear it said and another to hear what they were talking about. A recording doesn't allow you to forget about the flaws in your performance once they've vanished into air; they're there to hear over and over again.

So when Phil phoned the next day to ask how it was going, I said, "Not so well today," and told him why. "I've been listening to the recordings and they're really getting me down. I thought I was getting somewhere, but now ... Maybe I've taken this as far as I can. Maybe it's just too late ..."

"That's something I don't want to hear from you again." His stern voice.

"Well, but Phil, I don't understand why you're bothering with me. I play *terribly*."

The comeback was instantaneous. "*That's—why.*"

You asked for that, kiddo, I thought wryly. But immediately his voice softened as he went on, "It's normal to lose it and get it back and lose it again. You shouldn't be sitting down to the piano in the expectation that you'll get it the way you played it yesterday. You need to stop the intellectualizing crap—I don't mean *you*, it's something we all do. Stop trying to analyze what you're doing when it's working, or why it isn't working when you lose it. The big concert artists I've worked with over the years—if you ask them what it is that they're doing when they're playing really well, they all say the same thing. They say they can't explain it." A second's pause, then he went on, "It isn't *rational*. Got that? We're in a world, here, where rationality can't help you. Leave the other world behind and enter this one. It's real too, but it's a different reality. In every session we've had, you've reached a point where I can see something happening. There's always a breakthrough. You need to just keep at it till it becomes a part of you."

"But the recordings—I can't stand to hear them. I can't even begin to tell you how depressing it is for me."

There was a longer pause. "So you've hit rock bottom, is that what you're saying?"

"No, I wouldn't put it that way. I'm afraid it might be bottomless."

"Are you thinking of packing in it?"

The question surprised me. "No way—I can't. Not in a million years."

Then he laughed. "The bottom is soft," he said.

It was a landmark exchange, one I found deeply comforting. It reoriented me. At our next session Phil was gentle, reminding me of the way he was at some of my lessons as a young adolescent. He was patient. And suddenly it seemed I did understand what we were doing. I saw how he wanted me to be moving on the keyboard—"handing" instead of fingering—placing the hand so it was prepared not just for the next note but for all the notes it could reach before it needed to shift again. It was, as he kept saying, *simple*, a simple principle. Its purpose was to eliminate all sudden movements and the lurching accents they might create. I suddenly viscerally felt what he meant when he spoke of tension in the body creating interference; the importance of remembering to breathe, of letting the hand breathe. It all seemed obvious: requiring huge focus and attention, but no longer abstract or arcane.

After a week or so, Phil phoned again to see how I was doing. He had a radar for calling when I was at the keyboard.

"Better," I acknowledged cautiously. For the first time in a few days, the piano was actually sounding good. "Only I've been having to battle discouragement ever since hearing myself recorded. It doesn't go away."

"Throw out the recording," he said.

Throw it out? "But it was useful. Really—it made me hear all the things I mentally erase when I'm playing."

"Good, so you've heard them. Now, throw out the recording."

Self-indulgence, he had made clear, had no place in this whole endeavour. It was good to know that neither had self-flagellation.

IV   A TALE OF TWO TEACHERS

FOR MY FIRST COUPLE OF YEARS STUDYING PIANO
again, I had two teachers. Pamela saw me more or less regularly, subject to both of our working schedules; Phil saw
me from time to time, mostly over the summer and during
Christmas break at the university. In December of 2010, our
first session since the end of summer, I arrived with a folder of
materials I thought he might like to see. It contained a manuscript copy of my long poem, "My Shoes Are Killing Me," and
a visual arts feature I had written on David's photography and
the work of Montreal functional-object sculptor Tibor Timar,
who had spent a decade making one-of-a-kind chairs out of
scrapyard metal. I included some postcard reproductions of
David's more recent work. More and more, I found musical
principles animating my work as a writer, and when I talked to
David about them, he would often find a connection to something he was working on visually. I suspected all of this would
intrigue Phil. He could not fail to see the expressive use of
variation in the poem, in Timar's chairs, and in David's composite montages, which involved photographing a subject in
sections, from different angles and in different lighting, and

then assembling select prints to reconfigure it as a visually different "whole" each time.

Phil had something to show me that day, too: the box in which his partner Anna's finished dissertation was packaged, ready for submission. "Three hundred pages," he said in hushed tones, holding it up with such reverence it could have contained something alive. It was the culmination of years of research on "the pianist's signature voice," conducted under his supervision as part of the Leonardo Project. Knowing the project's mandate was to study variability in performance, I sensed we were all exploring similar territory.

Coming back to Phil after a lapse of any length was always an adjustment, and moving back and forth between teachers wasn't easy. After those Christmas-break sessions in 2010 I wrote, "Interestingly, Phil is now telling me to play with my eyes shut! Back to what I instinctually want to do—for even when my eyes are looking at the keyboard, they are not really *seeing* the keyboard; it's like I'm in a semi-trance. And with Pamela it has been all about *looking*—what she calls getting the glaze off my eyes and seeing my own hands, registering how they're positioned and where they're moving. This has helped greatly with my preparation. But Phil says I need to get away from the focus on accuracy, and concentrate on quality of sound, vibration of the key, smoothness of singing line. He feels this is best done without looking. Still, I think it was the work with Pamela that allowed me to achieve the continuity I now have."

Exactly a month later, after a lesson with Pamela on the slow movement of the Fantaisie-Impromptu, I was still trying to articulate how their approaches differed: "I grasped everything Pamela pointed out to me, easily and instantly. Things about keeping the bass line continuous, not letting the broken chord pattern break up into sections; not accenting the bottom note each time but using it as a passing note on which to make a turn. About including the 'after notes' when I practise an ornament. About finessing my pedalling—learning to release the pedal slowly, to half-pedal. Some of these things she has shown me before, like always including the next note when I practise a problematic group of notes, but this time I saw the reasoning: that it's not just *including* the next note; it's *focusing on* the next note—feeling it as a destination. Pamela is so much more precise than Phil. The things we're working on are always perfectly clear and make sense. With Phil, I'm usually in the dark. I understand things with my ear and body and hands but not with my brain. But there's a fluid, electric energy that goes with this, a state of mind, that I miss when I don't see him for a while."

More often it was Pamela, not Phil, who would identify the exact spot that was giving me trouble in a passage, and why. It was such a boon to have the reason for my difficulty articulated, the solution demonstrated. It seemed so much more efficient than Phil's way, which was more environmental—neither naming the problem nor isolating it from context, but aiming at a new *musical* approach to the passage that would make the difficulty solve itself. Getting there was much slower, often beset with confusion and misunderstanding, but it came (when at last it did) with that "something else" that seemed to come only from Phil, a feeling of vibrant mystery, something a little wild. It was as if a window into a different kind of consciousness would open, a flash glimpse into a whole other realm of musical awareness, beyond where normal intelligence could go. Even when he was being utterly opaque, a part of me was kindled to inarticulate comprehension, like hearing overtones of a pitch that was never actually sounded. Pamela's rational, analytical approach didn't touch that string, but it was putting more and more solid ground under me as a pianist.

The shift back to Pamela after a few sessions with Phil was always a jolt, too. Once, I told her I felt as if I'd been in another world, and she said, "Yes, it *is* like another world. Phil's world." I said it always took two or three sessions for me to get my bearings with Phil and then good things would begin to happen—"But it's always refreshing to come back to you, because you go straight to the point. Phil comes at things sideways. He doesn't explain what he's trying to help me with or why we're working the way we are. I'm never sure I understand what he wants me to do. If I ask, he says, 'It's not about what I want.'"

"Phil doesn't like to tell you what to do," she said. "He wants you to find your own way to it. I don't have any problem with saying *Do it this way*. I'm bossy."

%

Zeroing in on a passage I had just played, Pamela would still sometimes say, "So, tell me what's in your head when you play this part." I knew she was looking for a cue to begin talking about what she had heard, but the question always brought me up short. "*Nothing* is in my head" was the only honest answer I could give her.

"Oh, that's right, I remember," she replied once. And then, looking at me curiously, "Well, what *do* you experience when you're playing? If it's not in your head, where *is* the music, for you?" *Where was the music?* What a strange question, and my answer wasn't a thought I had ever framed before: "It's something I feel at the back of my nose. It's in my ears and in my hands, I guess, but not in my head—I mean, it isn't *thoughts*. Sometimes it's like colours at the back of my nose." I knew it sounded bizarre, but Pamela didn't blink. "Oh, you have synesthesia," she said matter-of-factly.

I knew the term; I also knew that the perceptual phenomenon it refers to is neither precise nor well understood. In the scientific sense, it describes a neurological condition in which activation of one sense triggers a secondary experience of perception in another: when used in connection to music, it usually refers to musical pitches evoking colours. I've always been skeptical about whether I have true synesthesia, thinking it likelier my colour associations were implanted in early childhood by old Mrs. Silverman's colour-schemed keyboard and notation. I've read that in neurologically-based synesthesia, the colours are unvarying: tested year to year, research subjects point to the same precise shade in response to the same pitch. That would rule me out: my associations aren't consistent, the colours are a general range rather than precise shades, and some are much more pronounced than others (notably the dark greenish-blue of E flat in the octave below middle C.) I don't actually "see" colours; it would be more accurate to say I infer them by a kind of sixth sense situated in the passages that connect ear and nose.

The location might explain why sudden strong smells interfere much more with my concentration at the piano than other intrusions such as a sudden loud noise, or ambient noise. To flash forward a year or two: for a time I had permission to practise piano at a local café before it opened, while kitchen staff were preparing the day's menu. At some point, trays of hot brownies came out of the oven and were carried past me with a powerful waft of chocolate, causing instant derailment in whatever I happened to be playing. Next time I played that piece I would smell chocolate as I approached the same point in the music, a triggered association that persisted for weeks, so that after a while there was hardly a piece in my repertoire that did not have a "chocolate moment" lurking in it somewhere.

If neurological synesthesia is relatively rare, moments of sensory overlap are not: memory, cognitive association, and imagination all play a role in our response to sense data. This accounts for the word's other definition: as a literary term, it means "describing one kind of sense impression using words that normally describe another"—for example, ascribing a shape to a sound (as when I called the tone of a clarinet "pear-shaped"). Such comparisons involve a stretch of the imagination, but one we seem to make easily: it's commonplace to speak of "loud" colours, describe the sound of a glockenspiel as "sparkly," or characterize a voice as "silken."

⁂

Phil had begun phoning frequently, asking how things were going at the piano. He told me he had read and loved my long poem. He seemed to recognize that some of his musical concepts were things I understood as a poet. He also said he could offer me more time through the winter, but didn't want to interfere with what Pamela was doing. I suggested they talk to each other.

When I next arrived to see him, he was quite animated: they had spoken, and developed a plan for me—Pamela working "pianistically" while he took an "orchestral" or "compositional" approach. Now that it had been put into words, he was suddenly much more involved. He had things to say about the folder I'd left with him, things he'd responded to in David's and Tibor's art work. My life *hors piano* had re-engaged his interest in me as a musician. He said synesthesia was something he'd studied for years: "I think the great composers all had it. I think all poets have it. This must be why you have trouble switching pianos—because the colours aren't right." I didn't argue; what mattered was that he now wanted to work with me in an ongoing way.

It was an extension of the contrapuntal learning already in process. There was the usual adjustment, with each switch, to Phil's way of working, often so bewildering in the moment. Coming home from our sessions, I first doubted whether I could even remember what we had worked on, let alone demonstrate it, but if I tried it out on David, he would remark at once, "Your sound in that piece has completely changed." Later, more details might come back, or I might simply find myself playing differently, a new flexibility animating the music.

These sessions, now that the semester had begun, were not at the studio; they were at Phil and Anna's home on a side street in Notre-Dame-de-Grâce, in a small front parlour. A brown shag carpet absorbed the dim winter daylight filtering in. A humidifier hummed loudly next to the piano, a Förster baby grand belonging to Anna. Also Anna's was the parrot whose cage stood by the window, a gorgeously coloured bird rescued from a lab by her veterinarian daughter. Phil loved birds. This one always replied to my greeting with a robust screech or two, cocking his head at me sociably. ("Don't pay any attention to him," Phil would say, "or he'll never stop"— but his tone was indulgent; he had stories about the parrot's intelligence and devotion to Anna.) There was other life in the room that winter in the form of a serious moth infestation— brought in by the bird's food, Anna explained. As I played, small soft brown moths cruised the air like dark snowflakes or the embodiments of notes that had flown off the pages of sheet music. Sometimes I'd try to zap one between my hands while Phil was talking, but they were devilishly hard to catch.

Winter into spring, we worked on Scarlatti sonatas: the A major I had begun with Pamela, and two new ones Phil had photocopied for me, K380 in E major with its processional fanfares and K322 in A major—his choices. Both were familiar. I recognized the first as one Bob Sigmund had played on harpsichord, but how was it that I knew K322? Reading through the opening, I experienced mystifying twinges of muscle memory, a ghost memory of playing it, but not on piano! Then I remembered I *had* learned a page of this piece—on the substandard classical guitar I bought on a whim in 1969. Fred had played a guitar transcription; it was one of the pieces he and Sigmund had committed to paper by ear, off a recording.

Unwittingly Phil had picked two pieces that were old friends, touchstones from a period of my musical life that still glowed in memory with a rainbow patina. I learned them quickly. The simplicity and clarity of K322, scored for just two voices, brought home the value of focusing on structure to get a piece securely under my hands. In this piece I could readily see when my movements weren't prepared, and the enhanced awareness proved transferable to other pieces. Phil now became more hands-on, cueing me physically rather than verbally, sometimes guiding the back-and-forth movement of my hand between white and black keys as I played, or gently swinging my elbow to get more of a dance into the rhythm. At home I found myself taking the initiative in changing fingerings and movements, making my own discoveries.

Phil was having a good spring. Anna's dissertation had been singled out as one of a number of highly original pieces of research from universities across Canada. Another of his students, Kasia Musial, "the-girl-before-me" in Hingston Hall the previous summer, had won a competition for which the prize was a Carnegie Hall recital. He invited me to audit a rehearsal he was coaching at the university's downtown campus, in a two-piano studio: Kasia as soloist with Anna's Vietnamese student Tram Minh Nguyen playing the orchestral reduction of Hindemith's The Four Temperaments. I liked the way Phil talked about the piece, contextualizing it historically, describing how the war years in Germany turned the world on its head, a distorted reality in which things became parodies of themselves: how this spirit, which pervaded the visual art of the period, was key to the circus feeling in parts of Hindemith's score. Phil looked happy working with these girls. I sensed how his presence was a ballast for them, a sort of benevolent *Geist*. His upturned, listening face in profile, his low-toned commentary alternating with bright bursts from the pianos, were their own kind of music. There was something so embracing, calm and sunny in that room.

With Pamela that spring, I was back on the Liszt Consolation. Contemplating the layers and layers that my work on this piece had gone through, I saw I was really just beginning to play it. Before, I had been on a comfortable plateau: playing from memory with good continuity and solid musical ideas. But now I was being alerted to so much that I wasn't hearing, or had stopped hearing! We also worked on the Chopin F minor Étude and the two new Scarlatti sonatas. For the first time it seemed we really were working towards performance—focusing on things like tone colour and musical character rather than minutiae of placement and phrasing. Pamela wanted me to play the Liszt in another mini-recital at the Westmount Studio she had scheduled for June, just five students performing for one another.

Sometimes moments of enlightenment came from sources other than my two teachers. My visits to Canal Street weren't frequent, but when Clive was around, he wasn't a neutral party. On one occasion I arrived to discover that in anticipation of my visit, he had disabled the una corda pedal on the Steinway as a means of thwarting my reflexive reach for it. I was miffed, but it didn't take me long to see his point. My normal touch on that piano yielded a warm *cantabile*, louder than I was used to— that was its "soft." To make that *seem* soft, I had to play more robustly for anything I wanted louder, and much more robustly for a real forte, just as he had told me. I had to learn to hear this dynamic range as normal, so I wouldn't feel compelled to mute it. Clive recognized that a bit of behavioural psychology might hasten the process.

Next visit, the pedal was still lying on the floor under the piano and I had to appeal to him to restore it: "Clive, I get the message, but I can't learn to use the una corda properly if it isn't there." ("Use the pedals *expressively*," Phil had begun to urge me, "don't just *use the pedals!*"—but he wasn't giving me much instruction in that regard, beyond saying I should let my ear guide me.) Clive obliged with a bow. Over the next few visits I discovered that a good piano is its own teacher. His Steinway was teaching me how it wanted to be played.

The day before Pamela's recital, I headed down to Canal Street to work on the Liszt. It wasn't a great day for me on the

Steinway. Clive couldn't stay—he had a construction crisis to deal with—but he kept being delayed by phone calls while I grappled first with the instrument and then with the piece I'd come to rehearse. I didn't think he was listening, but on the way out he asked mildly, "Are you going to *play* today? I was hoping to hear something before I left."

I had just begun to feel the Liszt was sounding a little better. "You just want me to play pieces *you* like."

"No, it's a perfectly good piece, but you aren't *playing* it," said Clive. "You're going *Da dee da da, plunk plunk,* like it's for a kids' ballet class. Where's the emotion?"

Actually, I had been concentrating intensely, paying close attention to everything Pamela had coached me on: pedalling, accentuation, dynamic contrast, differentiating between harmonic embellishments and melodic entries, varying the restatements of the melody. But Clive was right: my hyperconscientious rendition was dry and sterile. "Studied" is the right word for how I was playing this first-learned new piece on returning to "study" piano. Even after two years, Consolation #2 still felt newly learned; it had never acquired the unselfconscious fluidity Phil recognized when I played repertoire from my teen years. Later-learned new pieces were beginning to get closer to that level of naturalness; but the Liszt remained studied. Either I was too conscious and deliberate—giving myself instructions as I played—or, if I succeeded in turning off the prompter, my performance became mindless and automatic. Clive's question—"Where's the emotion?"—made me realize I had to forget about worked-out musical intentions and connect viscerally with this piece of music, find out what it meant to me. Phil, I now recalled, had characterized the Consolation as a simple "song without words" when we began working on it. I had to find a way to make that song mine, and *sing it.*

At my lesson the day of the recital, Pamela suggested I play all three of the pieces we had worked on most recently—the

Chopin Étude and Scarlatti Sonata K380 as well as the Liszt. The other two weren't nearly as prepared, but she said the recital would be very informal—"really just a chance to try out a few things." Apart from herself, and Phil and Anna, we would be just the five participants, but I was welcome to bring David, who was glad to come.

Three unexpected things happened when I played that evening. First, my mind went blank as soon as I sat down at the piano. For a few seconds I couldn't remember what note the Liszt started on or what key it was in. Having remembered, I didn't know what lay ahead: it was as if I was looking at the score in my head and there was a moving spot of whiteout continually obscuring the bars that came next. Yet my hands seemed to know where to go. Then, perhaps thirty seconds into playing, those seemingly reliable hands began to shake and I couldn't get control of the shaking. Lastly, I had no recollection afterwards of having played parts of the Chopin—had I somehow skipped them? Pamela reassured me I had played every note.

Apparently, forgetting what note a piece starts on is a not-uncommon way performance nerves can manifest; Pamela said she had experienced it. I thought my *post*-performance amnesia must mean I had lapsed into mindless-automatic mode, but Phil thought this inability to recall was a *good* sign. He was very upbeat: "The continuity was excellent, you played straight through, you communicated the music. The Liszt was best, the other pieces needed more preparation, but there were some nice colours, parts that came off very well. Some over-pedalling in the Scarlatti. But you gave a real performance of all three pieces." Pamela concurred, remarking that I hadn't had time to integrate changes we introduced in the Scarlatti. That night I wrote, "All three recitals I've played in have been good experiences. I never play my best, but enough goes well for me not to feel destroyed by my own perfectionism."

❧

This little recital in June of 2011 marked the end of my time with Pamela. She was away a lot that summer, and with the school year over, the Hingston Hall studio was again available. Phil began offering me time much more regularly, and this continued into the fall, though always on standby. He said my performance had impressed him enough to want to push me to a new level: "If I wasn't absolutely certain you were capable, I wouldn't waste a minute, I would refer you to a different teacher. I want to show you a new way of working. If it's uncomfortable, you should accept the discomfort and do it, because it will give you the solidity to be able to vary your performance—to adapt it to any piano, any acoustical situation, any physical or emotional state you happen to be in. I want you to be able to let go of *habits*, maybe I should say *memories*, in pieces you play, things you fall back on. It's not about playing piano *better*, I don't care about that. I don't want you to play like a good student. I want you to *play music.*"

But it wasn't a new way of working. It was back to square one, round three, on the warmups and exercises I had questioned and resisted and partially grasped, tried and laid aside and tried again, filed away as potentially useful to save for a rainy day. And sketching, sketching, sketching—did I, even now, understand what he meant by sketching? Puzzling over it again in my journal, I wrote, "He seems to mean focusing on just one voice line, or just two voice lines, taking a voice out or adding one, then taking out or adding another. He says, 'Sketch—don't *practise.*' But what should I *not* do—what does he mean by practising? Today he defined it as 'playing something over and over trying to get it right, maybe going over the rough spots a little.' I have thought going over rough spots in different ways was what he meant by sketching—turning a problem passage into an exercise by altering the rhythm, deliberately misplacing the accents, changing the note groupings.

But I see he means something more, he means *deconstructing the score*, reducing it in various ways to appreciate the relations between parts. In his words: 'Put yourself in the composer's shoes, try to retrace the steps the composer must have taken to flesh out a melodic thought. Recreate that process.'"

I had recognized that in achieving fluency in my haphazard way, I did tend to get fixated on the first musical ideas I brought to a piece, and that my grasp of the score fell apart if I tried to change anything. But it was hard to separate my own ideas from the bare musical structure, so strongly did the notes themselves suggest to me variations in tempo, dynamics, and character. And once a piece was memorized, those ideas became set—I thought they *were* the score. Was I to go back to working with sheet music in front of me again, on pieces I had finally brought to a level where I felt I could perform them? A local restaurant had offered dinner in exchange for an evening's playing; I had a lead on a retirement home looking for volunteer pianists to play Happy Hour in the lounge. Now such next steps would have to be put on hold.

At the same time Phil began insisting I warm up by improvising at each session. "Just establish a tactile, breathing, freely moving, gestural relationship with the instrument. Start silently, get a breathing rhythm going between the two hands, then improvise freely." *Freely?* I felt stupid and stiff doing this in front of him; I had never been able to improvise on piano and had no idea what he wanted. Typically I would just strike random notes like a child banging on the keyboard—a bit defiantly, as if to say, "See, I can't do this." Phil would observe me sorrowfully but keep his counsel. While the exercise remained profoundly uncomfortable, I relaxed a little once I understood there was no protocol he was expecting me to follow.

Could it be the same with sketching? The next time he asked whether I was sketching my Scarlatti sonatas at home, I didn't hedge. "Phil, no, I haven't been. I never feel like I understand what you mean by sketching. One week it's leaving out the ornaments, one week it's releasing some of the notes of a chord instead of holding them for their full value, one week it's connecting notes that aren't supposed to be connected. It's always different things, and I never know where your suggestions are coming from. Can't you put into a word or two what I'm supposed to be doing? Because the fact is I don't know." (There, finally it was out.)

Phil rose to the challenge. "Simplifying. It's about simplifying." (That word again!)

"Well, if it's simple, why don't I get it? Why is it so hard to see what to do on my own?"

"I didn't say it was *easy*. Simplifying isn't easy. The hardest thing in the world, for people, is to be simple."

We had different versions of this conversation over the next months. One day he put it more specifically: "It's about diverting ourselves from a difficulty—identifying what's difficult and getting it out of the way." That felt profound. *This may apply to human relationships*, I thought. (I had been fighting with my daughter that day.) Another variant seemed to go beyond deconstructing the score: "Get the difficulty out of the way. Turn it into something else." *The silver thread!* I thought, ambushed by the memory of how *imagination*—"visualizing" a sound—had once helped me on clarinet, when obsessing over physical technique proved inadequate.

Gradually I came to understand it was about eliminating struggle. I was acquiring a toolbox for dealing with impasse. Certain principles came up again and again, certain moves at the keyboard. They all involved removing a complication, the better to hear what it had been complicating. If a trill or ornament was hampering the flow of a melodic statement, the thing to do was not to practise the ornament compulsively, but to play the phrase without it. If one voice in a passage was giving grief, you could work on the passage with that voice removed. Instead of focusing on the hard part by itself, reinforcing its status as bugaboo, you could divert yourself by focusing on the *context* in which the trouble arose. Besides dispelling anxiety, what this does is to allow you to *hear* the underlying musical intent—the bare melodic line to be embellished; the other voice lines that give purpose to the one that's tripping you up—while experiencing physically how it feels to play the passage without struggle. When you reintroduce the hard part, your hands seem mysteriously to have figured out how to integrate it: without your conscious involvement, they find a way to correct the faulty movement, the misplaced or fractionally delayed accent, the unfortunate choice of fingering, that was getting between you and the music before. It feels like magic, but it's not. It's the Mindful Hand, bypassing your vexed brain, telling you what it has learned from your wakened ear.

%

Clive understood about getting a difficulty out of the way: his solution to my fixation on the soft pedal was to disengage it from the piano. But now Phil was after me about the other pedal. The function of the right pedal (damper or sustain pedal) is to extend the resonance of a note after the key has been released. It enables a pianist to connect notes the hand can't reach to connect, lend emphasis to select notes or give them a distinctive tone quality, create beautiful textures by allowing a series of notes to go on resonating simultaneously—in short, to enhance performance in so many ways it has been called the "soul of the piano." But that assumes it's beneath the foot of a pianist who knows how to use it. There's more to soul than sole.

The downside of this mechanical device is that it extends the resonance not just of the notes you want to sustain but of all the notes you play while it is held down, whether or not they harmonize with the ones you want. It takes precise and subtle footwork, and a sense of exactly *when* to release or partly release the pedal, to enlist it in the service of the music;

otherwise the effect can be an ugly, muddy blur of sound. The upside of the downside (but it is actually another downside, more insidious than the first) is that the blurring can be tempered by the soft pedal to create something more like a wash of watercolours bleeding into each other, an excellent smoke-screen for masking a pianist's inadequacies. Wrong notes, skipped notes, and botched runs aren't as noticeable against this sonorous haze, so why not keep things a little hazy?

I had a thirty-five-year habit of keeping things hazy. The pedal was my friend and sidekick; I *relied* on it to get me over passages I knew were shaky. Phil had been indulgent, probably because there were so many other issues to address in my playing, but "Too much clutch" was a comment I did hear from him frequently. ("Too much *crutch*," I'd translate to myself wryly.) "You're blurring," he'd say, or sometimes, "You're *shmearing*." Many of the "sketches" he prescribed involved getting my right foot out of the picture. But I hated the dryness of playing without pedal. It was like trading in a painter's palette for a hard lead pencil.

We had moved from Scarlatti sonatas to three jazz-style preludes by George Gershwin, a leap of more than three centuries—again Phil's choice. It was strategic in that parts of Gershwin are best played with no pedal, while other parts cry out for the colouring that generous use of both pedals can lend them. Perusing the edition I had bought, Phil said, "Let's begin with the middle one, the slow one. But for now, I want you to play it without pedal." He thought for a moment, then added, "In fact, this week, I'd like you to play *everything* without pedal. Play anything you like, but get your foot off the clutch completely. Will you do that?"

"Okay," I said, thinking cagily that I would try it a bit, for part of the time.

The very next night (synchronicity?)—catastrophe! David, vacuuming over-energetically, ran the Hoover into the heavy wooden piano bench and it tipped forward and over, hitting the pedals of the Mason & Risch broadside. They both snapped in two on impact. Metal fatigue? Worse news: my tuner was out of town for a week! (Phil laughed out loud when I told him the story later; he swore he had nothing to do with it.)

Having no choice, I began working as he'd asked, and discovered that thanks to all the focus on legato and singing tone, I could now play *musically* without pedal—something I'd been unable to do before. I went through my entire current repertoire, finding it a challenge, but richly instructive and absorbing. It showed me everything the pedal had been masking: rhythmic unevenness, awkward fingerings, overheld notes, clunky accents, insecure passages (and *why* they were insecure). It made me *hear* in an entirely new way. This was a priceless tool! In the best sense a remedial exercise, it was also a creative one; it showed me what I wanted, and gave me ideas. It was so enlivening of all my pieces that when my tuner installed two brand-new shiny brass pedals the next week, I was in no great hurry to use them.

During the following weeks I played through a lot of repertoire for Phil—old, new, some I hadn't played for him before. What he said he noticed most was that I was applying things we had recently been doing to pieces we hadn't looked at together in a while. It seemed to confirm something for him. "It's about letting one piece revitalize another. You're doing something I can't even explain, and you don't even know you're doing it!" But I did know. I could *feel* how things we'd worked on in one piece transmitted themselves to other pieces—could feel my hands making changes based on something they'd internalized from another context.

Not that there weren't still sessions when I wondered if this old dog was at the end of her capacity for new tricks. After one particularly disheartening session, I thought I had figured something out: he was giving me the prescription when what I needed in order to appreciate it was the diagnosis. *Why doesn't he say, "You're over-accentuating here" or "You aren't bringing out the counter-melody"? Then I would be looking to correct the problem. Instead, he jumps straight to a "sketch" and I don't know why I'm doing it. He wants me to hear what needs remedying on my own. But that's just what's not happening.*

Phil phoned a day later. "I know I gave you a hard time." I tried to explain my thoughts about prescription versus diagnosis, but he brushed that off: "It's okay," he said, "just do whatever you're doing. Just get back to the piano and we'll see how it goes." A pause; then an afterthought (he had heard me after all)—"What I'm giving you *isn't* a prescription. I'm not telling you what I want to hear. I'm nudging you in the direction of what I hear *you* trying to do. I hear what you're trying to bring across even though you aren't there yet, and I'm trying to give you what you need to bring it across." It was another watershed moment. Oddly enough my time at the piano since that session had been fruitful: much had begun at once to decode itself when I tried it at home, with all my doubts and irritation still roiling inside. *Bless the man,* I thought; *I don't understand his ways, but they work.*

The end of 2011 found us working peacefully and happily on Gershwin; then, seamlessly, on into a new year. New music, old music—letting one piece transmit its secrets to another. Reviving Mozart's A major Sonata, the elegant set of variations in the first movement. Working on the Pathétique Sonata again, the piece I brought to Phil for our first meeting in 2009. Now he showed me how, if I wanted to bring out the theme in the second movement, there were places where I had to *let go* of the melody notes, connecting them not to each other but to the intervening accompaniment notes. It sounded so beautiful when he demonstrated.

"I don't understand how you *know* to do that. It's totally counterintuitive."

"No, it isn't. It's contrary to logic, but it isn't counterintuitive."

His quiet voice at my elbow as we worked. "Listen to the decay, not to the attack. Follow the sound with your ear, hear the full duration of each note. What matters is the *length* of the sound, the *decay* of the sound, the *relation* to the next sound. Make the connections."

Now and then in the midst of a session it would strike me that here I was, back with my old teacher—back in the rhythm I remembered so well from my school years—week after week centred around these hours at the keyboard, cocooned, impervious to the world, in collusion under the spell of music. The return I had dreamed of for so many years, never believing it possible, denying myself even the right to wish for it, had actually come to pass, I was living it, how incredible, how fortunate. *This is not a dream.*

V BEST LAID PLANS

I HAD FOUND MY WAY BACK TO SOMETHING PROFOUND
and uplifting. To the cocoon in which an ongoing quest for
beauty unfolds: the quest to find beauty in every phrase of a
piece of music, to find it anew every day, to make it manifest
in the endless ways one can discover or devise to tease it out.
This is what, in the lexicon of music, we call "preparation."
It is what I had missed, at times grievously, and what I had
reclaimed as part of my life. It was enough, it would always be
enough—and it *wasn't* enough. The word implies a next step.
Preparation for what?

The idea of playing a full recital had not gone away. Beauty
in music wants to be shared. But musical performance happens
in the real world, not in a cocoon. In the real world, it is both
dependent on and affected by other human beings, human-
built instruments, human-made settings, human exigencies
and decisions. Adapting on the spot to unpredictables, the performer has one chance, in real time, to deliver the music to
listeners. Will beauty survive the stresses? Whatever the prepared intentions, however lofty the aim, what happens in actual
performance is often as not a compromise with conditions.

 All this was brought home to me in my first attempt (modest though it was) at a solo recital—beginning with an opportunity that knocked suddenly and too soon.

%

December 31, 2011. Seven of us are gathered for a quiet New Year's Eve at the home of our friends Roberta and Norman. We are three neighbourhood couples and Terry, a newcomer to Montreal whom Roberta met through a mutual friend and invited to join our Shakespeare reading group last June. Terry has cancer, diagnosed four weeks ago. She's just back from Vermont after a first week of chemo; it will be another month before she qualifies for medical coverage in Canada. She wasn't sure she was up to this evening's invitation, but Barbara offered to pick her up and has promised to drive her home when she gets tired. Roberta has installed her in the chaise longue in the middle of the living room, tucking a beautiful woven blanket around her, and has put on a CD of serene, otherworldly music, Arvo Pärt's *Spiegel im Spiegel*.

Terry sinks back into the cushions, looking small and wan in the big chair. She doesn't smile. In her group emails she sounds brave—candid, proactive, and practical, soliciting help as she needs it from friends in both countries. But seeing her face is different. She's all alone here, in the house she bought only months ago, realizing her dream of moving to Montreal after she retired following a late divorce. The house where we joined her in July to celebrate her sixtieth birthday. A house of many bedrooms, so friends from the States could come up in numbers to visit her in the city she fell in love with on a holiday trip some years back. She has made friends here quickly, but her young adult kids are in the States, working and studying.

It's a subdued evening, but with some lovely moments. Quiet talk, and each of us has brought a poem to read aloud. The Pärt recording is very beautiful. The bell-like triads are like crystalline drops of rain; the music seems to create an environment, a freshness like the beginning of the world. Now Roberta is describing gardens in England, where her family spent one sabbatical year. She becomes animated as she recalls how, on a ramble with her kids, she stumbled on a walled garden glimpsed through an open gate: "It was an amazing garden—full of contrasts, planted asymmetrically around a pond. It seemed there must be some pattern to it—we kept looking, but couldn't find one. Then a woman came to the door of the house and called, 'You're looking at my garden from the wrong place. Come up here and I'll show you.' The house was on a rise and had a big bay window. She explained, 'It's a reflecting garden. I planted it to be seen from these windows.' And we saw the garden was designed to be reflected in the pond, seen from above. You had to look at the reflection from that spot to see the pattern. She told us, 'It's a hidden garden. There's a whole concept of hidden gardens.'"

It's the kind of story Roberta loves to share. I'm intrigued both by the concept and by the poetry of the phrase. It evokes Phil's teaching. I think it is the hidden gardens in a piece of music that he seeks to illuminate—what he means when he says there are "secrets" in the score.

Terry comes out of her shell a little when I venture this. She has been following my late-life return to the piano with interest. She plays piano herself—not at a very advanced level, she has hastened to qualify, but it has been an abiding pleasure since she retired. Her youngest son, a cellist, is studying music in college and she enjoys accompanying him, playing arrangements of popular songs. Tonight she shares a new idea. Now that the cancer has waylaid her, she is considering using money she had set aside for travel to buy herself a baby grand. It will give her something to occupy her days; she can play duets with her son when he visits, and she can invite friends who play piano to come play for her. We applaud the plan.

Around eleven, Barbara drives her home and returns to see the new year in with the rest of us. While we await the eclipse of clock-hands, she asks if she may read a poem she has brought that she didn't feel she could read with Terry there. In her melodious voice, at the close of a dark cold day, she reads Auden's poem on the death of Yeats.

%

Terry may have been small and alone and seriously ill, but she packed a punch when it came to getting things done. With the same willful directionality she must have exercised in relocating to Montreal, she lost no time finding herself a piano and negotiating purchase terms tailored to her situation. She also contracted to have it repainted white (*white?*), and enlisted me to meet with her tuner-technician after delivery, to discuss whether any work on the action was desirable.

At this point the same thought flashed through my mind and Barbara's: perhaps Terry would be open to hosting a small private debut recital. By now I had over an hour's worth of repertoire, new and old, that I could prepare on short notice—a range from which to select a half-hour program. Barbara's conception was of musical selections framed by a talk, with readings from my book-in-progress. Terry could invite her Montreal friends; Barbara and I could each invite a family member or two, a manageable number for a home recital.

We were debating whether to make the proposal when Terry made it herself. Perhaps it was hasty on my part to agree at once: I hadn't tried the piano; in fact, we hadn't yet seen the piano, which was still at the dealer's being painted. And I didn't have much book-in-progress to read from or talk about yet; I would have been embarrassed to admit to Barbara how little I'd actually written, beyond tracking my return to lessons in a journal. But Barbara, ever the arts agent, was looking ahead, envisaging a series of "music and words" events for which the evening at Terry's could serve as a pilot. And Phil loved the idea—loved that what we planned was, in scale and intimacy, "true chamber music," and that it was not music alone.

The other thing none of us had fully taken into account was the wild card of Terry's illness and reactions to treatment. There were fainting episodes on the street, night visits to Emergency. There was a two-day hospital admission for rehydration. Terry decided we had best fast-track our event, given uncertainties that might lie ahead. We marked a late-March date on the calendar, halfway between scheduled treatments, and hoped it would be one of her good days.

Meanwhile the piano was delivered. I was taken aback by the white baby grand. It was the smallest grand piano I'd ever seen—not even five feet. I had assumed Terry would be giving her dining room over to the instrument, but no: she had chosen one that would fit her tiny living room and still leave space for bookcase, sofa, and three easy chairs. Perhaps the size accounted for two octaves in the middle register that sounded completely unlike the rest of the piano, or any piano I'd ever heard. The treble was full-toned and sweet, but descending the scale, there was a point where the timbre suddenly changed and the little white piano went off into some twangy twilight zone all of its own, emerging from it just as abruptly at the lower end. Terry hadn't noticed anything amiss, but she asked me to make notes for Murad, the technician, who was coming next day to do a first tuning. He had rebuilt this piano himself, she told me. This didn't sound promising (hadn't *he* noticed?) but I did as she asked and hoped for the best.

A week later, I returned on her request to retry the instrument and confer with Murad. I was playing the piano when he arrived. The uneven bass had been voiced to better effect, but I couldn't persuade myself there was any real improvement in the middle register. Murad, a compact dark-haired man with warm but melancholy eyes, sat down on the sofa and listened, toolbag at his feet. When I came to the end of the piece (the second Gershwin Prelude) he sighed and said, "What was that you were playing? Really, so beautiful. I could listen to it all day. So what do you think, how is the piano sounding to you now?" He cast me a cagey, appraising look. There was an elephant in the room and he could tell I knew it. I said tentatively, "The bass is better. But what's the story with those two middle octaves?"

Terry had gone out to the kitchen to make tea. With a glance towards the door, Murad acknowledged to me in an undertone, "I did the best I could. With an instrument this size ... You know, there are limitations ... this piano wasn't supposed to be for sale. We had it in the window just as a showpiece ... an oddity, not a standard design. But this nice lady, as soon as she saw it, she insisted this was the piano she wanted. She begged us to sell it to her. The lady told us her story, so sad. How could we say no? But the piano is what it is. I don't know how much more I can do."

It was my turn to sigh. "The pedal squeaks," I said. "Can you fix that? I'm playing for some people here in about three weeks. If you can come tune it again the day before, and fix the pedal, that would be great."

%

Not enough preparation time. Not enough time to finesse the pieces I'd chosen with Phil's help and begun rehearsing. Not enough writing time to etch out more than an opening "teaser" and a synopsis of what I hoped to include in my book. And I would be performing on a piano with major limitations. But by now the thing had its own momentum. Terry had had bad news: her tumour not responding to treatment; a last-ditch surgery cancelled as too risky. Waiting to hear whether anything further could be done besides pain management, she humbled us with her fortitude. She wanted to continue living as much of a normal life as possible. She welcomed a chance to be generous. Hosting us and sharing her new piano with friends was important to her.

A shift in perspective was called for. In my head, the pilot event became a "pilot for the pilot." The flawed instrument lowered the bar from the start, taking some pressure off. Instead of a practice debut, I was now thinking of it as "going over to Terry's and playing for some of her friends." Terry was doing this for us; we were doing this for Terry—it was just a good thing to do.

Phil was upset to hear of the piano's shortcomings; he had wanted me not to be too casual about this initiative—to present something serious and prepare properly. His consternation did ratchet things up a bit for me. I spent a couple of afternoons at Terry's, going through each piece to see how I could adjust my playing to offset the worst effects of the "Frankenstein register." Alternating with these afternoons, Phil set up two sessions so I could play my program for him on the Falcone—a full run-through, no talking between pieces. The greater formality of a mock performance, even for an audience of one, proved unexpectedly hard: the first try was a disaster, with a breakdown or major falter in every piece. Phil said I was reverting to old habits, forgetting to play laterally, losing the dance. But the second time I played as well as I ever had on the Falcone in his presence. He gave no feedback, saying only that I was ready to perform and should not think of anything but the music when I sat down to it on the weekend.

What made the difference between the two trial runs? I hadn't even touched the piano before going out to meet Phil the day of the second one! Al Fraser, sending zero-hour encouragement from Serbia, offered some explanation: "When you practise more, there's more chance you screw up in performance because you learned more, changed things, and the brain didn't get a chance to integrate it all into the performance situation. When you practise less, your brain is still working full-time to integrate everything. Not practising gives it that chance. But be aware that screwing up is an important part of preparing to perform. So is getting nervous. You need to screw up in order to *know that you can*. Good dress rehearsals make performers overconfident and then they aren't focused when they get on stage. A bad dress makes you get your act together." Well, I had had one of each. Did they cancel each other out?

No time to dwell on this. Terry was back on the medical roller coaster: that same week, sudden-onset pain took her to Emergency, where a CT scan was done. The doctor had no basis for comparison because her last scan had been done in Vermont, so she made an emergency trip across the border next day. She couldn't be sure they'd send her home in time for our event. Insisting we go ahead even if she couldn't be with us, she left keys with a neighbour.

It would have been a melancholy business to proceed without her, but Terry was home the same evening, on painkillers, with unexpected news. The tumour, though pressing on some new nerve, had grown very little; the team now thought it might not be the virulent type first diagnosed, but one for which there was a treatment that had a better chance of working. By luck, our musical afternoon fell squarely between her return and the start of her new treatment.

All was now in place. Barbara had printed a program explaining the book project and listing my musical selections: the Liszt Consolation, Bach-Busoni "Wachet auf," two Scarlatti sonatas (K380 and K322), Chopin's Fantaisie-Impromptu, and the first two Gershwin Preludes. Murad showed up on schedule to retune the piano; I almost forgot to remind him to fix the squeaky pedal, and had to leave before he was done, but he assured me he was on it. Terry's daughter arrived from the States and rearranged the living room under her mother's supervision to make space for "chairs in a row." And on Sunday afternoon, guests filled them.

Decades of teaching made it easy for me to start talking off the cuff about my return to piano as preface to reading the text I'd cobbled together. People seemed interested; I intended to pick up the talk again and invite discussion after playing my program. Announcing my first selection, I sat down at the little white piano. But as the poet said, *The best-laid schemes of mice and men / gang aft agley.*

I hadn't figured on mice. I hadn't anticipated playing the Liszt Consolation as a duet for mouse and piano. As became apparent at once, Murad hadn't fixed the pedal. Murad had clearly *tried* to fix the pedal, and in the process turned a mildly annoying occasional squeak into a much more frequent, considerably louder one. Nothing I did to try to silence it made a difference: easing up on foot pressure, wiggling the pedal sideways, one way and then the other, to change the angle when I depressed it. I could almost hear eyebrows going up, people shifting in their seats thinking *What the heck?* When with relief I reached the final cadence, there was no choice but to apologize and explain, "It's the pedal. It was supposed to be fixed yesterday, but the technician seems to have made it worse."

People wanted to help. "Isn't there anything that can be done on the spot? A band-aid solution?" "Is there a mechanic in the house?" "I fixed a Volkswagen once." "Would baby powder do the trick?" "What about WD-40—do you have any?"

Terry didn't want to try anything without asking her tuner. The little burst of audience involvement having de-formalized things, I proposed a pact: I would do my best to minimize the squeaking, and they should do their best to ignore it. Afterwards, people told me the squeak did become less obtrusive as they learned to focus on the music, but I wasn't as lucky—I spent the recital trying all means to quiet it, at the cost of my own focus on the music. Collateral benefit: thanks to the piano's challenges, I was *not at all* nervous. I was in problem-solving mode; there was no part of me left to be nervous with. And while it wasn't the performance I could have delivered on a better instrument, my hard-won continuity held in every piece.

To my relief people did seem to appreciate the music and talk. Over wine and cheese I heard some of them talking about serious interests of their youth they might like to get back to, or things they'd always wanted to try but never had. I heard, "Maybe it's not too late." And Terry was in her element— guests circulating in the dining room, new hope in the air.

Phil had asked me to call him next day to say how things went. After all our work getting ready, what could I say? Not much we'd done or discussed had even come into the picture. He laughed at the mouse tale. "You've learned a valuable lesson about performing. There's always *something*—and it's never going to be the thing you anticipated and prepared for."

It was a lesson I was to learn again and again on the next leg of my journey.

%

Terry died seven months later, in October. Towards the end of summer, I returned from a three-week piano intensive in Vermont to find her in the sunny, peaceful palliative care ward of the Montreal General. During her last weeks I visited frequently, walking over Mount Royal, cutting across a meadow of reddening sumac and bursting milkweed pods, down to the hospital on the lower slope. Terry wanted to hear all about my experiences at the summer piano session, and she wanted me to read to her from my manuscript, truly in progress at last. Some days she couldn't sit comfortably, or her feet would go numb if she sat, so we would walk slowly up and down the hall together, past the elevators, round and round the ward—I reading aloud, Terry pushing her IV pole. An intense, attentive, ambulatory listener in slippers, she was the first "reader" of what would become this book.

On my computer I still have home videos Terry emailed to friends soon after getting her piano—arrangements of "Moon River" and "Belle of the Ball" that she played with her son when he visited her during March Break. "The Belle" ended with a mix-up, Terry laughing and throwing up her hands as she hummed the final bars she was too late to play. There was something enormously moving about the videos: the purity of concentration in Joel's face as he played his cello, and Terry, in the trademark beret she'd adopted in lieu of a wig, looking small and frail but also brave and happy, at the keyboard of her little white piano. Terry, seizing the day.

VI   IN THE WOODS,
WITH PIANOS

ON A HOT, HUMID AFTERNOON IN MID-JULY 2012, I
dragged a much-too-heavy duffel bag over the threshold of
what was to be my room for the next three weeks in one of the
small residence houses at Adamant Music School in Vermont.
("Your mother's going to piano camp," was how David put
it to my grown progeny.) The weight in the bag was mainly
sheet music, carefully padded with clothing; I had brought
practically every piano album I owned to this summer intensive. Thanking the young man who helped me carry it from the
car—the school chef, who had picked me up, with three others,
at the local Greyhound station—I slid laptop bag and knap-
sack off my shoulders onto the low double bed and surveyed
my temporary domain. It was much better than I'd expected:
private, airy, with windows facing two directions. There was
even a little desk, for the late evenings and off-hours when I
hoped to work on my book. (*What* off-hours? I was soon to
wonder.) Late afternoon sun shone through the weave of the
curtain on the front-facing window. I tried the bed: comfortable. Framed on the wall was a calligraphed rendering of John
Donne's "No man is an island." Rather a solemn greeting

("Ask not for whom the bell tolls; it tolls for thee"), but it seemed right for a poet.

I *did* feel a bit like an island, though. I had learned, at check-in, that I was the oldest participant that summer—by thirty-five years. While I'd been warned this would likely be the case, I went on hoping one or two other old-timers would show up at the last minute—lifetime amateurs, lapsed pianists, late-starting retirees. The age range of my fellow students, hailing from across North America as well as Hawaii, South Africa, Korea, and China, was mid-teens to mid-twenties. Most had been performing and competing in festivals for years—even the handful who were still minors. Most were enrolled in or headed for degree programs in performance. I would soon learn from one of the teachers (Elaine G., sole other occupant of the little house) that my room was normally reserved for the program's coordinator, South African pianist and professor Franklin Larey; he had given it to me because I was the only senior participant. (A warm, personable man, he waved away my thanks when we assembled for supper that night in the dining room of Barney Hall, the school's main building. He said he was going to bunk in the main residence upstairs, where the under-agers were quartered; he thought they might need some supervision.) As it happened, I was to spend very few waking hours in the pleasant room he'd vacated for me, where night after night (if never for long enough) I slept the sleep of the dead. The schedule at Adamant was unremitting. The kids, being kids, seemed to be able to stay up all night, regardless. I'm not sure how much Franklin slept.

%

Synchronicity had set this summer's adventure in motion. Not long after my first visit to Clive's, another pianist showed up at our small synagogue. Over lunch after service, we traded piano stories. Elias Axel-Pettersson was from New Mexico, in his final doctoral year at the Université de Montréal. He'd had to choose between piano and violin for his performance major, having played both from an early age; he was also a chess champion. At peace with his decision to make piano his instrument and music his career, he had already cut a couple of CDs and distinguished himself in competition.

It was during this same week I first heard of Adamant Music School from an old friend going back to my teaching years, now a semi-retired librarian in Vermont. Hilari, a Celtic harpist, and her husband, an Irish piper and pipe maker, had become mainstays of the Celtic music scene there. During one of our rare telephone marathons, hearing of my return to studying piano, she exclaimed, "There's a wonderful summer school for pianists a few miles up the road from us here—you should come! There are practice huts with grand pianos all through the woods, you hear piano music drifting from them in this magical setting with winding walkways around flower gardens and ponds. They're open to pianists of all ages and backgrounds— their philosophy is non-competitive; the idea is just to provide community for people who love to play piano. There are classes every morning and public recitals in the evenings—it's billed as a local music festival. But playing in the recitals is voluntary."

Next time I saw Elias, I asked if he had heard of this place. "Heard of it? I've gone there—twice, in fact," he said. "It was great. I'm surprised *you've* heard of it. They don't exactly advertise. But if you're interested—do you have a car? As an alumnus I can bring you in for a day as a guest this summer. I can introduce you, show you around, maybe you can audit a class, we can stay for an evening concert. Their main session is three weeks, but if that's too long, they also have three master classes taught by some high-profile pianists. Those run for five days each, and if you aren't accepted as a participant, you can still go as an auditor."

Pamela hadn't heard of Adamant. Neither had Phil, but I felt his guard go up when I asked. "Not that particular place," he said. "But I know other ones—there are a bunch of them around. One or two asked me if I would come teach there, but I wasn't interested. They always want to know what school of piano playing I represent; they want me to talk about my method. They don't like it when I say I don't have one."

"I was thinking of applying," I said, going straight to the point. "Any reason not to?"

Phil hesitated; I could feel him searching for the right words. "Let's just say it might not be the time for that kind of input, with things still in a formative stage."

"I wasn't thinking of going for the instruction, Phil—it's the pianos—being able to play on a grand piano every day. And I thought the group classes could be a good opportunity to play in front of people. No one has to perform in the recitals unless they want to. This place is supposed to be different, it's non-competitive ..."

A twinge of impatience crossed his face. "Sure, I know. They all say that." *He's upset*, I thought. After a moment, stoically, he conceded, "If you want to go, you should go." But he wouldn't look at me. I wished I had never brought it up.

Still, on a Wednesday in August, David rented a car and we picked Elias up and drove out to have a look. It was as described. Thirty-three practice huts scattered across an idyllic site, each with a baby grand, many with two. A resident piano technician. A concert hall, a conference room, a music library. A dining hall serving home-cooked lunches and suppers. Thanks to Elias, I did sit in on a morning session with the teacher he'd worked with there, a retired music professor from South Carolina. Eugene B. was very hospitable, even offering me use of his reserved studio for the afternoon. Three of his students were rehearsing pieces they were to perform that evening, so I got to hear them twice (all played better on stage). After class, Eugene heard me play and confirmed I was up to the level required for the program.

At the faculty table over lunch, I learned that the main session at Adamant had at one time been two weeks, drawing the broad range of ages and backgrounds Hilari had described, but that when it was extended to three weeks, older pianists abandoned it for the master classes. The main session had become much more homogenous—what one teacher described a little gloomily as "summer school for Juilliard." This gave me pause, but I made the case to myself that attending the three-week session could add perspective to the book I was writing. Whatever else, it would be an inside glimpse of my road not taken as a pianist.

Adamant did not hold auditions. To apply by the April deadline, I would have to submit recordings of three repertoire pieces from different periods, transmitted as MP3s. My son, a sound technician, agreed to record me at Clive's and to format the files for transmission. This left one hurdle: I had to raise the subject with Phil again. And as I had expected, he wasn't happy. He didn't try to hide that he had reservations about these programs, and again he suggested it was premature: "It's one thing to go to a place like this when you're well-established in your working routines and can come to it with your own agenda, but that's not the case here."

"Well, I might not even get in."

"Don't worry," he said darkly. "You'll get in."

Did he really not understand that what interested me was access to grand pianos, away from the distractions and duties of home? "I'll take everything with a grain of salt, Phil. If something interferes with the way we've been working, I don't have to do it. And there's no pressure to perform. Phil! Don't you get it? *Three weeks in the country, with all my meals cooked, and nothing to do but play piano*—it's my dream vacation!"

This elicited a small smile. "Go, then. Just don't blame me if you come back messed up."

"Why would I come back messed up?"

"Let's just say I've seen things. Never mind, it's okay. Go. Play piano."

"But are you going to dump me if I come back messed up? If you are, I won't go."

"I won't dump you," he said. It wasn't exactly giving me his blessing. But it felt like pax.

%

Geese, a large flock of them, paraded around the verdant grounds of Adamant all day as though they owned the place, and not far behind, at a leisurely pace, wielding broom and metal scoop to pick up after them, strolled Frank S., the real owner of these acres, an affable man in his early eighties who had been a friend of the founders and was the school's president and ongoing generous patron. Three days into the session, when I was sitting by the pond after supper to catch the last of the sunlight before the scheduled faculty recital, Frank sat down beside me, greeting me by name—"You're the poet, aren't you?" One of the school's contacts had mentioned hearing Garrison Keillor read my poetry on radio; my other identity had followed me here. Still trying to get my bearings, I was feeling sufficiently unmoored to find that steadying.

I'd spent the first two days at Adamant in a strange blur, perusing the items in my orientation package, noting a new vocabulary (*play-ins, tryouts*), learning my way around the rambling grounds with the help of a hand-drawn map, locating as many of the practice studios as I could and trying the pianos in each so I could note my preferences before the lottery to reserve practice hours. Late at night in my room, I studied the Opening Week timetable and weekly program, trying to map out a personal schedule around the structured activities: classes weekdays from nine until twelve-thirty, meal hours, Monday evening *play-ins*, Tuesday and Thursday afternoon *tryouts*, Wednesday and Friday night concerts, and Sunday matinées (no one required to perform, but all required to attend). Rotating chores had also been assigned, and around all this, we had booked our studio practice hours. Where was the time to do anything else, if I wanted to take full advantage of pianos in the woods?

It was in this semi-dazed state that I had participated in the opening "play-in" at which we were each expected to perform one piece to enable faculty to place us with our teachers. Fourteenth in line out of twenty, I was more nervous than I expected to be—had a false start on the Scarlatti sonata I'd chosen to play, and my hands shook throughout. I wasn't able, ever, to forget that I was playing to a roomful of people, all pianists. But despite numerous small slips, I got through the piece without having to stop. I wasn't really able to concentrate on the others' playing; nerves and the newness of everything distracted me. An odd comedic moment sticks in memory: during a piece by Gabriel Fauré, all the geese came marching up the lawn of the rustic concert hall, right up to the wall of floor-to-ceiling windows that backed the stage, and assembled there in a row as if to listen. When the next participant launched into a Brahms Intermezzo, they all turned their backs and marched away in the direction they'd come. Someone quipped that they were Canada geese and preferred French music.

Our class groups and assigned teachers were posted in the dining hall when we arrived for lunch. I was happy to see I'd been placed with Eugene. He had this year's oldest and youngest participants. Xaviera, the youngest, was one of the others picked up from the bus station with me. I had taken her for college age, later to learn she was thirteen!—a precocious thirteen, inscrutable, preternaturally poised. It was her second year at Adamant. She told me she had started piano so young she couldn't remember a time when she didn't play; she'd been winning prizes in festivals since early childhood. "Now I wish I'd started later, because then I would be getting motivated now, like other kids I've met here," she ventured, confessing she didn't feel much incentive to work at the piano, or much excitement about playing—"It's just something I've always done." Her excitement was reserved for September, when she would be starting high school: "It's my first time going to school. I was home-schooled till now."

In striking contrast was Noah, also in our group, also home-schooled and still a minor. Noah was hyper-motivated. I had overestimated his age, too, at first taking this outgoing, articulate, robustly self-confident sixteen-year-old for closer to twenty. He was the first participant I had met on arrival. Tall and slim with a mop of fair hair and an open, untroubled face, he seemed to be everywhere and to have something to say about everything—a one-man ambulatory welcoming commit-tee, a bottomless mine of information about the school, other schools, music festivals, piano competitions, piano repertoire, recordings by pianists dead and living. Unlike the rest of us, he'd been at Adamant for the previous two weeks, attending two master classes, and would be staying on after our session to attend the third. He seemed so sure of himself and of his chosen path! *Is this kid capable of doubt?* I wondered. When I confided to him after the play-in that my challenge at the piano was a derailing insecurity in performance, his response was, "I'm really sorry, I can't relate at all. That's too bad. I wouldn't know how to help. It's a shame because it makes a waste of all your hard work." Then he was off to talk to some-body else. This could have been a bad moment, but I was too astonished by the tactlessness to be crushed by the dismissal. And Noah was too sunny and likeable to fault for being blunt; it was easy to believe he would have helped if he'd thought he could.

After supper that evening I finally got a chance to prac-tise, in the studio annexed to my residence house. It had two Steinways, both good, the newer one a dream. I didn't try to work on anything—just played through my current repertoire. Everything sounded so good on this instrument! For a blissful two hours I forgot how tired I was. I kissed the piano when I left, crossed the connecting corridor back to my room, and fell into bed like a stone.

%

Classes began next morning in a studio some fifteen minutes' walk uphill from Barney Hall, where breakfast fixings were set out at seven. Eugene gathered up most of his group and offered us a ride up the hill. After we'd all introduced ourselves, Noah kicked off our first session with the Presto movement of Beethoven's F major Sonata, Op. 10, No. 2—a spirited performance of a movement so full of exuberance and bonhomie I immediately wanted to learn it myself. Eugene suggested he work on giving it more dynamic contrast and shape—more building, more emphasis on offbeats—to avoid a rattling-through of undifferentiated repetitions. Xaviera was next, playing the third movement of Bach's Italian Concerto—a dramatically better performance than her first movement of Mozart's A major Sonata at play-in the previous day; her verve and assurance impressed me. Eugene again wanted more dynamic contrast: "You're playing it all in the mezzo-forte to mezzo-piano range," adding, "No one will arrest you for pedalling Bach, you know, as long as you do it judiciously." He had some comments on her Mozart from the day before, which she had also played entirely without pedal, and asked her to bring it to class next day. Xaviera told me later she was "finished" with the Mozart; she had performed it in competition when she was ten and had no interest in revisiting it. I realized this explained the clunkiness that was nowhere in evidence in the Bach. Her Mozart was truly still a child's playing; all the notes were there, but there was no sense that her understanding of the music had evolved since she'd first learned them.

I was the last to play before break. I played the Scarlatti A major Sonata; then Eugene asked me to play the E major I'd performed at play-in. His feedback was solid, though I didn't always agree with his sense of the music: he felt the opening three notes of the A major should be "trumpet-like," while I felt them as more elastic—perhaps because my first experience of playing them was on guitar? He wanted the four repeated notes staccato and perfectly equal each time they occurred, while Phil had been nudging me towards a more expressive, rhythmically flexible approach. But Phil had also recommended I regard this Adamant venture as an opportunity to try different things with my pieces; here was my opening.

The other two participants in our group, Kelly and Daniel, were enrolled in university performance programs; they were the most focused and sober in class, absorbing Eugene's input and applying it immediately to noticeable effect. After class, the three of us walked down the hill together. Kelly was one of a trio of Chinese girls at Adamant who were studying together in Los Angeles; she was a little shy, and her English was hesitant. She seemed thoughtful as we left, still turning over Eugene's suggestions for the Bach C minor Toccata. "My teacher in LA wanted me to play the fugue subject robustly. He wanted it very crisp. Eugene says to play it mysteriously." She liked the idea of mystery; it seemed a new idea to her. "Eugene says mystery is what makes music beautiful." (I had liked that remark, too, jotting it down in my class notebook. Another remark I noted was, "Everything is melody in Bach. Approach it by asking yourself how you would sing it." And then the name "Ebenezer Prout," an English music theorist who Eugene said had composed words to every fugue subject in Bach's Well-Tempered Clavier. I was curious about those words!) Daniel was quiet. He had played the same Brahms Rhapsody he'd performed at play-in, but much better this time; it seemed very realized to me. Eugene's focus with him was on pedalling: "Pedal *with* the bass notes, pedal *before* the melodic entry notes." And he had some suggestions for the ending: "Bring out the bass melody more—make the running figures more like smoke. Brahms's cigar smoke." Both Daniel and Kelly seemed pleased with the feedback they'd received.

There was no fixed seating in the dining hall. The first night, as groups of kids who knew each other from previous summers or current dorm assignments took tables together, I had looked longingly at the faculty table where my age peers were seated, hoping they might invite me to join them. This didn't happen, and soon most tables were full. I sat down at the only half-empty one, where four Chinese girls had gathered— then realized they had switched to English out of politeness to me, relinquishing a rare opportunity to relax into conversation in their mother tongue. At least I had classmates now, making it easier to find a familiar face at any table.

The conversation over lunch that day was mostly about our first class sessions, but by mid-afternoon, everyone was talking about tryouts, scheduled for the following afternoon—asking each other whether they were going to try out for the Friday or Sunday recital, discussing what they were going to play. (*Tryout*, to me, meant an informal run-through of a program prior to a public performance; here it clearly meant something more like an audition.) At dinner everyone seemed to be signing up for tryout times on a sheet posted on the bulletin board. I didn't sign up; performing in the recitals wasn't in my plan. But now I worried that if everyone else was doing this, I should too, or I would feel even more out of step than I already did.

The decision was taken from me by Eugene at breakfast. "I didn't see your name on the tryout list," he remarked as he passed my table. "You should sign up. You're definitely ready. I'm encouraging everyone in our group to try out." In class he looked at the list of pieces I was working on and asked to hear the Bach-Busoni, "Wachet Auf," then the first movement of Beethoven's Pathétique. His suggestion for "Wachet Auf" was to make sure I knew every place where the chorale subject entered: "You should go over the score and separate out all the chorale notes. You need to be aware of them so that each time the chorale shows up, you can make sure it sounds out over the counter-melody." I saw I was indeed losing clarity because of being hazy on these entries—hearing the beginning, but not following the melody all the way through with my ear. As for the Beethoven, I was just pleased to get through it in front of the class, even if it was my usual "curate's egg" playing. Eugene's verdict, that it wasn't ready to perform—"but it could be, in a week"—was gratifying. He thought I should try out with the two Scarlattis.

After lunch I signed up for a 3:30 tryout slot and filled out information sheets for my selections. I had thought this would be like play-in, with everybody in the hall for the duration, but we were only expected to show up at our scheduled time to play our pieces for a board of three: Franklin and two of the teachers. This gave me a couple of hours to practise. Approaching my set time, I came back to Waterside Hall, where I could hear an audition just ending, but when I went in, it was to learn there were still two ahead of me. Sitting at the back I heard Eben, Franklin's Cape Town student, and then Noah; both played beautifully.

I was surprised at how nervous I was this time. There was something about the formality of presenting our sheet music to the three auditors, who glanced through it impassively and handed it back with a courteous "thank you" that was scarier than the whole roomful of people at play-in. But the concert grand sounded so beautiful that it kept me focused; I got through both pieces without serious mishap. When I exited, still shaky but proud to have carried this off, the outer passage was full of kids, some waiting their turns, others finished but staying to hear a friend. Noah was among them. He had asked if I would talk to him after I was done; he wanted feedback on how he had played as compared to that morning in class. "Was it still too loud?" he wanted to know; and had he successfully integrated Eugene's input? Everyone was sitting on the floor, half-listening, half-whispering, an ambience suddenly companionable that seemed to include me as one of them for the first time. The performance situation was equalizing. Later, when Franklin came up to the supper table to tell the four of us sitting there that he had enjoyed hearing us, and "You're all playing," there was a feeling of satisfaction and inevitability.

When I returned to Barney Hall that night to access WiFi, Franklin stopped by my table to say I was scheduled to play both Scarlattis on Friday—not Sunday, the day I'd asked for. Dismayed, I said I'd been counting on the two extra days to rest and prepare.

"You played beautifully today," he said. "Just do the same tomorrow. You'll be fine."

"I have no experience, Franklin, you don't know how easily I can lose it under pressure."

"Have you practised left hand alone?"

"Only in places." It wasn't the time to admit I had never been able to play a left-hand part alone from memory unless the other hand was playing along silently.

He said, "I can play left hand alone, without the score, in any piece I play. Try doing that tonight at practice and you'll feel more secure."

%

The humidity had finally broken and the weather next day was exquisite, but we spent the morning cooped up as usual in a shadowy studio. Eugene worked with me on the Liszt Consolation I'd never been happy with. He said it needed to be more rhetorical. "Excuse me for putting it this way, but you shouldn't feel you have to play it like a nun. Think of it as a series of dramatic statements. Liszt was a showman, a ladies' man. If it's a song, let it be a song he's singing in a boat, to a woman he wants to seduce." I had been resisting the melodrama, wanting to understate, not to risk slipping into the ready clichés of a more romantic reading. But maybe it was a matter of that tightrope Phil had once described, the one between the sublime and the ridiculous that art could sometimes walk: "You mustn't fall off on *either* side." Something to think about, once this evening's trial was behind me.

An afternoon spent quietly wrestling with myself, working in unaccustomed ways that felt very uncomfortable. I practised in two different studios, then lay on the grass outside Waterside Hall, resting my back and dozing in the sun, waiting my turn to rehearse on site. I had taken Franklin's advice and practised both Scarlattis with left hand alone. I had taken Eugene's advice and practised both very slowly. And I was starting to feel like I didn't want to play my Scarlattis anymore. And to feel cheated out of a beautiful day: the performance looming had turned it into a chute I was travelling down. I lay gazing at the cloudless sky thinking, *This isn't a life I would like.* It wasn't even that I was seriously nervous. *It's this pressure I feel to be on the* qui vive. *I can't lose track of time, digress to follow an impulse, wing it through my day as a writer can. The hour of performance is like a semaphore blinking. It doesn't leave me alone.*

Oddly, I didn't feel nervous even as the time got nearer. I was resigned to my fate (which included not having brought proper concert clothes). In a detached way I noticed symptoms that were a flashback to my clarinet days—a suddenly-dry mouth, cold hands—but they were divorced from emotional anxiety. Watching the audience arrive, there seemed nothing to fear here: casually-dressed country folk, friendly faces, many grey heads—I knew if I could only give a poetry reading, they'd be with me all the way. Early evening sunlight was still filtering into the hall through the wall of windows where the geese had lined up to hear Fauré. Franklin, as he'd promised, sat with me in the last row, along with the others playing before intermission. It was only when my turn came to walk down the left aisle towards the stage that a moment of pure panic overtook me as I realized I was empty-handed. *Where was my instrument? I had forgotten my clarinet!* My heart did a quick flip-flop, but then I was back in the present, the piano waiting.

What I was prepared for—shaky hands—didn't materialize. I told my hands not to shake, and they didn't. What I did get, and could never have anticipated, was shaking *feet.* Especially my left foot, which I needed in the first Scarlatti to create an echo effect in the fanfare repetitions. This was no mere tremble: it was like a palsy—a slow, wide vacillation, as if I had Parkinson's. I had no control over it at all, and it was monumentally distracting. I derailed, as feared, having to stop and pick it up again, and small slips spoiled favourite moments in both sonatas. Though I managed to hold it together to the end, it was disappointing not to have played better, or even as well as I had at play-in and tryout.

Everyone was very supportive—Franklin, all of the teachers, my fellow participants, the audience. Franklin said it was a good performance despite my screwups: "You played very musically." Eugene said, "You should be proud of yourself, you've taken a major step." At the reception afterwards, a couple of local women told me they admired my "bravery" in coming back to music at my age and getting on stage. Too tired to know how I felt, I wondered if formal performance could get easier with experience, as playing in class had quickly done.

%

It's one thing to go to a place like this when you're well-established in your working routines and can come to it with your own agenda, but that's not the case here. Phil's words. When I arrived at Adamant, I thought I did have my own agenda. I was going to play piano every day for as long as I liked, on good pianos, blissfully uninterrupted by household routines and editing work. I was going to take long early morning walks in the peace and beauty of a country setting, lie in the sun and dream, float on my back in the pond watching clouds. I was going to hear a lot of piano music and gain some experience playing regularly in front of a small group of fellow students. And I would try to spend a little time each day working on my book. What I was *not* going to do was perform on stage in a public recital.

As things panned out, I wrote hardly a word of the book, took all of two morning walks, lay in the sun once only (with an eye on my wristwatch), and never so much as dipped a toe in the pond—but I performed five times in three weeks, with audiences of fifty to eighty. Besides the two Scarlatti sonatas, I played the Liszt Consolation, I played the second Gershwin Prelude, I played the Debussy Arabesque. At tryouts, I also auditioned Bach-Busoni, Beethoven (Pathétique first movement), and Chopin (Fantaisie-Impromptu). Adamant's agenda trumped my own before I could recognize what was happening: from the moment I wrote my name on that first sign-up sheet, it was like a snowball rolling downhill. What began as "When in Rome ..." moved swiftly to "Personal Best," wavered briefly at "Quit While You're Ahead," but concluded in a spirit of "Carpe Diem." The Adamant program was built around three recitals a week. How could I hold aloof from the main focus here? How could I pass up on this opportunity to develop as a performer, and where would I find a more supportive environment? Finally—when, if ever, would I get a chance to do something like this again?

※

We had a class on Saturday morning that week, to make up for ones missed during orientation; after that, we were free. Many left campus for the afternoon, singly or in groups, if they could get rides to town. I would have visited Hilari and Benedict, but they were away for a few days. "I'm a little lonely tonight," I wrote in my journal that evening. "The kids are back from town and the movies, but they have bonded, they have their generational activities, their iPods and cellphones and video games and cards. I can talk to them about piano but not much else." Conversations happened anyway, here and there. Korean-born Jade, who at twenty-seven was next oldest to me at Adamant, also seemed a little adrift that night, though it wasn't her first time there and she seemed to know everybody. She told me she had a bachelor's degree in music but had left it for a few years to study and work in the sciences. Now she was studying piano privately with one of the Adamant teachers. She understood the sadness I described when talking about my own break with the music world; she, too, had been unable to listen to music during her years away from it. She seemed a little haunted by my story of coming back at fifty-nine.

On Sunday morning I spent some of my practice time on "Wachet Auf," trying to *sing* the chorale melody as I played; discovered I couldn't do it. My fingers got hopelessly mixed up on the counter-melody as soon as my voice came in. At the end of an hour I could sing the first phrase and sometimes get halfway through the second before losing it at the keyboard. Sobering! But I enjoyed the challenge. In the evening I practised again, in a studio that quickly became my favourite: Edgewood, situated at the end of a flagstone path that skirted pond and layered gardens before turning off where landscaped terrain gave way to woods. The piano was a sweet-toned Baldwin with wonderful resonance. The only other furnishing was a sagging, threadbare, gently mouldering psychiatrist's couch; I laughed out loud when I recognized what it was. A room at the edge of the woods, containing a grand piano and a psychiatrist's couch—surely this studio was meant for me. I worked on Liszt that night, on a particular harmonic shift Eugene had pointed out, saying, "If something pretty magical doesn't happen when you come to this chord—if you don't highlight it somehow—you're losing the meaning of the passage." He suggested a *piano subito*, a sudden drop in volume, to dramatize the shift.

It was well past eleven when I left Edgewood. I had forgotten to bring a flashlight. There was the barest fingernail of crescent moon, but so many stars, and so brilliant! As my eyes adjusted, I could just make out the path. Frogs were singing up a storm as I skirted the pond; then isolated lights from windows reached out to show me the way to my residence. "I can't say that the time is flying," I wrote in my journal before switching off the bedside lamp. "My first week here has felt in some ways like a month. But I'm ready for more."

※

Week Two. In Monday's class, I play Liszt and then Bach-Busoni; Eugene still thinks I could bring out the chorale notes more, asks to see the score, tries reading through it himself and acknowledges it's harder to do than he thought. "You can try out with the Liszt tomorrow," he says. *Am I really going to do this again? It seems I am.* Before the audition next day, I practise in another favourite studio, the Rose Room—door flanked by rosebushes; painting of cut roses above the piano, wine-red curtain lending a rosy cast to the room. I work on Liszt, then digress to read through a Chopin mazurka I first played in my teens. One thing I'd hoped to do here was revive a number of mazurkas I learned or re-relearned nearly a dozen years ago, in the weeks following 9/11. (Was it the lurch in the rhythm, the wildness of the folk dance pulling against the courtly ballroom form, that drew me to them at that time?) I also memorized a number of Shakespeare's sonnets. *When sometime lofty towers I see down-rased.*

Not very many signed up for Tuesday tryouts; at supper we learn we're all playing in the Wednesday recital. I mention to Eugene, in passing, that I have not heard a single Chopin mazurka at Adamant. "Are they out of fashion?"

"It's because everybody wants to play a Big Piece," he says in a slightly aggrieved tone. "It means all the work we do is technical work, just rising to the demands of these long, difficult pieces kids bring here to perform. They consider short, simpler pieces beneath them."

"But the simpler, shorter pieces allow you to pay attention to the details and feel the music. They *demand* it, to make them interesting." He agrees. "Exactly."

By evening I have a grievance of my own, recorded in my journal: "The reason we're all playing is they need to fill a program. I'm not ready. I'm just beginning to grasp the kind of preparedness required to perform, and I don't have it with *any* piece I play—there are accidents waiting to happen all over the place. I can't integrate what I've learned here in a day's lead-up to performance, but it's there to confuse my hands as it mixes with what I'm used to doing."

%

I've made it my habit after supper to sit alone by the pond for up to an hour and write, longhand, in my journal while the sun goes down. My seat is a long-dismantled porch swing of weathered greyish wood, set at a slight tilt on uneven ground. Between the lateral lean and the deep incline of the seat-back, it's not very comfortable, but the spot is peaceful and private, the evening light bewitching. Long grasses by the water's edge bend in the breeze and gleam in the last low rays of sun; wavelets sparkle as rushes of wind ruffle the surface of the pond. There's a faint distant twittering of song sparrows, sometimes the elastic twang of a frog among the lilies, or a splash on the opposite bank. The flag on its pole beside me, Stars and Stripes against a cirrus-stippled sky, makes a fluttering sound like a wood fire. If it's a concert night, I join the drift of walkers towards Waterside Hall before the sun has dipped behind the trees; other nights, I sit on until the light is too dim to write by, then trek off to a practice studio. Pond Hour has become very important to me as a time to catch my breath. Later, after practising, I spend a half-hour on the internet in Barney Hall, catching up with family by email. This is my writing life at Adamant. The scribbled pages and saved emails are all I will have, once back home, to track my trajectory as the pace of the session accelerates. From this point they speak for themselves:

JULY 24 *(from an email to my daughter, who competes in martial arts)*

So, I'm playing again in tomorrow night's concert, the Liszt Consolation #2 (console me, please! I don't feel ready at all). I was nervous just trying out for the board of three, even though one of them was my teacher here and I play for him every day!

(Her reply, same day):

Enjoy! I survive tournaments and anything else stressful by firmly refusing to think about upcoming nerve-wracking event AT ALL until I'm in the middle of it. Maybe you can use this approach to nerves inspired by Tilopa (an 11th-century Buddhist monk I met on the internet):
Six Words of Advice
1 Don't recall—Let go of what has passed
2 Don't imagine—Let go of what may come
3 Don't think—Let go of what is happening now
4 Don't examine—Don't try to figure anything out
5 Don't control—Don't try to make anything happen
6 Rest—Relax, right now, and rest

JULY 25

*11:30 p.m. It's over. It was like last time. A little better:
no shaking. I got off to a good start, but nervousness built
as I played, and I blew my two best moments: that harmonic shift I worked so hard to highlight, and the final
cadence! All I could do was laugh, it was so infuriating.
Elaine G. gave me hell for that, afterwards: "It's a performance. You should have remained poised." She says
I gave myself away to people who wouldn't have known
the difference.*

*But many people complimented me. Hilari said,
"You made the piano sound beautiful."*

*The kids tell me you never stop being nervous, you
never know how it's going to go, and there's never a
perfect performance. "All you can do is know the music
really well." People have different tricks. Noah practises his program right up to the moment it's time for the
concert to begin. Kiana says she practises anything but
her concert piece in the hours before the concert. Poppy
also would not play her concert piece on the day of a concert—"I don't want to disturb the shine on it. I want it
to feel new." People deep-breathe. Many swear by eating a banana to calm the nerves. I did both tonight, and
maybe it helped—there was no shaking.*

*Hilari says there are two kinds of performer, those
who play better than usual on stage, and those who don't
play as well. And there are those who are nervous beforehand but calm down once they begin to play, versus those
who start out okay and gradually begin to feel nervous
as they're playing. What bad luck to be the second sort!*

JULY 26 *(from an email to David)*

I'm trying out again in a couple of hours—second
Gershwin and Pathétique first movement. Why am I

putting myself in this pressure cooker? One girl was taken
to hospital this morning after getting dizzy and falling
on the stairs. They said she was dehydrated, but it isn't
even hot here anymore. I think she's overtired. We all are.
Classes are a yawnfest lately.

JULY 26

*Franklin has asked me to play the second Gershwin
Prelude at the Sunday matinée. Class today was rough.
Eugene didn't like the way I was pulling the beat in the
opening figure of the first Gershwin. I was taken aback,
because Phil was tickled by the same thing—maybe
because he has worked a lot with jazz pianists? When
I said I was playing it the way I felt it, Eugene was cat-
egorical: "I don't care how you feel it. There's a score.
Play it as written—that's how I want to hear it. I can be
as stubborn as you." But I wasn't trying to be stubborn.
I was just surprised.*

*Noah was oddly friendly today. He said I have a spe-
cial sound—"There's a warmth and richness, but also
an* AIRINESS *in your chords that doesn't sound like
anybody else. It's like your sound has texture ... how
can I put it? Not exactly silk—more like suede." Another
oblique compliment at breakfast: somebody at the next
table called across to Eben, "I enjoyed your Liszt last
night," and Eben called back, "I didn't play the Liszt.
Robyn did."*

*All this week, Noah has been carrying around a
book called* Performance Success: Performing Your
Best Under Pressure, *and I have been eyeing it surrepti-
tiously. Should I be reading books like that? Is it a genre,
a subcategory of self-help book? If I order one, can I ask
to have it shipped in a plain brown wrapper?*

JULY 27

*End of Week Two. A terrible night—foot and leg cramps,
I couldn't sleep despite being almost hysterically tired.
But got up at 7:00 to practise before breakfast. I took
my plate out to the porch to get a bit of sun before class.
Eugene was there with his coffee. When I took the deck
chair beside his, he greeted me with, "I hope you're not
going to talk. No, I mean it—I don't mind if you sit here,
but I'm not having a conversation." As a former teacher
I could sympathize—I used to hate it if I ran into one of
my students on the metro before my eight o'clock class—
but it felt like a rebuff after yesterday's exchange. I think
the teachers are tired, too ...*

JULY 29

*Sunday matinée. Despite banana and deep breathing, I
was nervous beforehand, my hands shook, and so did my
foot. But that wasn't what defeated me: it was inatten-
tion in the home stretch, just as with the Liszt. I muffed
the last few bars of Gershwin and had to backtrack.
(Will I ever get on top of this? Or am I just not cut out to
be a performing musician?) After the concert, a couple
of people sought me out, shook my hand and thanked
me, saying they found it inspiring to hear me play. One
was a man around my age who played in his twenties
(jazz) and said he was going to order the music for the
Gershwin Preludes.*

 *I feel this time at Adamant is the last chance I will
have to do anything like this—to practise six hours a
day and live with other musicians and perform with
them. These three weeks will become dreamlike, fading
as my years at Conservatoire did, only faster. I want to
remember walking down from Edgewood tonight in the
wet grass ... an almost-full moon against bands of cloud,
the frog sounds, little toads hopping away from my feet,*

*pond reflecting the moon, islands of water lilies ... such
stillness, the wet flagstone path, rainwater pooled on
some of the flagstones, the moonlit shapes of sculptures
looming ghostly in the sculpture garden ...*

JULY 30

*A good day. Played the Chopin Fantaisie-Impromptu for
class in Waterside Hall this morning; Eugene coached
me on pedalling and tone, projection, dynamics, transitions. He said I can try out with it—not tomorrow,
but on Thursday. After lunch I somehow ended up with
Noah in the sunny piano salon in Barney Hall, where we
fell into a conversation about piano playing, teachers,
practising. I played the Chopin F minor Étude for him,
showed him my pedalling, talked about the trouble I've
had with it. He said he really likes my playing. Coming
from Noah, who listens obsessively to recordings of the
greats, this was quite a compliment. Franklin too has
been encouraging. He says I've covered an impressive
amount of repertoire, and that the more experience I can
get, the better chance I have of overcoming performance
problems.*

JULY 31

*Audition the usual mess. But I'm to play the Debussy
Arabesque in tomorrow night's concert, and to retry
Bach-Busoni on Thursday.*

AUGUST 1

*Well, I did it. On the day when it was hardest for me
to get on stage, I performed for the first time here without losing it anywhere. The feeling is more relief than
elation. It wasn't the best I've played the Arabesque
by a long shot, but I'm still in a state of disbelief that
I pulled this off. My little fan club of audience regulars*

high-fived me when I stepped down from stage. The kids were happy for me too. But the lead-up to this perform- ance was nightmarish. Our group was in Waterside this morning so I had already done one run-through on stage, but when I went back in to rehearse, the piano keys felt slippery. Work I did yesterday on a shaky run wasn't kicking in. Thanks to pedalling changes, the Arabesque suddenly felt like a whole new piece. Spent two hours in the Rose Room afterwards, playing slowly with the score, and couldn't get through it a single time, tripping up even in places where I never had trouble before. The whole thing seemed to be deconstructing. The thought of playing it on stage in a few hours was terrifying.

All during dinner tonight I was thinking I should not try out tomorrow, maybe not even a practice try- out without intent to perform, and take the last few days here to relax. But now that I've broken the pattern of derailing, I think I should play again. It's the last chance to audition any new piece for the Friday recital or Sunday's closing matinée, when everyone who wants to participate will play a short piece. David will here on Sunday; he's driving out to get me.

AUGUST 2

After all the wavering, I went for broke and auditioned all three remaining pieces. "Wachet auf" was a dis- aster (yet again); the Beethoven had some very good moments but also some muffed runs and at the end I had a memory lapse, froze, and couldn't play the final chords! But the Fantaisie-Impromptu went well—bet- ter than in class.

What I have learned here is how much I can't do. I have enormous abilities but the underpinnings for solidity in performance are not there. My playing is still a house of cards, despite progress I've made in the last three years. It's okay for background music, but not for the hush of a concert hall. I have a sense, now, of what the life of a concert artist must be, and it's a life I'm unsuited for: I do not have the drive, the competitive spirit, the single-mindedness, the hooked-on-adrenalin nerviness, the compulsive self-discipline, the sheer stamina—I don't have, never had, any of the things I see it takes.

Franklin looked abstracted after tryouts. He told me not everybody would be able to play on Friday: too many tried out, most with long pieces, including several concertos. "We can't have a five-hour concert. We have to choose only the best." My guess is he may ask me to play the Chopin on Sunday; it's just at the limit of what is considered a "short" piece.

11:45 p.m. Adamant shows a different face. I was down tonight, did not feel like practising, but played a couple of hours anyway. At 10:00 I went to Barney Hall to check email. The list of people scheduled to perform tomorrow night was posted on the fridge, and none of our class was on it: Kelly won't get to play her Beethoven concerto, Noah won't get to play his Mozart concerto. Kelly and Noah were at a table near the back, both looking dejected. Noah wasn't able to get through the Rachmaninoff G sharp minor Prelude from memory— he'd been hoping to play it at the closing concert—and he was already upset about that, even though the panel is giving him a second audition on Saturday. He and Kelly had noticed (I hadn't) that most of those on the list to play Friday are students of the two teachers on the panel. After a moment's glum silence Kelly said, "Well, anyway, I'll be playing my Beethoven with the orchestra in a few months, at my university. I don't care!" But she did care.

Franklin passed our table on his way upstairs, and I asked how my Chopin sounded at tryout. He had only criticisms: left hand overpowering the right in the slow movement, rhythmic unevenness in the fast. He said I should play Scarlatti again on Sunday, and only then did I realize how much I'd been hoping to play the Fantaisie-Impromptu at the closing recital, with David there to hear me. Many kids waited till this week to get serious about tryouts, giving themselves extra time for the longer pieces they were working on. So a lot will not get to play the pieces they most wanted to perform. Now I understand why Eugene pushed me to try out the first week. Suddenly this Friday concert seems to be a much bigger deal than the others: the earlier ones were like play tryouts, and this one, without our knowing, turned out to be the real thing.

It's very late. I have hit a low, but it's not just me— some sort of watershed has been passed in the dynamic of the session.

AUGUST 3

I had a quiet, "thinking" sort of day. Feeling a deep nostalgia for the days when I was first distancing myself from the Conservatoire and McGill music scenes. Those summer nights in Bob Sigmund's apartment—four or five of us playing for each other on different instruments, playing together, improvising together, listening to jazz into dawn. Days of sharing music for the pure love of it, no ambitions, no other agenda. It was hearing a recording of Ravel's Sonatine in class today that brought this back—our last class, a winding-down session listening to CDs from the school's library. Remembering Bob playing Ravel, summer of '69.

Thinking about teachers. Eugene is deeply conventional. He believes firmly in the value of scales, arpeggios, metronomes. He's a stickler for the score. He has an incredibly sharp ear for wrong notes, overheld or underheld notes, missing notes in chords, missed rests, rhythmic infidelities—I've been surprised to discover my errors, chronic inaccuracies that crept in over years of playing from memory. A lot of Eugene's teaching here has been about making things technically easier: dividing difficult runs between the hands, relying on the pedal to connect far-apart melody notes. The first time I played the Liszt for him, watching me transfer from one finger to another to maintain legato in the melody, he shook his head and said, "Really, that sort of thing is hardly necessary if you're using pedal." His view is that substitution fingering "ties us up in knots for no good reason." But I think if it ties us in knots, it's because we're thinking about fingering instead of focusing on the moving line. The "good reason" for this choreography is that it enhances awareness of melodic movement by enacting it with the hand.

I appreciate Eugene's honesty. This week he has spoken to the value of playing pieces one knows one can play, and playing them well, rather than exceeding one's grasp with repertoire one isn't technically up to. He says there are pieces he knows he will never be able to play—"I could struggle and get the notes down, but I would never be able to make MUSIC of them, so it doesn't make sense to give my time to them." Today he gave us each a personalized list to take home: suggested repertoire, tailored to our abilities and needs. Everyone was touched that he took time to do this. The class (except for me) compared lists over lunch.

Thinking about Phil, I have a sense he works with the genius, as in animating spirit, of his students, rather than with their skill base. He gets at the latter through the former. He gets in touch with the individual genius

*and speaks to it, prompting the skill base to rise to its
demands.*

AUGUST 4

*Huge doubt has crept into everything I play. I feel I'd
have done better with my time here just to learn some
new pieces. Or to relearn those mazurkas. I could have
created my own program in this beautiful setting. Did
I make the wrong choice? I pushed myself—I put myself
to the test. For two weeks, the novelty and challenge of
auditioning and performing provided momentum. Then
somehow, in the third week, it began to feel like a forced
march. Practising changed—it became an imperative,
"I have to practise"—where before, as at home, it was
"playing piano," a series of happy islands in my day.*

*Everything is very subdued here now. There's a kind
of dissipated energy, everyone a little at loose ends. Some
people have started packing.*

At the final Sunday matinée at Adamant, despite what I
thought was solid preparation on the Scarlatti, I derailed in
exactly the same place as I had the first time. It was utterly
demoralizing. Noah did get to play the Rachmaninoff prelude;
I was glad for him.

I had so looked forward to David coming out to fetch me. I
wanted to show him my favourite studios, my favourite pianos,
play on them one last time. But when he arrived, I couldn't
summon much feeling for it. The allure of the pianos had worn
off. Suddenly I was tired of all my pieces and had no desire to
play them. It wasn't only the pieces I had performed; it was
everything I had auditioned and worked on during the session.

I came home to my little upright and could not get through
a single piece with attention and fluidity. The Mason & Risch
sounded so thin and tinkly—and out of tune, to boot. My hands
had forgotten their cunning; they were leaden and lumpish.

Mindless hands! I felt betrayed: the thing that had been making me happy was now making me unhappy. Inexplicably and without warning, the joy had gone out of playing piano.

Phil was away on vacation, but we did talk on the phone. I had emailed him weekly, so he had a sense of where he might find me when I emerged from the woods. But now I was at a loss for words. "I don't know where to start, Phil. Tell me what you want to know."

"I don't want to put words in your mouth."

"Well, it isn't good." *Out with it, kiddo.* "I came home and I can't play. It feels like there's lead in my hands."

"Uh-huh. That's what I thought."

It wasn't as if he hadn't warned me. "But how did you know this would happen?"

"Because I've seen it so many times," he said quietly. "Going from playing an hour or two a day to playing four or five hours a day, with the pressure of performance ... it turns playing music into a test. And sensitive people, unless they're very strong in their work habits, are almost always messed up by it. No matter how informal the performance situation seems to be, it's a performance, and it brings a whole different kind of anxiety into playing."

"*I pushed myself—I put myself to the test.*" My own words. I knew I was doing it. But I didn't know it would put lead in my hands and rob me of my feelings for the music.

Phil seemed to understand all of this. "It's common. It's a thing that happens to musicians, for different reasons. Think of it as something like a writer's block." He did have a suggestion: "Here's an antidote, I call it the counter-repertoire. Learn a new piece, something you have no intention of performing. Just pick something you'd like to play, read through it a few times, play around with it. Then go on to another."

Instinct had already nudged me in this direction; I had begun revisiting Bach preludes and fugues from The Well-Tempered Clavier that I hadn't played for years. But I was finding I had to relearn them virtually from scratch. My fingers were spastic, tripping over one another in "ghost" muscle-memory as I tried to read from the score. The written notes seemed totally unfamiliar. I could neither read them fluently nor play so much as a line *without* the score.

From Novi Sad, Al Fraser emailed a reply to my distress signal: "Robyn, this is normal—it happens to me regularly. It means you need a break! The subconscious needs downtime to recharge. This is no cosmic catastrophe, it's part of the artistic growth process. You know this."

It was a full month before I recovered my stride at the piano. The desire was there, but when I tried to play, my focus was fractured. There were moments when my hands came back to life: the first came when my visiting baby grandson crawled over to the piano bench while I was playing Scarlatti, pulled himself to standing, and flexed his knees in a baby dance, bobbing up and down at my elbow as he grinned his delight in the music. I felt the dance jump like a spark from his legs to my hands. There was the relief of getting the piano tuned, of seeing Phil again; the satisfaction of getting the Bach A flat major Prelude and Fugue back under my fingers, playing them for him, hearing him say of the fugue, "It's good ... it's *dangerously* good, you know what I mean by that, don't you? The danger is you might be content to stop there. You might miss the secrets in the score, the multiple hidden possibilities ... you might stop experimenting with the music ..."

By mid-September I had come back to myself as a musician. And in the meantime, I had made some progress with my book: I was starting to feel a shape to it. In my three weeks at Adamant I had experienced a condensed and speeded-up version of my decade in music school, the gradual disillusionment that led me to throw in the towel on a musical career. Had I not just been moved to reaffirm the rightness of that choice for myself, once and for all? I had become a writer. I was still a writer, and happy to be one. Some kind of closure there, some coming-to-terms? I thought I saw how I could package this—a handy story arc, a tidy ending.

But no. Too handy. Too tidy. And not the end.

The danger was that I might be content to stop there. It wasn't that the story wasn't true, but it wasn't the *whole* story. There was a second storyline running under it, a counter-melody—something ongoing, still coming into its own.

It's not about finishing something. It's about keeping it alive.

VII REALITIES, REFLECTIONS, WRONG NOTES AND CRAZY CADENZAS

OUR FRIEND ELIAS COMPLETED HIS DOCTORAL PROGRAM in piano performance the year we met him, played his graduation recital, and at once began mailing out application packages to music faculties across North America in hope of securing a teaching position. More than a year later, with some eighty lines in the water, he hadn't had a single bite. Undaunted, he sent out more. Meanwhile he was eking out a living teaching piano privately, mostly to children, mostly in their homes, sometimes in after-school programs. To help make ends meet, he sometimes taught chess as well. Negotiating the city by bicycle until winter forced him onto public transit, living in small apartments, practising wherever he could get studio privileges, he was glad of the occasional opportunity to perform in a church concert series, a community centre, a private home, or a piano store—somewhere to connect with an audience and sell a few CDs. Twice a year, winter and summer, he travelled for several weeks to give master classes in places where he had built connections, lining up as many recitals as he could in each location, subletting his apartment if possible. It was at once inspiring and sobering to observe him year to year as he agented for himself, finding venues, managing his schedule, doing his own promotion, juggling all this with teaching, his personal practice time usually having to come last.

"How many pianists are there at any one time majoring in performance in the program where you studied?" I asked him once, out of curiosity.

He did a quick calculation. "Around ninety, I'd say." His was just one of Montreal's four universities offering music degrees or diplomas. And this was only Montreal. I thought about all the other universities with music programs, in cities and towns scattered across North America, all graduating aspiring pianists year after year. What kind of future could these graduates realistically hope for as professionals? Never mind a concert career—how many would succeed in finding or creating a niche that would offer income stability and a measure of musical satisfaction commensurate with the years of dedication they had committed to their art?

Another time I asked Elias if, based on the level of my playing, he thought I would be accepted into a university performance program myself, were I of an age eligible to apply (I knew age would have disqualified me even thirty years earlier).

"No. You wouldn't get in," he said, bluntly but not unkindly, a simple statement of fact. I put the same question to Al Fraser, and he concurred: "Sadly, I'd have to say you wouldn't. The standard is so high these days. There are all these Chinese students who are technically off the charts, they start studying over there at the age of three, they come here head and shoulders above most applicants in terms of their proficiency and experience."

Just some basic realities. Phil once remarked, of his university students over the years, "For some, it's all over the day they play their graduation recital. They're finished the degree, they have their piece of paper, and they're never going to touch the piano again. I can always tell which ones won't continue."

※

Before my return to lessons at fifty-nine, I played piano a few times, spontaneously, in the atrium of Toronto's Baycrest Centre, the seniors' residence and hospital near my parents' condo where I stayed on visits to the city. When my mother began volunteering there, she gave me a tour of the highly regarded institute where, two afternoons a week, she interviewed new volunteers. Last stop was the skylit atrium, where she led me over to see a donated baby grand piano with a beautiful chestnut finish. "Why don't you play something? This piano is for residents and visitors. A couple of locals come in once a week to play old show tunes, but I don't think anyone is scheduled today."

At the time it was so rare for me to get a chance to play on a grand that pleasure overrode shyness about playing in a public space. But soon passersby began to gather; some pulled up chairs. They were hugely appreciative, but I kept having to stop: "I'm sorry ... I don't remember the rest ... I should have brought my sheet music ..."—a convenient fib, as I knew it would not have helped. It wasn't memory failure causing my falters but all the issues Pamela and Phil would later address with me. Still, it became routine on Toronto visits to accompany my mother to Baycrest and play piano while she conducted her interviews upstairs.

The atrium was a hub, with staff and workers continually passing through, visitors browsing an indoor bazaar or bringing coffee and snacks to the small tables, caregivers with their charges seeking a change of scene. Sometimes a little group of chairs and wheelchairs would gather by the piano, especially past four o'clock when the day's programs ended. Later my mother would come down and listen too, often inviting a friend to join her. It was *de rigueur* for me then to play the Fantaisie-Impromptu; if I made no move to do so, she would request the showy piece herself, calling it "I'm Always Chasing Rainbows" after the popular song cribbed from its slow movement (or, remembering how that used to irritate me in my teens, "Play the one you know I'm waiting for.").

Those early experiences at Baycrest—seeing people respond to the music, feeling their disappointment when I couldn't finish a piece they recognized—were part of what prompted me to reconnect with Phil in 2009. And it was my experiences playing at Baycrest in ensuing years that best furnished the model for what performance could be, what I wanted my performance to be: not a personal proving ground, not a showcasing of skill or a feat aimed to impress, but a sharing of something I loved. It was performance without the formal trappings. The piano was not on a stage. I came in unannounced and unscheduled, without a program. I played what I felt like playing; people could come and go as they pleased. They could also interact with me—and did. Distracting as that could sometimes be, I learned things from it. Engaging with listeners—*listening* to listeners—gave me insight into different ways music can reach people.

Once, as I concluded the slow movement of the Pathétique Sonata, an old woman with a wonderfully alive rosy face wheeled up to the piano with her support worker. "Oh, I love this so much—you don't know how happy it makes me!" Her eyes shone as they parked themselves to my right, at the treble end of the keyboard, to hear more. She knew the Chopin pieces I played—sang with them and played "air piano," pointed to herself, she kept losing her words but it was clear she was saying she used to play. After each piece she stood up from her wheelchair to hug me, sometimes weeping a little, but face still radiant: "Happy, happy time! Don't stop!" Then, as if foreordained, another woman made her way towards the piano with her walker, stationing herself to my left, at the bass end. She told me she had been a ballet dancer; she knew and identified the Fantaisie-Impromptu. As I continued to play, flanked by the pair, I had the sensation these two women were channelling energy into me, giving me new powers at the keyboard. Rather than inhibiting me, their close presence enhanced my attunement to the music. The sound of the piano soared and floated in that huge space, familiar phrases taking on new colours as I poured heart and soul into them. I felt as though it wasn't just *me* playing; the three of us had fused somehow. Two separate listeners seemed to be playing *through* me. I was giving voice to the music *for* them, and this had made us one.

Another time, a man in a wheelchair with IV rolled up to the piano and asked if I knew the Chopin C minor Nocturne. I didn't, but when he mentioned first having heard it in a movie, I said, "Wait, do you mean the C *sharp* minor Nocturne?" and played the opening phrase. "That's it!" he cried. He was effusive when I played it for him; told me that after hearing it in Polanski's *The Pianist*, he had listened to every YouTube version he could find. Then, "I have to leave in a few minutes to go for my treatment. Could I ask you to play it once more? It's the first time I've heard it played live—this is healing for me." His face glowed as I repeated the Nocturne, again playing unusually well because I was playing *to* somebody. A month later, back in Toronto for work reasons, I came in to Baycrest and this man reappeared as I was playing the same piece: "I heard the notes as I was coming out of the elevator and I knew it was you—what a pleasure!" He stayed listening for an hour, then asked, would I be there a while longer? When I assented, he raised a just-a-minute finger and left, returning shortly with a thick binder of reproductions of his paintings he wanted to show me: Byzantine-style portraits of historical and mythical figures. Vividly coloured, meticulously detailed, it was stunning work; the originals were huge panels in oils, he told me, each a full year in the making, each researched in depth—the personality, the life, the historical context. As I leafed through the binder, marvelling, he added, "Often my ideas for subjects are inspired by music. And I listen to music while I'm painting." We never exchanged names; I have tried since to find out who he was, whether his paintings are represented anywhere, but haven't been able to learn anything.

By 2013, I had built up more than two hours of repertoire I could deliver from memory, and whenever I came to Toronto, I would install myself in the atrium and play all of it. Sometimes a small crowd would gather, treating it as a concert; other times, individuals came up to the piano between pieces, wanting to connect, to share their own musical stories. Once, I felt the dynamic of the lobby change from its usual busy ambiance: a hush came over it as all attention seemed suddenly to have shifted to the piano. This might have been unnerving, but instead it seemed to waken my own ears. The next afternoon the same thing happened; both days, the piece that brought the hush was the first movement of the Pathétique Sonata. I recognized, maybe for the first time, the astonishing power of this movement—the genius of Beethoven. It was as if I was telling a story and everyone was listening, captive, waiting to hear what happened next; I knew I had a responsibility to tell this story with no holds barred. In the presence of such active listening, some kind of daemon had entered the music. It pulled me out of the private bubble in which I had been communing with Beethoven, and I began to play to my listeners, to *communicate* Beethoven. The rapt collective focus had turned the performance into something reciprocal, an exchange of energy.

The composer creates the music—the performer creates an experience of the music—it's the listener who interprets. Phil's words took on new meaning for me at Baycrest. Over the years, people who worked there came to recognize my playing: after a piece or two familiar faces would appear, staff passing through on their breaks, or leaning over gallery railings of floors overlooking the atrium. My repertoire consisted overwhelmingly of classical favourites: others who played on the Baycrest pianos surely played many of them, too. Yet staff who knew my mother would come up to me and say, "I heard the piano from my office and I knew right away it had to be Toby's daughter." I took it as a sign I had communicated something at once universal and personal: I had given voice to the music in a voice of my own.

%

What is it that makes performance into a test, instead of that other thing—that mysterious and wonderful reciprocal thing? What is being tested? Why are we nervous? Is it the thought of "audience" as a collective judge? Is it the ordeal of formality—donning concert attire, the backstage wait, rituals of bowing and applause, the stage lighting, the discomfort of having to do one's private "preparation" under scrutiny of strangers? Is it the artificiality of the situation—the performer exposed and alone, on a raised dais in a pool of light, the audience anonymous and plural, a level below in the dark—divided from each other, each in a way dehumanized to the other by this separation? (Argentinean pianist Martha Argerich has spoken of feeling enormous loneliness while performing on stage.) Is it knowing that one has just one shot at delivering the music one has worked long and hard to prepare? (Glenn Gould, who called solo concert-hall performance "the last blood sport" and abandoned it early in favour of the recording studio, referred to the concert stage as the "No Take Two place.")

What are the stakes? Obviously there's fear of failure— of botching that single shot in some horribly conspicuous, irredeemable way: fear of public humiliation, of disappointing or embarrassing family and friends; fear of fallout, of a blot on the track record if the performance isn't up to scratch. Normal human feelings. Supposing you could rise above them, though, and completely let go of such concerns, which are basically self-involved (as implied in Phil's "You need to get off *yourself*, as a performer")—are there not other, even higher stakes? A whole other kind of pressure comes with wanting the music to *mean* something—feeling a responsibility to the composer whose creation you are representing and to the audience who (for better or worse) will experience that creation through your mediation.

⁂

Flashback: Eugene, at Adamant, talking about the standards to which pianists are held in the major competitions: "If you skip notes, that's enough to get you eliminated. Even a note that doesn't sound fully is regarded as if you played a wrong note." I wondered if this was why so few competition-winning pianists I'd heard on radio over the years had excited me, despite their dazzling facility. Since they all have that, one looks for something they don't all have. What does it take for a human being to acquire the skill to play with that kind of precision, even under pressure? We are not machines; why aspire to play like one? What may get lost in the process?

Flashback: my son, in conversation—"But aren't the best pianists, the ones who play with real emotion, also the ones who play wrong notes?"

Arthur Rubinstein. Vladimir Horowitz. Alfred Cortot, my great-grandteacher. Rubinstein's cavalier attitude about his wrong notes was legendary. Still, most seem willing to grant the last word on the subject to celebrated pianist and pedagogue Rosina Lhévinne, whose take on them was to sigh, "Ah, but *what wrong notes!*"

What are wrong notes, anyway? *Real* wrong notes, where the pianist is mistaken about something in the score, are rare in professional performance. Generally what we mean by "wrong note" is not a mistake but an accident: the player knows what the right note is, but misses it. When did this other kind of wrong note, a misstep in execution, became a sin? As many have observed, recording technology changed listener expectations. All music was once live: it wasn't so long ago that this changed. Music, whether it happened in a private home, a village square, a church, a theatre, or an emperor's palace, was experienced by listeners in real time, presented in person by musicians visibly engaged in a human activity. Occasional slips were seen as inevitable; it was the spirit of the performance that communicated itself to the audience. There was showmanship, there was improvisation, there was novelty—many conductors and pianists were also composers, often premiering their own latest works. And when a performance was over, it was over: it continued to exist only as a memory for those who had heard it.

Recording made it possible to preserve a performance for a mass audience who could hear it again and again. But slips that barely register on one hearing become an irritant when heard repeatedly. Sound editing made it possible to "correct the record" by replacing flawed passages with clean retakes. Marvellous developments—but they changed the experience of listening to music. Tolerance for anything less than impeccable execution in live performance diminished. An obsession with perfect accuracy as a *sine qua non* for the aspiring concert artist dominated the competitions and filtered down to the listening public.

An emailed thought from Al Fraser, in response to hearing about my Adamant experiences: "You don't realize that for the listener, it is *really* not important if you screw up here and there. How you are playing when you are not screwing up *is* important. It's clear your playing gave listeners something that distinguished you from the others—enough to catch the attention of individuals who were moved to tell you about it. Your occasional stumbles did nothing to prevent you from getting your very fine musical message across."

In fact I *do* realize this. "They're not what's important" is the message Phil always gave me about stumbles. But let's face it, *too many* wrong notes do mar a performance. And even a single wrong note—say, in a particularly beautiful lyrical passage, or at a moment of high drama in the music—can be a major spoiler.

A memory: Phil, back when I was in my teens, quoting what he said was a Chinese proverb, "A mistake is a danger and an opportunity." We must have been talking about wrong notes, for he went on to tell a story about playing lounge piano in his twenties: "I hit a clinker in a piece by Chopin—not just a wrong note, but a highly prominent one, the top note of a virtuoso run up the keyboard, really the climax of the whole piece. And I don't even know how, but on the spot I realized I could turn the mistake into something else—I could use that note as a pivot, and improvise a crazy cadenza back down to where I needed to be next."

Can we do the same with the "wrong notes" we hit in our lives?

In more recent years, Phil once said something similar, something I wanted to kick myself for not having written down. It was something like, "Mistakes are the rough edges our imagination can make something of."

Actually we learn by imagination, not by experience. Suddenly this old dictum of his comes back to me—one of those enigmatic remarks I've carried through the years and puzzled over. Phil Koan. Am I finally making the connections? Experience is what we acquire through practice, under a range of conditions; it brings us to a place where we're comfortable with what we've learned. Imagination is what can take us beyond that.

※

"Improvising is all about hitting wrong notes. The thing to get rid of is your fear of hitting wrong notes."—My son's advice, at a time when Phil had been nudging me towards improvisation.

It was something that continued to defeat me, much as I wished I could do it. My son could do it. Had been doing it since before he turned three, first on a two-bit harmonica bought in Chinatown, then moving to the piano, sometimes playing both at once. It was all Leon really wanted to do at the piano—that, and play by ear. It was *reading* music that gave him trouble.

How can you hit a wrong note while improvising, one may ask. If you're creating something never played before, making it up on the spot, how can any note in it be "wrong"? A simple answer is that melodies and chords follow standard formulas: to make musical sense to our ear, the notes must belong to a particular scale that determines the tonality or key. The odd note that doesn't belong may occur, but unless it behaves according to conventions that our ear recognizes, it announces itself as an outsider. It jars us; we hear it as a mistake.

My recoil from rogue notes was indeed inhibiting me. Rather than risking them, I was avoiding improvising in a recognizable key: if the music isn't based on any scale, no note can be heard as wrong. (The trouble is, neither can it be heard as right. No wonder I was frustrated.) Leon's email continued, "And it isn't always fun. Sometimes nothing good happens. Think of it as gambling a bit. I usually know within thirty seconds if it's going to be a good or bad session."

Many years down the road, I'm still learning to improvise. Little breakthroughs happen, where for a few weeks I'm on a roll; then the luck changes and I lapse for months when I should be cultivating a gambling habit. Ironically, the first breakthrough came on a day when I vented to Phil that it was futile to expect me to improvise; I just couldn't do this thing. That night I sat down at the piano to prove it to myself one last time, and suddenly found I could. Stranger still, what was coming out sounded like jazz. Without ever having learned jazz progressions, I was finding them blind. Not without missteps—but like a kid managing to stay upright on a two-wheeler for the first time, I felt a momentum I could coast on.

Riding this little wave (it lasted perhaps three weeks) I wrote to Leon, "It's so strange—not only am I not afraid of hitting wrong notes, but I'm hardly hitting them! Any note seems to be able to heard as a 'right' note or a passing note. If I hit a clinker, I play it again on purpose and try to do something with it, and that makes it sound like it was intentional the first time. I don't know the chords I'm playing, my hands just find them—basic blues chords, I think. I bonk away wildly, and it makes sense! But I've noticed I'm incorporating bits of stolen stuff from music I know or have heard recently. It's pastiche, but I could never do this before."

His reply: "Yeah—that's what jazz is. Jazz players talk about chords or modes as 'colours,' it's like you develop a box of crayons you can dip into and draw with. Your newfound ease is probably just the result of learning so much new music. If you're learning romantic pieces you have every jazz colour imaginable—most of the early jazz greats were classically trained, so they were mixing those colours with the rhythms of barroom blues. So it was pastiche for them too. You're experiencing what it might have been like to invent jazz."

It was nearly a year before the next breakthrough, and again it came via my son. It was late December. I had relearned most of the Chopin mazurkas I'd wanted to revive at Adamant; Phil was excited by this, and wanted me to work towards a performance, but I was feeling depressed about piano. The mazurkas felt stuck where they were when I'd last relearned them ten years earlier; the glow of renewed fluency faded as no new perspective emerged. Into this slump came a link from Leon: Jimmy Yancey playing boogie-woogie in the 1930s.

I'd gone out to an event that evening, ignoring a weather alert, and had just walked five miles home through a snowstorm after waiting nearly an hour for a bus that never came. Exhausted and half-frozen, I checked email before bed, clicking absentmindedly on the link. What I heard was like a jolt of electricity, an instantaneous reboot: suddenly I was dancing all over the house to Jimmy Yancey. The next day I dug up a 1943 "teach yourself boogie-woogie" manual Bob Sigmund had passed on to me decades earlier. I began learning the genre's template, chord progressions, and standard left-hand rhythm patterns as I read through the Leamjo Boogie, a model piece the author, Sharon Pease, had composed to illustrate them.

Playing a jazz piece from a written score is not improvising. But playing it from memory, once it was fluent, gave me the *feel* of improvising—that happy-go-lucky feeling of "bonking away wildly," having fun with formulaic progressions and rhythms. I spent Christmas break playing it obsessively, in alternation with Chopin mazurkas. The spontaneity and rhythmic vitality of boogie-woogie began at once to infuse the Chopin. When Phil called to set up our first session after the holiday, I wondered if I dared let him know what I'd been up to, but once in the studio, without preliminaries I played the Leamjo Boogie. He was surprised but couldn't conceal his delight. He offered some pointers on style, then asked to hear a couple of the mazurkas we'd last worked on. The difference since the last time I had played them for him was palpable.

"This is brilliant," he said, shaking his head. "How did you hit on the idea of bringing these things together?" I couldn't take credit: chance, not imagination, had brought me to Jimmy Yancey. All I could say was, "Well, they seem to have something in common."

"It's because of the beat," he surmised, "the *timing* of the beats," but I thought it was more than that. Both are highly structured, using formulaic material in similarly idiosyncratic ways—each is like a language of its own with a limited yet infinitely versatile vocabulary. It was again a matter of one piece revitalizing another, though it wasn't an obvious pairing. There was spinoff, too: Leon, inspired by the revitalized mazurkas, began learning a couple of them himself.

⁂

January 2013. My stepdad was ninety-three. To my mother's relief, he had come out the other side of a difficult few months—a spell of depression, punctuated by four falls—and was in a sunnier place. Visiting for a few days, I found him mellow; he had given up driving with good grace and was content to stay home, enjoying the large-screen TV and home entertainment unit that my youngest brother had bought for our parents and installed in the den on his own last visit. The classical music station was playing on it when I arrived; my stepdad said it was what he appreciated the most. The "surround sound" really was superior. A couple of years earlier, my mother had bought an electric piano, thinking she might like to play again, maybe learn simple arrangements of show tunes to play at Baycrest herself. Her motivation soon flagged, but she loved to hear me play when I visited. There had been no piano in their home in all the years since they'd shipped me the Mason & Risch.

On my last night in Toronto I played for her while she was preparing dinner in the next room, and to my surprise my stepdad, hearing me begin, left his customary chair in the den where he liked to doze (opening one eye periodically to explain to anyone there, "I'm not asleep, just thinking") and came into the living room to listen. I was playing a favourite of his, Beethoven's "Moonlight" Sonata, and followed it with the Pathétique, suddenly remembering I first heard both on a Rudolf Serkin recording from the 1950s that had probably been his purchase. He was more animated and responsive to my playing that night than I could remember him ever being, and more communicative than he had been for some time. "You're playing really beautifully," he said over and over, in a marvelling voice. "It's wonderful to hear these pieces. Terrific playing, dear—a pleasure. You know, you should really record yourself."

It was an unexpected moment of connection to have the music reach him in this way, to be able to play him the pieces he loved. Sheldon had broken contact with him some twenty years earlier, a breach that seemed irremediable and appeared to extend to me and to my youngest brother, the two siblings who had kept up, intermittently, with this brother who never shared our roof. My stepdad was stoical about the rift, laconic on the subject if it came up, and after a while it stopped coming up—a private family sadness, like so many family sadnesses people feel helpless to redress. We knew Sheldon had abandoned piano for organ in his twenties, had continued to compose, and had enjoyed a long and successful teaching career. He and I never crossed paths. But he did cross my mind, fleetingly, as I played piano that night.

It turned out to be the last time I saw Dad outside of hospital. Three months later he was diagnosed with inoperable cancer, and he died that July.

VIII   EXPERIENCE: VARIATIONS

WHAT MAKES US WANT TO PERFORM? WHEN WE SAY someone is a "born performer," we are speaking of a personality type—an extrovert, someone who enjoys the spotlight, whose motivation to perform comes of a natural inclination towards showmanship. Not the case for an introvert, whose motivation may be equally strong but comes from a more guarded place, and whose aversion to the spotlight is at war with it. The extrovert has to resist exhibitionism and cheap theatrics; the introvert may have to be pushed onto a stage. But I think each must have a bit of the other inside. At Baycrest I first began thinking about how to cultivate my inner extrovert.

I wanted to play for others, but didn't want my person to be the focus of attention. I didn't want the stress of being on stage. Back from Adamant, I knew I needed to build up more experience playing publicly, but I wasn't ready for formal performance. The next phase of my musical journey played itself out in local cafés.

Bistro Philinos, right around the corner, was a place we'd frequented for years. Harry, owner and chef, is a silver-haired Greek with deep-set, melancholy, sea-blue eyes, a man whose moods play his face like an instrument. His bouzouki and guitar sit atop the upright piano against the rear wall. Having seen children fooling around on that piano while their parents dined, I didn't feel out of line asking if I could try it sometime, which led to being told I was welcome to play it anytime. Harry and George, his then co-owner, had rented the piano, an Essex made by Steinway, from a local piano store, and while they hosted the occasional concert of Greek music, it was primarily for their own use before and after hours, sometimes in company of other Greek musicians. After my summer at Adamant I approached Harry about playing on a regular basis, and for a few months I played on Tuesday nights in return for supper.

It wasn't a very clear arrangement. The staff usually had the radio on or Greek music playing when I arrived, and if Harry wasn't there, they didn't turn it off. I was too shy to announce myself except by beginning to play, so the piano at first had to compete with whatever else was playing, as well as kitchen clatter and loud-partying diners. I didn't mind; it gave me a chance to warm up before anyone noticed I was there. The Essex was the best upright I had ever played. The piano seemed to like me, too; I could play more accurately on it than on any other.

On busy nights at Philinos, the first challenge was to project my sound to a level where it would prompt staff to turn off the other music. The next was to play dramatically enough to persuade groups of boisterous diners that the piano might be worth listening to. Musically, this was a great workout for the inner extrovert. I thought about the difference between playing for "chairs in rows" and playing somewhere like this— between playing for people who have come for the music and playing for a captive audience I have to win over. Philinos was always noisy, but typically some people would begin to show interest in the music, the manager would switch off the radio, and the room—at least briefly—would go quiet as attention moved to the piano. The feeling of being "outed" mid-piece rattled me, sometimes to the point of having to stop and start over. Yet at Baycrest a sudden hush always galvanized my focus on the music. Why was it that a dawning awareness of audience could push me either way?

Even on rowdier nights, listeners at Philinos did make themselves known. Once, a whole table burst into applause after I played "Wachet Auf"; another time, a long row of tables did the same after the Fantaisie-Impromptu—this, after I'd been playing very well for half an hour under the impression, from the noise level, that no one even knew I was there. Once, when I took a break to eat my salad, the waiter told me, "You see the Italian gentleman over there with his family? He keeps asking, *Why did the lady stop playing*? They love your music." But noise, even with lulls, was a constant, and in the surges, there were times when I literally could not hear myself and lost my bearings. It wasn't the right place to be playing classical repertoire.

My next opportunity came through literary channels—a newsletter for local writers announcing a new performance series at a café that hosted arts events. What caught my eye was that the venue had a nine-foot concert grand—unheard of!—and that the address was on my neighbourhood rounds! I'd missed noticing when the semi-basement storefront, last remembered as a tango club and then empty for a long time, reopened as the Café Résonance. Its mandate was unusual: vegan restaurant and internet café in the daytime, jazz bar after nine in the evening.

Martin, the primary owner, happened to be at the counter when I went in to see the place. A young jazz bassist with a warm, lively face, he told me he and his co-owners had met in the jazz program at McGill. Their idea was to create a music venue and support it with the café, but running a restaurant was more demanding than they'd anticipated, and they were still trying to find a balance that worked. Nearly everyone involved with the place was a musician or artist of some kind;

the kitchen and counter staff were all part-timers, working in rotation. The piano, which I would not have noticed had I not read about it, was tucked away at the back of the long, narrow space on a low black-painted platform serving as stage. I was excited to hear it was a hundred-year-old Chickering, a make I knew was a favourite of Phil's; Chickerings of that vintage aren't easy to find. "We were lucky with this one," Martin said. "We bought it from a recording studio that was downsizing." Seeing my interest, he asked if I was a pianist.

"Yes, but classical."

"Go have a look, try the piano if you like. We're actually looking for some classical music. We do one classical concert a month, usually students from U de M, but not many are comfortable with this sort of venue."

I was just going to *try* the piano, but it was such a pleasure to play that I continued for nearly half an hour. Martin seemed interested in having me perform, but I didn't feel ready to sign on for a scheduled event. When I explained I was just looking to gain experience by playing somewhere informally on a regular basis, he suggested I try Sundays between four and five, and after my first Sunday he said, "Any time you're ready to do an evening event, just let me know—then I can announce you and we can put out the can for contributions."

I'm not sure why I never did get to that point at Résonance, though I went on playing Sundays, off and on, over a period of nearly three years. Martin remained wonderfully supportive, offering me time at the piano before opening, while the first shift was setting up for the day; later he even gave me a key so I could come in before staff arrived. On mornings when I did go in early, I sometimes played on into the first hour after the doors opened.

If noise was an issue at Philinos, the opposite was true at Résonance. The regulars were almost all students, writers, and young professionals who came to the café not to socialize but to work on their laptops. Some wore headphones; some even put in earplugs, since the staff played recorded music all day. It often took people a while to realize there was someone back there in the shadows, playing live piano. The temptation was for me to be similarly oblivious—not an ideal situation for boosting the inner extrovert. But in other ways the Sundays were a boon. I learned to stay unfazed when I derailed, and got better at recovering without having to stop. I could try out new pieces in a relatively relaxed situation, or try out something like a program, playing all three movements of a Beethoven sonata, or a pre-chosen sequence of Chopin mazurkas. I could even have a stab at improvising.

I learned some ins and outs of café playing. I found out that if you announce to friends you have a weekly gig, they will feel no urgency to come out and hear you because they know they can always come another week; it's better to invite individuals on specific days. I learned that the presence of even one interested friend can make a significant difference to morale and focus, and that if a couple of friends are there to applaud your first number, other people will automatically join in and are then likelier to applaud subsequent pieces. I learned that applause makes a difference—especially, spontaneous spatters you know are not cued—and that a stranger's thank-you, a compliment, a smile, or a thumbs-up makes a difference.

I learned that performance and response to performance are equally unpredictable. Sometimes I played unexpectedly well on a day when I had to force myself to show up. If I was well-prepared, things could go very well—*or not*—and sometimes I played well when I hadn't prepared at all. The piece I had worked on most could be a disaster, while a piece I hadn't played in months, or one I had no business performing in public yet, could come off beautifully. Audience reaction was just as hard to anticipate. I played some of my best Sundays to zero response—just a roomful of people in their own worlds behind their laptop screens. Other times, applause came after every piece even though there were fiascos and my playing was sloppy throughout. Now and then there was a chemistry—a listening audience giving me energy I could give back. That was always wonderful, but it could never be counted on.

I loved my time alone with the Chickering. To be able to explore its colours all by myself, in the quiet of the empty café in the hour after daybreak, was an inestimable gift. But it felt unearned. At some point I should have claimed the role of performer at Résonance, instead of clinging to the safety of "background music." Having failed to make that move, I found myself in a holding pattern that was less and less comfortable. Insecurities set in. Were people getting tired of my same old pieces? Even with rotation, did I have enough repertoire to play week after week for so many of the same regulars? Could I learn enough new music, quickly enough, to justify continuing to play here? My physical distance from people in the café was turning into an emotional distance. Sometimes I even felt intimidated by the Chickering. (*Such a big piano. Such a serious piano. Who am I to be playing such a piano?*)

The antidote to this malaise was my next venue. Le Dépanneur on Bernard was the other café in the neighbourhood that hosted musicians, a homey, "alternative" breakfast-and-lunch place that featured live music all day. Singers, guitarists, pianists, and other instrumentalists signed on for three months, playing a scheduled hour a week. The café had WiFi, but the ambience was social: young mothers took over the sofas and easy chairs with their infants and preschoolers, artists and writers sketched and scribbled at small mosaic-topped tables, young entrepreneurs worked on cooperative projects at larger tables in the cave-like back room. The owner, an amateur guitar builder, grew his own salads and herbs and kept bees on the roof.

The café piano was an old dark cabinet upright with no name—presumably it had been painted over—and no high B-flat: a string was missing. It wasn't a good piano but neither was it terrible; it was never serviced, but held its pitch through thick and thin, as some old cabinet uprights do. While it was a comedown from the Chickering, I welcomed the change: it made me realize my nervousness in performance was directly proportional to the seriousness of the instrument I was playing. This wasn't a problem with No-Name.

The challenges here were different. The café had a front that opened to the street, with the piano just a few feet inside. If it started to rain, I felt drops. It was an exercise in concentration to have to compete not only with kitchen racket but with the traffic on Bernard passing within a stone's throw of where I sat. Whether it was the cappuccino machine or a garbage truck, something always seemed to drown out the most expressive passages as I came to them. And if distance from the audience was an issue at Résonance, here there was a table near enough to the bass end of the piano that I worried I could knock over a coffee with my elbow in an energetic passage. But I liked that the piano was right in the midst of things here; I could feel people listening. Their faces were friendly when I turned to acknowledge them; many expressed pleasure at hearing classical music in that venue. I felt comfortable and relaxed playing on the No-Name in a café full of suntanned bodies and summer-happy voices.

Around this time street pianos reappeared in the neighbourhood, a city initiative begun the summer before to make pianos available outdoors and in public spaces for anyone who wanted to play them. The pianos were donated and given to local artists to decorate; they were old uprights, junkers, some more playable than others. It was fun to play these pianos if I found one available when walking by. Hearing others play them was fun too. Who would guess there were so many pianists in a city, eager to share their playing?—classical, popular, jazz; some serious students, some penniless music graduates, the occasional retired professional, gifted amateurs of all ages. The pianos were like magnets, drawing all of these as well as children taking lessons, toddlers with their parents. Small dramas happened around them every day.

One morning in August, in the little square called Parc du Portugal—across from Leonard Cohen's house, where three years later Montrealers would gather in a spontaneous vigil to mourn his passing and sing his songs—I took turns playing one of these pianos with a young man who told me he was self-taught except for a few months of lessons as a child. The park was quiet that morning, but we had a rapt and loquacious audience of one: hunched like a small gargoyle on the edge of the gazebo where the piano had been placed was a skinny woman in jeans with a scraggly grey ponytail, rough skin, and a missing tooth. She told us she was going to sit by the piano all day, as she had been doing every day, "*parce que* j'ADORE *la musique, j'adore écouter les personnes qui peuvent jouer.*" She said she had lived forty years in the neighbourhood after growing up in Northern Quebec, her parents were very poor—no money for music lessons, no piano—but they could get records by mail-order subscription, and she sent away for every single one, listened to them "*réligieusement—c'était ma passion.*"

She wanted one of us to show her how to play Chopsticks, which she had once learned from a friend as a child. But she was hard to instruct. We both tried, but she gave up quickly, shaking her head. It was as if she thought she didn't have the right—that pianos were for people who "knew how." Suddenly I had the idea of asking her to play piano with me. She came shyly but with childlike delight in her face, and I showed her (as I had done with my younger siblings, later with my children) how to play an alternating fifth on low F, repeating it in a steady rhythm. Once she had established the beat, I began playing the melody of Albert Ellmenreich's "Spinning Song," for which her part was the bass line, and as soon as she heard it she cried in astonishment, "*J'accompagne!*" Her excitement was contagious. In French, I told her she didn't need to play

Chopsticks, she could just play piano—that anyone could play, the way anyone can make a drawing, given paper and crayon. "Music is drawing with sounds. Try it—just doodle something on the piano, and I'll draw with you." I showed her we could have a dialogue on the piano, responding to each other's musical doodles, and that she could also do this by herself, one hand answering the other. "You see? You don't have to wait for somebody to come play the piano. You can play too! Listen to the sounds you make. Let the piano be your teacher." Almost at once she began to imitate figures I was playing, and to explore a little. "Oh," she kept saying, "*Vous m'avez fait tellement heureuse aujourd'hui!*" She had made me happy too.

%

In my closet pianist years, I rarely played on a piano other than my little upright. Since emerging, I have played on such a range—from century-old concert grands to some distinct oddities. I also had the uncommon luck to play on three pianos I could never have imagined laying hands on.

In 2011—thanks to our friend Elias, who introduced me to Adamant that summer—I was given a totally unexpected chance to play the two concert Steinways the Montreal Symphony Orchestra had acquired for its new concert hall: a Hamburg-built Steinway chosen by Till Fellner and a New York-built one chosen by Emanuel Ax. With last-minute renovations at the hall still in progress, the instruments were housed at Prestige Piano on Sherbrooke Street, and the tour manager for the orchestra had put out a call for "high-level" pianists to help break them in: each piano needed to be played for ninety minutes a day over the next three weeks. Elias, who had signed on to participate, emailed me a link to the notice he'd received. He meant only to ask if I'd like to meet him at the store and try the pianos, but I didn't realize that, and somehow found the nerve to respond to the call myself, giving his name as referee. A reply came at once, offering me a slot to play the New York Steinway. Pianists didn't seem to be falling over each other to fill these slots: later in the week I was offered time on the Hamburg, and the next week, thanks to a cancellation, a second session on each.

The New York Steinway had a brilliant sound, but I was smitten with the Hamburg. I couldn't believe how responsive it was—the buttery mellowness of tone, the evenness between registers, the way I could feel the vibration in every key under my fingertip. The piano seemed to read my mind; the sounds, exactly as I wanted them, came almost before I touched the keys. Was I playing this piano, or was it playing me? The chance to play these instruments was bittersweet for me, as if the gates of Paradise opened just long enough for a glimpse, then shut.

In 2015 my tenth poetry collection won the Governor General's Award for poetry. This proved my ticket to another noteworthy piano experience. After the presentation and gala buffet in Rideau Hall, guests were invited to explore the main floor of the Governor General's residence: a guide offered tours of the library, greenhouse, and drawing-room where the Queen is received on visits to Canada. I had invited Barbara Scales as one of my guests for the evening, and when she saw me looking longingly at the baby grand in this salon, she asked our very amiable guide if it would be possible for me to try it.

"Are you a pianist?" he asked me. "Wouldn't you rather play Glenn Gould's piano?" We had not known that Gould bequeathed one of his three pianos to the Canadian government, on condition it be housed somewhere where it would be played. In fact it had been played earlier that evening, in a chamber ensemble to accompany the processional of laureates to their seats before the ceremony. Now, as the evening wound down and staff began clearing tables out of the reception rooms, I had a rare opportunity to play Glenn Gould's piano in Rideau Hall. ("Will you play Bach?" Barbara whispered. But I didn't dare risk Bach after an evening of free-flowing wine.) A handful of guests gathered as I played Scarlatti, Chopin, and Debussy for about twenty minutes, on a piano with a touch like velvet and a matchless sustain in the treble. "Did you feel a mystical connection to Glenn Gould?" people asked me afterwards. Perhaps I should claim writer's prerogative here and make something up, but I think it's enough to say I felt blessed.

Something I don't have to make up is that I didn't remove the wrist corsage women laureates had been furnished for the ceremony. A full-sized rose affixed loosely to the back of the wrist while playing piano weighs more than one might guess, plus it wobbled—I thought it exactly the sort of exercise Phil might come up with for mysterious pedagogical reasons of his own. The poet in me suspected there might be a metaphor to be gleaned from this (something about honours sitting heavy?)—but I won't pursue it here. Enough to say a rose is a rose.

IX   RETRIEVALS

THE DOORS HAVE JUST OPENED FOR THE DAY AT CAFÉ Résonance. Time to leave the Chickering I've been practising on since sunrise—working the last movement of the Beethoven E Major sonata (which I'm relearning) and Debussy's "Clair de lune" (which I'm trying to memorize); cleaning up the last rough passages in a Brahms Intermezzo I've been learning on my own—all in hope of having something new I can play here on the weekend. The morning's "chocolate moment"—hot brownies shattering my concentration with their all-pervasive aroma—is past; the regulars waiting outside have begun to file in. It's time to put on my other hat: establish myself at a table, order breakfast, and start working on my book. Yesterday I came to the end of a section; today I'm casting for what to write next. *All beginnings are hard* ... Out of nowhere I find myself typing the sentence, "How I loved my clarinet!"

It isn't really where I want to go, but I write another sentence, and another, and suddenly I'm writing in a white heat. Maybe this is where I *had* to go. I'm writing about the clarinet I remember from when it was new, not the tarnished one I last played in Winnipeg with Eli (that day itself now ten years past). As I conjure the instrument back to life, I fall in love with it again. On the way home I feel an irresistible impulse to get out my old Buffet and blow a few notes.

Minutes into the house, I'm in the walk-in closet, pulling the dusty case off its shelf. Greasing the corks, assembling the sections; wetting the ancient reed I played on in Winnipeg, tightening the ligature—all the familiar preliminaries I could do in my sleep—but oh! so sad. I can barely get a sound out of the thing. It obviously has leaks, it must have several to be so difficult to blow; the keys feel misaligned and they're sticky and sluggish. I can't play *anything* this time, not only because my embouchure gives out after less than a minute and my head swims from the effort of controlling my breath, but because the clarinet won't "speak." Putting it down I notice something else, something strange: the barrel has changed colour, gotten much lighter, dull tan with a milky tinge. I look up "grenadilla wood" online and learn this can happen as it ages. The metal rings around barrel and bell are loose, too; the wood has shrunk. I've lost everything—not just my once-prodigious facility as a clarinetist, but the instrument itself. For a desperate moment I toy with the idea of having both clarinets completely overhauled—a major investment, no doubt, assuming they're even worth overhauling; then I can decide either to play them again or sell them. (Play them? Am I crazy? No, not *that* crazy.) For the rest of the day I'm in a subdued state of mourning for something I finally understand is gone for good.

※

Three years after losing her second husband and partner of nearly six decades, my mother is still living independently in their condo, insisting she isn't ready to move in with my sister and her family uptown. She still has a life of her own here, she says. For a while nothing changed in the condo, but recently she has begun going through a drawer here, a box there, sifting and sorting—"I need to start getting rid of things. I don't want you children to have to deal with this later." The condo is blessed (or cursed) with many large closets. Out come old winter coats, household appliances in varying states of repair, obsolete computer manuals and hardware; boxes of my unsold books stored here to lighten my luggage when I travel to and from Toronto for literary events. Then there are the shelves of books, records, and cassettes to weed out—a few treasures amid much junk we cannot fathom why she kept. Papers keep surfacing in unexpected places: some of my father's surviving papers; my stepdad's diplomas and commendations; school records, writings from my childhood and my siblings' childhoods, shoeboxes of old photos, wedding invitations, birth announcements. Every time I visit, she has a pile for me to go through: "These are yours, or maybe they would interest you, take what you want."

It's hardly surprising pieces of my lost music life should turn up here. Certificates from the Kiwanis Music Festival attest that I won competitions I barely remember playing in; there are concert invitations, programs, clippings of reviews and articles. As I get deeper into writing about those years, forgotten facts, names, and dates resurface, enabling me to confirm chronology, fill in blanks, and process unexpected information (was that really André Laplante who shared my debut recital?). On one visit, pages of a 1965 photo feature on the Masella family, clipped from the *Montreal Star*'s Weekend Magazine, take me back.

The Masellas were something of a legend in the Montreal music world: an immigrant family, a father determined that all eight of his sons would become professional musicians. Here, photographed on a staircase in their parents' house, are my teacher and his seven brothers, one on a stair, each with instrument in hand: Rafael at bottom, then in descending order of age Pietro (oboe), Joseph (French horn), Rodolfo (bassoon), Alfredo (violin), Paul (French horn), Mario (violin), and

Giulio (French horn). On the next page, an aerial-view photo of the Montreal Symphony in concert, an occasion when all eight brothers were performing, along with their father, Frank (also a professional clarinetist, though a tailor by day) and Rafael's wife, harpist Dorothy Weldon. Ten small white circles highlight each Masella on stage that night. Most poignant for me is a photograph of Rafael with his father. Frank is piecing together a coat he's sewing for a daughter-in-law, while Ralph, pipe in mouth and wearing a familiar-looking vest and bow tie, is holding a clarinet sideways in his hands—his father's, according to the caption—eyes downcast as he tests the key action. Even though he is not looking at the camera, his thoughtful mood comes through; the picture evokes him so tangibly that a whiff of Balkan Sobranie seems to rise from the page. Out of nowhere, a memory: how, on days when I had to perform in the evening, he would schedule a lesson in the early afternoon, a chance for a final run-through, some encouraging remarks, a few reminders—ending the session always with the same words: "Good. Now, *go home and eat a steak.*"

This wasn't the first time the Masellas had been featured in print. Later I track down a much longer article, published in *Maclean's* magazine in 1954, detailing the family immigration story and various skirmishes as different brothers locked horns with their father before acquiescing to his will that they become musicians. Who would have thought that just three years after the feature in *Weekend*—glorious proof that Frank's vision for his boys had triumphed—five of the brothers would be summarily dismissed from the Montreal Symphony?

I'm sorry I lost touch with Ralph Masella. I think my second Concours recital was the last time I saw him. He continued to teach at the Conservatoire for years, but I never went back there after graduating, never thought to seek him out. It must have been shame that kept me away. Once, he told me I had the makings to become one of the best clarinetists of my generation. Today the shame is not so much that I failed to fulfill the promise he saw as that I never thanked him for the years he worked with me and believed in me—work that had its own validity regardless of where it led or failed to lead; years that I don't regret.

※

On another Toronto visit, a frayed manila envelope that escaped earlier notice awaits me; in it, among extras of concert programs I find a second review of my Sarah Fischer recital. I had forgotten there were two reviews. An earlier batch of papers unearthed one by Jacob Siskind, who criticized my choice of a Brahms sonata—really a chamber duo— as recital piece, implying that my pianist-partner, a girl my age at Conservatoire, wasn't up to its demands, but conceding that I had "managed to make the very best of the situation." André Laplante came in for much rougher treatment. The second reviewer, Francean Campbell, gave Laplante a rave ("When critics disagree, the artist is in accord with himself," as Oscar Wilde put it). She was generally complimentary to me, but the first of her three short paragraphs seems worth recording: "Young Robyn B— took us by surprise by being a Miss. I don't know just why one never expects clarinetists to be girls. Perhaps marching bands, Benny Goodman, and the New York Woodwind Quintet have something to do with this habit of thinking."

Took us by surprise by being a Miss? Her comment certainly took *me* by surprise at the time. In our high-school band almost all the clarinetists were girls; the boys wanted to play brass instruments, percussion, or saxophone. And hadn't my teacher placed me in first chair with the Conservatoire Orchestra, my very first year playing in it? This review must still have been on my mind a year later, when the subject of women wind players came up with the *Ottawa Journal* interviewer following my *Matinée Symphonique*. The eye-opener for me today is not only the thought expressed but the belittling tone—and coming from a woman! It underlines a climate that must have made itself felt, at least subliminally, all during my music years.

I've begun to re-establish contact with a few old Conservatoire friends, now widely scattered, for help supplementing what I remember of those years. One of them sends me a photo from his own archive: the Expo Band on stage, summer of '69. There I am in the front row with the other clarinetist— not a "Miss"—and it is he, not I, in the concertmaster's chair. There are only three other women on stage. I don't remember the imbalance registering with me at the time; probably I already took it for granted. A journal entry from the same year does mention "being the only girl in the common room" during rehearsal break at an orchestra gig, a church performance of a Haydn Mass. Another friend, a talented horn player who gave up performance to study sound engineering around the time we lost touch, now writes me that she soon discovered prospects for a woman sound engineer were no better than for a woman wind player. While she had long since left the music world, she kept up with it much more than I ever did; from her I learn it wasn't until 1975 that the first woman clarinetist was hired by a Canadian orchestra—"and she got in by connection, not by audition."

All this has changed, but change came slowly. At the time I abandoned ship, *circa* 1972, we were hardly on the cusp of it yet; there were only four or five women in the Montreal Symphony, one being Ralph's harpist wife, the others all string players. As late as 2013, the *Harvard Crimson* ran an article entitled "Still a Man's World?," maintaining that challenges continue to face women in the world of classical music despite substantial progress made since the 1980s. The author points out that while gender equality has improved in terms of headcount, certain orchestra sections remain male-dominated, citing basses, oboes, clarinets, trumpets, trombones, and percussion. Oddly I don't remember concern about gender disadvantage figuring consciously as a reason for my defection. I never saw it as something that could bar the way for me. Yet looking at my three-item press kit today, it's hard to imagine it didn't play a role.

Was there more? There may have been. Perplexed by a cryptic journal entry from 1970, I ask James, now a retired organ builder, whether he can remember anything that might shed light on why I thought a certain administrator at Conservatoire was trying to undermine me.

"Well, yes, in fact," James says at once. "Didn't you once tell me he made a pass at you? This would have been a couple of years after the fact, but I recall your mentioning it."

I'm dumbstruck. "I said that? Are you sure?" But now something stirs, a vague memory of making an appointment with this man to ask about applying for a teaching job. Did he say something about there being a procedure to follow before I could apply—then walk me to the door with what I first took for an avuncular arm around my shoulder, suggesting with a parting squeeze that if I was seriously interested, I could come back to talk with him at end of term? Did I only afterwards recognize this as a veiled proposition? I didn't go back. I don't want to make too much of this: a passing embarrassment at my own naïveté, a small sinking of the heart. I took it as a singular disagreeable incident. Only now do I wonder if I was being given a message about what it might take for a woman to advance in the world I was about to enter.

Almost inadvertently I've become a sleuth, fitting together fragments of a nine-year paper trail leading up to my graduation from Conservatoire—noting gaps, grappling with riddles. I'm trying to pinpoint where I disembarked—to get to the bottom of why I never wrote a word about my two Concours recitals, a year apart. How can it be that I remember nothing about playing them—not where they took place, not who accompanied me on piano, not my programs, not whether anyone came to hear me other than my teacher and the panel of judges? Concours recitals were held in the daytime, on weekdays, but they were open to anyone who wanted to attend. Did I not invite anyone? Not even my husband? How can I have cared so little about the culmination of nine years of study? I stare at my handwriting of forty-five years ago—the half-sentence with which I dismissed that culmination—as if it will disclose its secret if I read it a sufficient number of times: "The week runs itself through my mind, from the night we moved house ... *through the hectic week of my Concours recital—I somehow coming out with a Premier Prix*—then the taping session of a recital for CBC Radio, then the circus of landlady, carpenter, plumber, gas company, roofer as we try to get the new flat organized ..." It's a half-sentence more than I wrote about my first Concours.

And then—it comes like a bolt—I do remember something.

... The second Concours. I have saved two favourite pieces to end my program. One is the Debussy Rhapsodie for clarinet and piano I first learned with Bob Sigmund; the other a sonata by an Armenian composer, Edvard Baghdasaryan—the edition, in Armenian and Russian, given me by a fellow music student during my first year at McGill; given him by someone he had met in Russia who knew the composer and hoped it would find its way to a clarinetist in North America. It excites me to think that my choice of this piece as a Concours finale might constitute its North American première. From my place on stage I glance over at Mr. Masella, a few rows back in the hall, for a cue to begin the Debussy, but he raises a hand signalling me to wait. The judges confer with him briefly, then he comes forward towards the stage and calls up, "They're asking us to stop here. They say the program is too long, they're behind schedule, they want to break for lunch before the next Concours."

I can't believe what I'm hearing. "But I saved the Baghdasaryan for last! And the Debussy is one of my best pieces." He goes back and confers again; there's some arm-waving, I'm too far away to hear anything, but it ends with a shrug, then a

handshake, he's coming towards the stage again, then he's up on
stage. "Don't be upset … They said they're too far behind sched-
ule to hear any more. But they say they don't need to hear more,
they heard enough to judge, they're giving you a Premier Prix.*"*

The memory slams me now almost with the force I felt
then: stunned disbelief, then a wave of helpless rage. Whatever
that *Premier Prix* might still have meant to me (already deval-
ued as a "Deuxième accessit," a second try)—it was taken
away in a stroke when I was told they didn't need to hear the
rest of my program. It felt like a consolation prize. Like a bone
I was thrown, appeasement for their abdication as listeners.

※

Deep into the book that has morphed into a musical autobiog-
raphy, I've been writing of happier times at the Conservatoire:
years when the clarinet was my life, my joy, my identity—*my
axe*; when my whole heart was in the breath I blew into the
instrument day after day, and the school was my second home.
I've been reliving those years, but the experience is tinged
with sadness at the thought of my two clarinets stowed away
in disrepair, the knowledge that I will never play them again.
Thoughts of all the music I played on them: lost, irrecoverable,
vanished into air!

One day it occurs to me that a recording of one or both of
my radio performances with Sheldon might still be archived
at the CBC. A website search yields nothing (later I learn that
had I tried just a few years earlier, I might have been able to
recover them, but the CBC had since dumped all its audiotape).
As a last resort I try googling "clarinet" and my name, on the
off chance that some CBC tapes could have been moved to
another archive before the purge. Up comes the website of the
Conservatoire de musique du Québec (well, *of course* the school
would have a website now!) with two entries under my name in

its library catalogue: *Concours de clarinette du Conservatoire,
enregistrement sonore, 1972* and *Concours de clarinette du
Conservatoire, enregistrement sonore, 1971. Deux rubans.*

There it is in black and white, yet I stare at the screen,
unable to believe my eyes. They have two reels of audiotape
under my name in their archive. They have recordings of both
of my Concours! Did I know the recitals were being recorded?
I have no memory of being aware of it. I click on the entries,
and my programs come up—substantial programs, longer than
I remember preparing, and not the same both years—only one
piece in common, the Debussy Première Rhapsodie. Wait—I
never got to play the Debussy in 1972; wasn't that where they
stopped me? But the program lists the piece as third out of
five selections, *not* penultimate selection as I'd remembered.
Maybe I did play the Debussy. And the Baghdasaryan is also
listed! Is it possible the panel relented and let me finish my program, and what I'm remembering is just the outrage of being
asked to cut it short? Or was the program submitted in advance
of the event and catalogued that way, rather than as actually
recorded? Yes, that could explain it.

I share all this with Fred, now living in Sweden, and ask
what he remembers of my two Concours recitals—was he
there? He replies that he was at both recitals; says they were
in Plateau Hall, says my pianist the first year was Marcel
Lachance (how could I fail to remember that? And why, hearing it now, do I still not remember it?). He doesn't recall who
the pianist was for the second Concours, nor does he remember
if any friends came, either year. Then: "But yes, I can confirm that bit about the second Concours. Absolutely appalling.
They stopped you and said they didn't have time to hear more.
And then gave you a *Premier Prix*, for godsake."

So it did happen. But my amnesia regarding the Concours
is depressing me. Suddenly I'm feeling I did not value my own
musical gift. I took it for granted; I was cavalier and flippant
about it. I think I was not a serious musician—or not serious

enough to take charge of the musician I could have become. No one but myself to blame for that.

The existence of the tapes overrides all else on my mind as it sinks in that this piece of my past has survived. Those elusive two hours, a year apart, that I've struggled to remember—they're there to be recovered, if I can just get a guest pass to the library, if the staff is willing to set up a listening station. It's so unexpected I feel quivery at the thought—like being given the key to a time machine. The Bibliothèque is closed for vacation but I email the librarian, explaining I'm an alumna from forty-five years ago who did not continue in music, and asking if I may come listen to my Concours recordings. Two weeks later comes her reply: regretfully, they cannot play the recordings for me, the equipment they have is old and in poor repair, there's too much risk it could destroy the tapes. I ask if they would be willing to digitize the recordings if I paid; she replies that the Conservatoire does not offer this service, but they could lend me the tapes for a couple of days to take to a studio to convert. She warns that it could cost a few hundred dollars and adds that she cannot guarantee their condition. It takes all of about five minutes for me to decide I will do this.

Mark Corwin, professor of electroacoustics at Concordia University, has worked closely with Phil Cohen since the 1980s, recording musicians for the Leonardo Project; he seems like the right person to ask where to get tapes digitized. My timing couldn't be better. It's still summer, classes won't be starting for two weeks, the studios at the university are empty, and Mark says he really enjoys digitizing old reel-to-reel; he offers to do the job himself. He admits forty-five-year-old tape is a wild card: "It may be too corrupted to work with, but it could be fine, depends how it's been stored." I ask if my son can come observe the process, and he says, "By all means. It will be good to have another sound man to consult with."

Conveniently, the Conservatoire is now less than a half-hour's walk from my home. After several moves the school is finally in a permanent home of its own—a block-long, gleaming modern building with every amenity we lacked during the Show Mart years, plus facilities for new disciplines involving technologies that didn't exist then. Vaguely I recall reading of the inauguration of this space in 2009 (by coincidence the year I restored contact with Phil Cohen), but I never found occasion to walk over for a look. Now, entering the airy, light-flooded building, the first thing I register is the name of the concert hall: Salle Gabriel Cusson. I'm catapulted back to my last semester at Conservatoire, a day when I exited the elevator on the third floor of the Show Mart to see a discreet typed notice on the hall bulletin board, informing us of *"le décès de M. Gabriel Cusson, Professeur au Conservatoire de plus de 25 ans."* It had by then been four years since I'd completed my *dictée musicale* requirement; seeing his name on that notice felt like a goodbye that hadn't been spoken. Today, seeing his name above the door of the concert hall feels like a greeting. I seem to hear his voice again, the familiar words that signalled he was about to play the next four bars of dictation: *"Bon! On continue."*

Twenty minutes later, having left a small security deposit, I walk out of the Bibliothèque with a bag containing the two precious reels of tape, labelled and dated. Retro objects, these Scotch Tartan boxes, standard packaging for an obsolete technology. My Concours programs are printed in ink in the space provided, but the names of the pianists are not given. On the way home I think about the reels sealed inside for all these years, in an archive that was moved and moved again—who knows how long in storage between locations, who knows where and under what conditions? Summer humidity. Winter dryness. The tapes have to be played to be digitized. The quality of sound might not be good enough to warrant their preservation, or portions could be deteriorated. At any point in the playback, the tape could stretch, permanently distorting the sound; at worst, it could split or break. I'm trying to temper my hopes.

※

August 30, 2017. In the sound studio where we've arranged to meet, Mark sets up the machine his technician has delivered and he and Leon examine it together. It's a half-inch machine, and the tape is quarter-inch. "It might work anyway—if not, I'll get another machine," Mark says. "I'm not going to do a test run-through; I'll digitize while we listen. If the tape breaks, at least we'll have a sound file up to that point. I don't want to take a chance on playing these more than once." My heart is in my throat as he threads the tape. Seconds later, we hear music: a truncated piano introduction, then like a miracle the sound of a clarinet fills the studio, clear and full-bodied, as if being played live in the room. I'm electrified. I recognize the sound as my own, though the Karl Stamitz concerto I'm hearing isn't one I remember ever performing, and the music is only half-familiar. Beautiful tone. We marvel at the fidelity. It's unbelievable to me to be hearing this; it's also very strange. The cadenza, played with dazzling facility, comes as a complete surprise—*when did I ever learn that?*—and the Stamitz is followed by a Hindemith sonata I not only don't remember learning but don't even recognize as something I've heard before! Early into it, there's an extraneous sound, a muffled crash with some echo—we look at each other and speculate, did someone knock over a chair? Somehow I seem to know it's one of the adjudicators dropping her clipboard. The intrusion lends the performance a shocking immediacy, a reminder that we're listening to live footage, recorded on site. That is, Mark and Leon are listening to live footage. I've been teleported back to site: for me it's May 5, 1971.

"Plateau Hall, right?" says Mark. "I recognize the acoustics." We listen to the Hindemith, remarking on its features as a composition; I'm pleasantly surprised at the quality of the playing. But right around this point, something goes wrong, suddenly we're getting bleed-through from the tape's other side, Brahms on top of Hindemith. So soon in the process! My disappointment is acute: "I knew it was too good to be true." Mark is more sanguine. He stops the reel and goes to fetch a quarter-inch machine. Anxiety again as he rewinds, re-threads, forwards to the Hindemith ... and relief again: no bleed-through on this machine. Hearing the opening movement a second time, I recognize a phrase here and there, and the same in the subsequent three movements, but the sonata is largely terra incognita. Mind-boggling that I could entirely forget a piece I learned and rehearsed with a pianist, probably performed more than once, and played so well.

The whole morning is unreal for me, a little like twilight sleep. I'm aware the tape could break at any point, this could be my only chance to hear it. I don't want to miss a note, but there's another track going on: Mark and Leon chat through the whole procedure—technical talk about equipment and software, speculation about what kind of cleanup should be done on the sound files. I hear the conversation and sometimes even participate, but in a sort of dream state, the way when you're semi-anaesthetized you can hear medical technicians talking, and even answer them if they ask a question. The windowless studio with its machines and blinking lights is like an artificial womb in which a lost part of my life is being rebirthed by extraordinary means. My private focus is on the music: silently applauding a passage well executed, disappointed when something doesn't come off as well as it could have, gratified by unerring intonation and beauty of tone in places, piqued elsewhere by misses of one sort or another ... exactly the responses I would have experienced while actually performing.

Neither the quality of the tape nor my playing is as good in the second reel. I can tell right away I had a less than perfect reed. The pianist, whoever it was, isn't at his best. My own playing in the first movement of the Mozart concerto, then in the three Schumann Fantasy Pieces, is competent but uninspired. The Debussy (it would seem I *did* play the Debussy) was better on the first reel. But the Stravinsky that follows, three short pieces for unaccompanied clarinet that I remember as devilishly hard, come across as effortless and wonderfully spirited—this despite some distortion on the tape and a break between the second and third piece when I had to stop to clear accumulated moisture out of a burbling tone-hole by blowing into it hard and repeatedly. I had forgotten this quirk of clarinet-playing: in cooler temperatures, condensed breath builds up inside the instrument and sometimes runs down in a little track until it hits a hole where it begins to pool. "I'll edit that out of the file," says Mark, but I'm glad to have heard it. I feel about it as I did about the dropped clipboard; it's the anomalies that transport me back to the moment with the most immediacy.

As we approach the end of the reel, the tape begins to wobble; Mark is now guiding it manually, and again I'm holding my breath. Though the program lists Baghdasaryan, it doesn't look as though there's room for another piece on the reel, and as far as I know, I didn't play the Baghdasaryan, so I'm dumbfounded to hear the opening notes. But watching Mark's hand steadying the tape as it winds to its last, I see there's no way it can accommodate more of the sonata. The first movement finishes barely two inches from the end of the reel. And with this, one mystery is solved. It wasn't my last two pieces that the panel stopped me from playing; it was the last two movements of my "finale" piece. And now I see why: the tape had run out. It made a good stopping place. They didn't want to wait while the reel was rewound.

I knew I would not be totally pleased with my performances, but Mark and Leon both say I will be getting a nice CD out of this. Mark will clean up the files and send them to Leon, who will press me a CD (Mark's newer machine no longer has a CD drive; technology has already raced on). Emerging from the studio, I'm surprised it's still daylight. I hardly know where I've been or for how long. Back home, trying to process the experience, I write, "Hearing myself play those pieces on tape didn't really trigger memory. What it did was evoke my visceral, physical connection to the instrument. Tongue. Reeds. Breath. The struggle with my slow tongue, its lag in staccato passages—I heard it and felt the frustration of it. The struggle to coax beautiful tone out of a resistant reed. The effect of nerves on breath control: failing to take a deep enough breath for the length of the phrase to come, or forgetting to clear my lungs of stale air before taking a new breath—then having to pay for it. The almost giddy relief of making it though a passage of multiple register shifts without the sound choking up somewhere. What I experienced was not a *memory* of performing but a physical reliving of it, alongside an anxious weighing of my strengths and weaknesses."

Two weeks later Leon drops off the CDs. Hearing them on our sound system is very different. The sound coming through the large speakers is so vibrant. Instead of finding glitches the more irritating for hearing them again, I'm more forgiving. In the studio I didn't appreciate how well I was playing, worried as I was about the tape breaking, and caught up in the physical response to what I was hearing. Now as I listen to the recordings by myself, with family, with friends, I'm happier and happier to have them. It's like getting back a part of myself I had thought gone for good. It's like discovering that back in the 1970s, I cut two albums I didn't know I was making, on an instrument I no longer play. Hearing them, and knowing I have them to listen to again, is healing: finally I'm at peace with what I've lost. I don't have to play clarinet any more, I don't have to play any of those pieces again, I have the recordings.

And I have a piano.

Bon! On continue.

%

It doesn't escape me that I owe the Miracle of the Concours to two generations of technology. The first made it possible to preserve my musical performance by recording it. The second made it possible to preserve the recording, nearing the end of its life in one form, by recreating it in another. As I package the reels to return, it's strange to think of the half-life of these recordings, archived in institutions that no longer have equipment to play them or reason to do so. Mark says Concordia has no plan to digitize years of recorded graduation recitals: too much work, no demand. The librarian at Conservatoire says if they had had equipment they could trust to play the tapes there, I would not have been allowed to borrow them: an exception was made for me. Yet she, too, says there is no plan to digitize their archive. Why are the reels being kept? For how much longer will they be kept? What secrets are they keeping? These are my thoughts as I walk east along Villeneuve to my old music school. I have been lucky.

It's a beautiful sunny morning. Arriving at the Conservatoire, I notice what I did not notice when I came here to borrow the tapes three days ago: there's a text in large white lettering on the wall flanking the entrance. It stops me in my tracks:

je ne suis pas
revenu pour revenir
je suis arrivé à ce
qui commence.
Gaston Miron

(I haven't come back to come back. I've arrived at what's beginning.)

I stand reading the words again and again. It's as if the quotation, from Quebec's best-loved poet, was placed here for me today. It sums up my moment and could equally stand as an epigraph to what I have found myself engaged in these past several years. A homecoming, but not for the sake of coming back. A return to a home ground where something is beginning.

Whoever chose those words to emblazon on the wall of a music school understood something about music.

X   BRIDGE

MUSIC WILL SAVE US. IN FALL OF 2016 THESE WORDS
appear in giant graffiti on the boarded-up façade of a burnt-out
building that once housed Dusty's, a venerable Montreal diner.
For the weeks that the message remains legible, I smile each
time I walk by it and say *Amen*. Music did save me. In adolescence it saved me from social isolation; playing in the school
band gave me, for the first time, a collective enterprise I could
fully embrace. In the years since, music has saved me again
and again: from tedium, from anxiety, from loneliness, from
emotional turmoil. It has saved me from the slough of despond
that is writer's block, from the shipwrecks of a life's crises and
reversals, from idling away hours on inane distractions and the
blandishments of technology run amok. If anything can save
us going forward as a species, music will.

%

Phil was winding down. By 2015 I was seeing him much less
frequently as exigencies in both of our lives made themselves
felt. His back injury from the long-ago car accident had come

back to haunt him, causing misalignment and chronic pain. On my side, travel to promote the new poetry collection disrupted routine, and tendonitis, that bane of musicians' lives, had manifested in my right arm. I could still play piano with minimal interference, but felt the effects later: weakness, aching, tingling, swelling. I took a long break from Sundays at Résonance. Eventually I realized the cause was not playing piano but working on computer at a new desk of the wrong height.

Unlike my physiotherapist, Phil never suggested I stop playing altogether to allow the injury to heal. Given his knowledge of physiology, I expected he would have an explanation for what was going on in the arm, but he neither attempted a diagnosis nor advised me to seek one; he simply observed me closely for signs of strain while I played, showing me new movements, angles and positions I could try in order to avoid it: "There's always another way to do a thing, to bypass the difficulty. Your work at the piano isn't seriously compromised—you're managing to keep going and even gain ground. Just pay attention to your body's messages—stop if you have discomfort and try to identify the trigger. Find what works—it may vary from day to day. It's *theory* that can get us into trouble." My osteopath was on the same page. Her approach was to listen to the body (she used the word "listen") and base her treatment on how the injury was presenting in the moment. She suggested things I could do between visits. When I asked if I should get an MRI to identify the issue, her reply was, "Not unless *you* need that definition. I don't need to know what the problem is in order to work with it—I go by what's in front of me. You seem to be doing well with the arm—it hasn't worsened in function or mobility."

During this period, I was in Toronto for my mother's eighty-ninth birthday and found myself at the piano in the atrium at Baycrest one afternoon. It felt good to play in front of people again. I realized performing had become important to me. It had become part of my musical identity, part of my "walk" as a musician. It was no longer enough to play for my own ears. That day, I felt again how the presence of listeners allowed me to lose myself even as it prompted *me* to listen—to concentrate—not to let a line or a phrase go by with my mind elsewhere. It spurred me to follow the music.

Hard as it was to lose the regularity of working with Phil, it was a relief to have the extra hours to devote to writing. Journal entries tracking our work sent me back to the piano: as I revisited early sessions to bring them to life on paper, much that had baffled me became clearer, motivating me to relive them at the keyboard. On my own now, I was tracing the circle deeper, bringing new awareness to old questions. What does it take to be *present* in one's hands? I puzzled over the phenomenon we call "automatic pilot," the ability of the hands to play from pure muscle memory while the mind wanders off on its own track, totally disengaged from the music, thinking idle thoughts. "Don't *think*," a watchword of Phil's, wasn't about this kind of thinking; he meant *don't think about what you're doing at the piano, don't watch yourself; let go of self-consciousness, SELF consciousness, as you play.* He was invoking a state where the player is *one with the music*, singing along silently—where *inner singing* replaces thinking of both sorts. But what does it take to *sustain* that singing, to keep the mind from wandering? I grappled, too, with my antipathy to a program: if I prepared specific music to perform at a specific time, I could be pretty sure that when the time came I would feel like playing something else. How does one enable *spontaneity* when there's a program, especially one played repeatedly—and how bring freshness and surprise to what has become routine?

When I did get to see Phil—in shorter sessions, ever farther between—all I wanted was to play for his ears, get his input on pieces I had been working on without guidance. Anxious not to waste time, I'd balk at his insistence that we go back to some of the old warm-ups. Sometimes our exchanges were heated: "Phil, if after seven years I'm still not understanding what you're after with this exercise, why can't you accept that I'm never going to understand it?"

"I don't *want* you to understand it. I never wanted you to understand it!"

"That's right, and you've been giving me stuff you don't want me to understand since I was eleven years old!" After one exchange came close to a fight, distressing to both of us, he spoke more gently. "I'm just trying to help. I'm doing this for *you*. I want to make sure you have all the tools you need to be your own teacher after I croak." The word choice surprised me and didn't. It was the first time he had voiced the thought, but I knew it was where we were.

A fall landed him in hospital the week that MUSIC WILL SAVE US appeared on the wall. I visited him there, and again in rehab where he spent four more weeks—joined on one occasion by Al Fraser, in Montreal after a playing a recital in Ohio. Phil was tired that day and not at his most articulate, but there was something he was struggling to get across to us, something about what was important to him in music. Al kept trying to formulate it for him, but each time he would say, "No, not exactly," or "No, that's not it." We waited; he tried again.

"They all have *answers*." He didn't say who they were. "Answers don't interest me. Analysis doesn't interest me anymore. These days, it's just the direct experience I want—just to hear the music ..." And he began to describe something he'd seen recently on television, village musicians playing in ensemble: "They weren't trained, most of them couldn't even read music. There was a score but they had learned their parts by ear, they had a conductor who sang the notes for them. And what came across when they played together was something so wonderful ... how can I put it ... there was no interference. It was direct communication. They were just playing the music— playing for joy." He inclined his head as if still hearing it, an almost childlike sweetness to his smile: "That's all that matters to me now. That's what I look for."

I had been summoning courage for months to ask him something, and it suddenly felt urgent. When Al left the room to respond to a phone call, I moved my chair closer. "Phil, I know you don't like to answer questions, but there's something I need to hear from you." At once his face became serious and focused; he must have felt the gravity of it for me. "Go ahead."

"I need for you to tell me that you trust me to learn new music on my own. That you believe I can do it."

There was a second's hesitation as he took this in. Maybe just long enough to weigh the risk of not replying against the risk of replying. Then, without altering his expression, he looked me steadily in the eye and said, "I do."

※

Phil was home by year's end. For his ninetieth birthday, a snowy Sunday in February, Anna organized a buffet brunch at a restaurant with wheelchair access, but she had bigger plans for spring: a surprise gala concert and reception, free and open to the public, honouring Phil in his Jubilee year at Concordia. She put out word to see who of his students over the years might participate and booked the university's concert hall for May 17, 2017, the date favoured by most. How to organize such an event and publicize it locally while keeping it a secret from the honoree? Conscripting him as coach, she disguised it as a four-hands concert for Pamela and herself. Meanwhile fourteen more performers signed on—pianists, instrumentalists, singers, sound artists, some flying in from the States and overseas. Grandson Graham, now seventeen, composed a Fantasia for viola and piano, dedicated to Phil, to perform with his father for the occasion. I was relieved when Anna asked if, instead of joining the roster of pianists, I would read something I'd written about Phil, to give context to the evening.

At the chaotic dress rehearsal (people just off the plane, some seeing each other for the first time since student years)

it became obvious the program was much too long, and everyone agreed to jettison at least one piece they'd wanted to play;
I went home and abridged my abridgement. The concert the
following night came together like a charm: spirited performances, a full house of enthralled listeners. At the end, Phil was
brought on stage in his wheelchair to join the performers for a
standing ovation that went on and on.

Handed the mic when it subsided, our friend and mentor
looked out into the hall at a multitude of adoring faces. "What
a mob!" he said, to a low ripple of laughter. And then—simply,
addressing all of us—"Thank you."

Phil Cohen at Loyola Campus, late 1980s (Courtesy of the Leonardo Project/Concordia University)

Phil Cohen at Loyola Campus, late 1980s (Courtesy of the Leonardo Project/Concordia University)

CODA: DEAR PHIL

Dear Phil,

As I write this, late at night on May 5, 2018, you are in a small private room on the fourth floor of the Montreal Neurological Hospital following a massive stroke yesterday. I knew nothing until this morning, when Anna phoned me in tears; in a while she called again with the latest scan report. It showed a worsening. She said if I wanted to see you I should come, but by the time I got to the hospital I had missed the period when you were still responsive.

Anna had gone home to pack an overnight bag, Pamela keeping vigil in her place. We took turns holding your hand, we spoke to you; no sign you could hear us. When Anna returned, I sat with her until Kasia arrived in late afternoon, and stayed on with both until dark. All of us numb, mute, in shock. Later, as I walked from hospital to bus stop in rain-freshened, suddenly balmy air, the streets were strangely quiet for a Saturday night so close to McGill. Almost no traffic; few walkers; moisture in the air making huge golden haloes around the streetlamps on Prince Arthur. A hush over the whole downtown. I remembered lying awake last night as unprecedented high winds swept suddenly over Montreal, ninety-kilometre gusts that rocked the city for hours, roaring in treetops, whistling past the planes of high-rises, rattling roof-flashing and windowpanes, knocking down anything unfastened—a chaos of random bangs and crashes outside in the dark. Prodigious weather. I wondered if you heard those winds.

In the rhythm of my walking, each step drove further home the truth that although you are still alive, you have already moved beyond reach. All along, all these years, I thought I would get to know you better, Phil; I thought there would be time to find out who you really were. All the unfinished conversations, subjects we touched on but left hanging, intuitions I've wanted to share ... all the half-memories, things I've wondered about and meant to raise at a propitious moment ... What was I waiting for? When did I imagine those propitious moments might come? Now we will never talk about the things we didn't talk about. From here on, the conversations will be one-sided, in my head or on paper.

I stood at the bus stop in the soft spring night, negotiating a new reality. Already talking to you silently, I climbed onto the nearly empty bus that pulled up, and when I got home, I picked up my pen.

%

JULY 14, 2018

... Picked up my pen, but soon put it down. More than two months have passed, I hardly know how. But I've begun learning a new piece, another Brahms Intermezzo (Op. 118, No. 2). *Teneramente.* The soaring melody says what I have to say right now in a way words can't.

Your leaving felt so sudden, Phil. You made it through one more day, unresponsive. You died on Sunday night, the sixth of May—just one week after the lively lunch Anna hosted at the apartment for a handful of friends in honour of a weekend visit from your long-time student, New York jazz pianist Jeff Franzel. Before sitting down to sushi, we took turns playing for you and for each other. The mood was celebratory. Seven weeks home following another two-month stint in hospital and rehab (the second in less than two years), you were doing well, gaining in strength, even working at the piano again with your stalwarts. The physio team had been dubious about whether you could recover enough mobility to come home this time. But here you were, and Anna had plans to host lunches like this weekly through the summer.

You were quiet that day but looked happy, sometimes conducting us from your wheelchair as we played. We thought we had a season's worth of these gatherings to look forward to as the days grew longer and warmer.

%

JULY 22, 2018

Phil, I hoped one day to put this book in your hands, and that is now one more thing that won't happen. The book I thought I was going to write, a book about a year of piano lessons, evolved into something much more complicated. It was a while getting off the ground, partly because I was hesitant about what I could include. Would I have to change your name, replace real details with invented ones? Could I strip away the particulars that coloured my experience of you, yet still convey something true to that experience?

This went beyond the normal hesitancies of memoir. I knew you to be intensely private, reticent, a dodger of personal questions. Perhaps you felt "getting yourself out of the way" was as important to your teaching as you insisted it was to musical performance. Recently your student Peter Robinson, who credits you with getting him back on stage after more than a decade's struggle with intractable tendonitis, described how he confronted you in his home city of L.A. during one of your regular trips to coach pianists there: "I said to him, 'Phil, I've known you for eight years, you literally saved me, you've mentored me musically and personally, you know my entire history and I don't know the first thing about yours—I don't even know where you live. Is that normal? Who are you? Where are you from? Are you married, do you have children? You've told me *nothing* about yourself.' Phil didn't answer, but late that evening—he was staying at my house—I found him sitting by himself in the kitchen. He heard me come in and said without looking up, 'All right, Pete, I'll tell you.' He must have been thinking about it all day. 'I live in Montreal. I'm married. I have children.'"

Was this someone who would take comfortably to being written about? Yet when Al Fraser told you two chapters of his own new book were devoted to you, your response was, "Only two?" We had a laugh about that. Finally I realized the only way out of my impasse was to write freely, and hope to earn your trust by writing truly. You did know I intended to write a book; I must have had some sort of faith you weren't unfriendly to the idea. Still, it was with trepidation that I first read a few pages aloud to you and Anna at the apartment, after a session there a couple of years ago. While she prepared lunch, I sat beside you at the dining room table, next to your better ear, and read my account of the first piano lesson I had with you as a child. I felt it necessary to preface my reading: "You have to understand, Phil, this is a personal story. It isn't a book about piano pedagogy. It isn't even about your teaching. It's about how I *experienced* your teaching." And you nodded, your expression sober.

Then I read. I glanced at your face as my words called up your living room on Mountain Sights in 1960, through the eyes of the eleven-year-old I then was. Everything seemed to surprise you, yet also to be familiar. You became more and more animated as I described the strange exercises you showed me at the piano that day, until at one point you turned towards the kitchen doorway, exclaiming, "Anna, are you listening to this? It goes back *that far*, I was already onto it, so early!" Your excitement made me feel I was on the right track.

Not long after, you and Anna invited me to read the whole chapter to a group of friends assembled in the university's concert hall to audit one of Jeff's recording sessions. It was like a plunge into cold water to launch into my narrative, knowing where it would take us; only the pin-drop quiet of the listening gave me courage to let my own words carry me. When I came to the end, you motioned me over, your face already telling me what I needed to know. You said how touched you were by what I had read, and how much it meant to you that I had written about Gordie. A weight came off me then, but the writing went no faster.

Perhaps three weeks before you died, I asked if you remembered I was writing a book; it had been a while since I'd mentioned it. The immediacy of your reply surprised me: "Yes, and I can't wait to read it." I know you weren't speaking literally, but it turned out to be true: you couldn't wait, and you didn't wait. It's some consolation to remember I read many later portions aloud to you in hospital. What more can I say ... I'm reminded of your own words when I approached you nine years ago with the goal of playing a recital in a year's time: *It's like any creative process. It can't be forced, it doesn't work by deadline.*

%

JULY 30, 2018

Some might say I missed your most important years, Phil— your career years. I missed your defection from McGill (legend has it that while serving on a panel evaluating final piano exams, you stood up, broke your pencil in half, and walked out when it became apparent political concerns were going to determine the grade of one student). I missed your subsequent hiring to create a music division at what would become Concordia University. I was briefly party to the heady period when you were single-handedly laying the groundwork for a visionary music program there, but when I left for the west coast in 1974, it was to lose sight of you completely until that May afternoon in 2009 when I played for you again for the first time.

In the years between, while I juggled raising a family with writing and teaching, you developed the diploma program at Concordia and co-founded the Leonardo Project, real-time research that became the centrepiece of your professional life. Partnered with a psychologist, you explored creative musical performance as art and science, measuring those "subtle differences in timing" that could shed light on the magic that stirs listeners. Participants in these programs echo those of us who knew you only as a private teacher: they say the experience was both unique and uniquely inspiring. It was only when our regular sessions came to an end that I realized I had missed the chance to hear more about this work from your own perspective.

As your hearing worsened, phone calls stopped, to be replaced by hospital visits. On good days, I could read to you; sometimes we could even work a little—the Geriatric Institute had a serviceable baby grand in the West Lounge. Some startling moments of connection; some days when you spoke in riddles—unfinished sentences, non sequiters. You kept coming back to certain tropes, familiar ones: I heard "No *answers*"; I heard "Turn it into something else." Once, out of nowhere, you said in an unusually strong, clear voice—not your usual *sotto voce*—"I thought it could be measured. I was wrong. It *can't* be measured."

You were looking straight at me with an expression I couldn't read. Was this something you were saying to me, or were you concluding aloud something you had been turning over in your head? It did sometimes seem as though you believed I could hear your thoughts. Could you have been recanting a premise of your own research? You knew I was writing a book; was it possible you wanted me to record this?

Your physiotherapist arrived then, and the moment passed. Later I remembered, and wondered. It was one of the things I meant to ask you about. But would you have answered?

Fifty years after the Kennedy assassination, I was still second-guessing.

⁂

AUGUST 2, 2018

You were alert and engaged the last time I played at any length for you, Phil—a last session, of sorts, on the piano in the West Lounge. I played piece after piece, and you had something to say after each. Mostly you wanted me to play with the music more: to let the unexpected happen—an unpremeditated change of pace, a *piano subito* where one would expect a crescendo. You said, "Don't go into it with intentions, don't say 'I'm going to play that part *this way*'—that will never work. Just be open to doing something different." Later, as I wheeled your chair into the elevator to go upstairs, you remarked, "Nothing I said today was intended as criticism of what you're doing—you know that." Back in your room, as I was readying to leave, you waved me nearer, there was something else you wanted to say. I had to lean in close to make it out; you were tired by then, speaking barely above a whisper. It was "Find your freedom."

The Geriatric Institute is on Queen Mary Road—strangely enough, right across from The Chantilly, site of my high-school piano lessons. After visiting you, I'd cross the street to get my homebound bus in front of the very building where those transformative lessons unfolded, week after week, half a century ago. It was the same bus I took in high school, but going the other way. Waiting for the 51 that afternoon, as then, I pondered the words you'd left me with.

Find your freedom. At our first encounter in 2009, when you described the cartoon of the man with the ball and chain, puffing contentedly on his pipe—when you said I was going to have to break the chain—I balked. I didn't feel chained. What was the chain? You didn't answer, and I now know you weren't talking about a single impediment or a one-time jailbreak. The chain is different things at different times, different things for different people. That I didn't feel chained was the whole point—we so often *don't* feel chained, until by chance we pull against a chain we didn't know was there, or notice one we hadn't recognized for what it was.

The man in the cartoon was Everyman, the chain his comfort zone of the moment. I've come to see that growing as a musician is a largely a matter of recognizing when comfortable habits we've settled into, whether of playing or thinking, have become a form of restraint. You unsettled us, nudged us out of our comfort zones, to keep our relationship with music dynamic. It was always about breaking the chain. "Breakthrough"—your word for those moments of seeing another way—was your aim with everyone, a process in which we grew not only musically but as human beings.

%

AUGUST 3, 2018

Today I'm remembering how you turned to me after a session last year and said, "You know, you have *tremendous* potential. You should use it." Forgive me, Phil, I think I laughed—to hear that at sixty-seven! I should have felt honoured that to you, my age was irrelevant. You spoke as if I were ageless, just as you never talked down to me as a child.

At this stage it's moot whether I can break the chain that has kept me from getting on stage in a more formal way. But

I think you knew I would not stop playing piano. That I will continue to look for opportunities to play for others, to share the repertoire we worked on together these past several years. And new repertoire—finally with confidence that I can be my own teacher. I'm back at the piano for life: *Da Capo al Fine.* I'm open to wherever it takes me, for as long as I have left to pursue it. The joy with which you infused piano playing is what kept me at it over the decades and brought me back to you so late in the game. You transmitted that spark, but it doesn't depend on you. The flame is mine to nurture, as it was during my thirty-five years going it alone at the keyboard.

Still, I know that whenever and wherever I play, I will feel you as a presence, as I so often did during those years. As I do now. How can I describe that presence?

It isn't a memory. It's something *present.*

I hear you listening.

NOTES

36. "A mistake is a danger and an opportunity": Phil's quotes were often approximations, and rarely sourced. I assume this was his version of a remark J. F. Kennedy made in a campaign speech in 1959 or 1960: "In the Chinese language, the word 'crisis' is composed of two characters, one representing *danger* and the other, *opportunity*." Kennedy's words have since been widely cited in business and political contexts, though some have claimed they are a Western misreading.

39. Pischna (Josef Pišna, 1826–1896) was a Czech pianist and composer who performed and taught in Moscow for thirty-five years. His *60 Daily Studies*, widely used in piano teaching, appeared in several editions. (Mine was a revised edition by Willi Rehberg.)

45. At the bottom of the key, ff: The verse lines that end the chapter are from the poem "The Cyclist Recovers His Cadence" in my 1981 collection *The Space Between Sleep and Waking*.

67.   Alfred Cortot (1877–1962) was regarded in Europe
      and internationally as one of the finest pianists of his
      day. Born in Switzerland, he studied and later taught
      at the Conservatoire de Paris and founded the École
      Normale de Musique de Paris, which trained both pian-
      ists and piano teachers.

67.   Yvonne Hubert (1895–1988), born in Belgium, studied
      with Cortot at the Conservatoire de Paris and gradu-
      ated in 1911 with a *Premier Prix* in piano. Already a
      distinguished performer when she came to Montreal in
      1926, she founded the Alfred Cortot School of Piano in
      1929 to promote the French tradition, and later taught
      at the Conservatoire de Montreal and the École de
      musique Vincent d'Indy.

92.   The poem is "The Orchestre du Conservatoire
      Rehearses in Salle St-Sulpice", from my collection *A
      Day's Grace* (2003). It is reprinted here with gracious
      permission of The Porcupine's Quill.

95.   "It was a make-do home for a music school," ff.
      The description of the Conservatoire's quarters in
      the Palais du Commerce appeared under the title
      "Requiem for the Show Mart" as a Balconville feature
      in *Maisonneuve Magazine*'s inaugural issue, 2002.

131. Busoni, Bach-Busoni: Ferrucio Busoni (1866–1924)
      was an Italian pianist, composer, conductor, editor,
      writer, and teacher. His piano transcriptions of Bach
      works written for organ and other instruments are
      called "Bach-Busoni Editions."

165. "No surprise for the writer, no surprise for the reader"
      is from Robert Frost's essay, "The Figure a Poem
      Makes."

186. *All the instruments of joy* ff: lyrics from "Sound the
      Trumpet" in Come Ye Sons of Art by Henry Purcell
      (1659–95), a school choir favourite. The words are
      thought to be by Nahum Tate.

196. Katie Ford's essay was first published in *West Branch*,
Number 67, Fall / Winter 2010, and is quoted here
with her permission.

197. The poem "Carried," quoted in full, is from my collection *Becoming Light* (1987).

209. shofar: The blowing of the ram's horn punctuates the
morning service for the Jewish New Year. Some skill
is required. It is a religious obligation for the congregation to hear the blasts, sounded serially in a prescribed
pattern. If not perfectly executed, a series must be
repeated as many times as necessary to fulfill the obligation, deflating the drama of the moment.

214. "unwanted accents": In his wonderful presentation,
"The Transformative Power of Classical Music" (TED
Talks, June 2008), British conductor Benjamin Zander
illustrates these in a way anyone can understand with
his comic impersonation of a child pianist at different
ages playing the opening of Mozart's Sonata in C, K545.

241. W. H. Auden's poem, "In Memory of W. B. Yeats
(d. Jan. 1939)" concludes by repeating the last line
of the first stanza, "The day of his death was a dark
cold day."

266. *When sometime lofty towers I see down-ras'd*: this is
line 3 of Shakespeare's Sonnet 64 ("When I Have
Seen by Time's Fell Hand Defac'd").

292. Jimmy Yancey: James Edwards Yancey (1901?–1951)
was a Chicago-born pianist, composer, and lyricist,
considered one of the pioneers of boogie-woogie style.
He was influential as a pianist from an early age,
though he did not begin recording until 1939.

293. Sharon Pease (1903–1959) wrote a monthly column
for *Downbeat Magazine* for twenty years, interviewing
famous jazz pianists he had first heard in dance bands
on the Mississippi River boats in his youth. His instruction books, *Boogie Woogie Piano Styles No. 1 and No. 2,*

contributed to the barroom genre's gaining respectabil-
ity with mainstream jazz pianists.

323. Gaston Miron (1928–1996): A central literary figure
in Quebec's nationalist movement, Miron was a poet,
writer, and publisher, a founding editor of l'Hexagone,
Quebec's first press dedicated to poetry. The text I saw
by the entrance of the Conservatoire is from the title
poem of his collection *L'homme rapaillé* (Université de
Montréal, 1970). The same text appears in giant letters
that encircle the building's lower exterior, as part of a
public art project. I have reproduced the verses as they
appear by the entrance. In the printed poem the lines
are broken differently:

je ne suis pas revenu pour revenir
je suis arrivé à ce qui commence

ACKNOWLEDGEMENTS

MUSIC, LATE AND SOON WAS A LONG TIME IN THE WRITING and in the living, a full ten years from conception to completion. Along the way, many more individuals than I can acknowledge provided vital encouragement simply by the lively interest they showed in my late-life return to music. Those most directly involved appear in these pages. Some, sadly, are no longer living, among them my longtime friend Eli Herscovitch, who set the return in motion, and my primary piano teacher and mentor, Philip Stanley Cohen, who is so much at the heart of the story.

Thank you to friends both musical and literary who took time to read and comment on portions of the manuscript-in-progress, or who responded to portions read aloud: Sharon Bourke, Alan Fraser, Barbara Scales, Roberta Frohlich, Jack Hannan, Véronique Robert, Pamela Korman, Anna Szpilberg—and special thanks to Joan Eichner and Marc Plourde, both of whom read every word. Conversations with Jeff Franzel, Kevin Austin, and Stewart Grant helped me fill in some blanks. I'm grateful to Al Fraser for permission to include excerpts of our email correspondence, and for persuading me that if I wanted to write an honest account of music in my life, I could not reduce my ten years as a clarinetist to a single paragraph in the first chapter.

Among those who lent support to the musical part of my journey, again I owe much to Al, Pamela, and Anna, as well as to Elias Axel-Pettersson, Clive B, and the late Terry W; to faculty and fellow participants at Adamant Music School, summer 2012 session; to Martin Heslop and staff at the Café Résonance. I thank the Bibliothèque of the Conservatoire de Montréal for allowing me to borrow audiotape of my Concours recitals, and Mark Corwin for his digital rescue job.

Writing grants from the Canada Council for the Arts and the Conseil des arts et des lettres du Quebec provided essential financial support at various stages in the process of completing this work; I thank them for their programs.

Dan Wells, my publisher and editor both, showed great patience and faith in the project, remaining loyal to it through an unusually long gestation, then working under all the constraints and pressures of 2020 to see it through the next stages. John Metcalf provided input at a critical juncture. Vanessa Stauffer's calming presence and steady attention to details was a balm. Warm thanks to these three, and to the rest of the team at Biblioasis

Finally, I am grateful to my family for giving me their blessing to reclaim and pursue an old passion, for their belief in the value of writing about it, and for their acceptance of the demands this made on my time—most of all to my husband David, who suffered through all the ups and downs with me, tolerated far too many late nights and burnt dinners, yet listened with full attention to each newly-finished chapter and pronounced it good.